ULTIMATE SELLING POWER

How to Create and Enjoy a Multimillion Dollar Sales Career

Donald Moine, Ph.D.
and
Ken Lloyd, Ph.D.

CAREER
PRESS

This edition first published in 2002 by Career Press, an imprint of
Red Wheel/Weiser, LLC
With offices at:
65 Parker Street, Suite 7
Newburyport, MA 01950
www.redwheelweiser.com
www.careerpress.com

ISBN: 978-1-56414-641-0

Library of Congress Cataloging-in-Publication Data
Moine, Donald J., 1953-
    Ultimate selling power : how to create and enjoy a multimillion dollar
sales career / by Donald Moine and Ken Lloyd.
        p. cm.
    Includes index.
    ISBN 1-56414-641-3 (paper)
      1. Selling. I. Lloyd, Kenneth L. II. Title.

HF5438.25 .M63 2002
658.85—dc21

                                                      2002073822

Cover design by Cheryl Cohan Finbow
Interior by Eileen Dow Munson

Printed in the United States of America
IBI
10 9 8 7 6 5 4 3 2 1

Ultimate Selling Power is dedicated
to the tens of millions of bright, hard-working
sales professionals around the world who
contribute so mightily to the economies of
every successful country.
In every nation, not only do you get the leads,
you take the lead in making sure that
the goods and services produced by your
fellow citizens get sold.

As sales professionals
(and as sales millionaires and
future sales millionaires),
you have made a dramatic positive
difference, not just in the world of business,
but in the world itself.

Acknowledgments

In doing our coaching, consulting, and research work in sales and marketing for the past 20 years, we have had the pleasure of working with numerous sales superstars and marketing geniuses. We would like to give a special acknowledgment to the outstanding contributions that these remarkable individuals have made to our lives and to the sales profession. With this in mind, we offer our ultimate thanks to L.K. Lloyd; Steve Adler; Donovan Greene; David Fahey; Ted Thomas; Mark Magnacca; Geoffrey Pickworth; Tom Gau, CFP; Phil Kavesh, Esquire; Larry Klein; Ken Unger; Jerry Richardson; Edward Hunt; Eric Lofholm; Olivia Barbee; and Jerry Kerns of Morningstar.

In addition, we offer a major thanks to Gerhard Gschwandtner, publisher of *Selling Power*, the number one magazine in the world for sales professionals, for all of his support, encouragement, and advice over the past 20 years.

We would also like to thank Cary Fulbright and Marc Benioff of salesforce.com, the company that has created the most powerful and flexible customer relationship management solution in existence. Cary and Marc were patient, understanding, and insightful when guiding us through the exciting and challenging world of CRM.

And finally, we thank the entire Career Press team for their support throughout the writing of this book. We offer special thanks to Ron Fry, Mike Lewis, Anne Brooks, Stacey Farkas, and Jackie Michaels. We regard you as the ultimate publisher.

Contents

Chapter 5: How to Develop and Use Your   113
Unique Selling Proposition

Chapter 6: The Pre-Sale Warm-up   133

Foreword

In just a moment, you will learn why I am such a fan of the work of Donald Moine and Kenneth Lloyd.

You may have heard of me. My name is Ted Thomas and I am known as a master marketer. I made a fortune early in my life, lost it, and now have rebuilt another fortune using insights from Donald and Ken.

My story is so incredible that you might think I made it up. As you will see, there are thousands of people around the country who can validate the facts of my life. These are the people who knew me then and who know me now, and they've seen what I have been through and accomplished.

In the 1970s and 1980s, before I knew Donald and Ken, I was one of the most successful real estate developers and syndicators in California. I made tens of millions of dollars for my investors and, through much hard work, made several million dollars for myself. I lived in a custom-built home in an exclusive country club in northern California and became one of the major benefactors of a symphony orchestra.

All of this success came to a screeching halt in the mid-1980s when the tax laws affecting real estate syndications were suddenly changed. Overnight, all of the economics of syndication were wiped out. I used my net worth to try to prop up and save the jobs of the 246 outstanding people who worked for my company and to save our partnerships. I used up a million here and a million there trying to save the company. Then, I reached into my own pocket to try to help the investors in my real estate partnerships.

It was all to no avail. I went through every penny of my $11 million personal net worth before conceding defeat. I am proud to say that I was able to help many of my investors retrieve some or all of the money they had put into the real estate partnerships. Unfortunately, I was so busy helping everyone else, I didn't have time to help myself. I lost everything and ended up in bankruptcy. In fact, when I went to file bankruptcy, some of the attorneys with whom I spoke said I was too broke to declare bankruptcy! I didn't even know how I would pay my legal fees.

I had to rebuild my life and my career starting with nothing. Nada. Zilch. Zero. The only thing I knew at that time was real estate. But how could I do anything in real estate without a dime to my name and with horribly ruined credit? I decided to get into the foreclosure business. I actually figured out some ways that a down-and-out person such as myself could acquire real estate through foreclosures. Through optimism, study, and hard work, I mastered the foreclosure business. I even wrote several books to teach others how to profit from real estate foreclosures.

Discovering
Unlimited Selling Power

I first learned of Dr. Moine in the early 1990s. At that time, I had largely transitioned out of the foreclosure business and was focusing my energies on selling my books, tapes, and seminars on real estate foreclosures. Donald had been hired to coach one of the most famous infomercial gurus and seminar leaders in America. I was amazed that this multi-millionaire guru was hiring someone to make him even better. Being a superstar already, why did he need, or want, a coach? I was stunned to see that with Donald's coaching, feedback, and instruction, this guru became even more powerful and successful.

I was one of the speakers that this famous guru allowed to make presentations at his events. While the guru collected hundreds of dollars per person in registration fees from each person who attended his seminars,

I was paid nothing! Why did I do it? Because after I gave my one- to two-hour educational program, I was allowed to sell my books and tapes. There was only one problem: Hardly anyone bought my books or tapes!

Seminar participants loved my educational programs on foreclosures. In fact, I sometimes received standing ovations. The problem is that they weren't motivated to buy my educational products or to pay to attend my seminars. My closing ratio was only 2–3 percent. Although money was tight, I decided to hire Dr. Moine to coach me as soon as he had an opening in his schedule.

Over the coming months, I spent several full days with Dr. Moine. He patiently watched videos of my presentations and we went over them minute by minute, starting and stopping the video recorder so many times I was surprised it didn't break. Donald rescripted my presentation and reengineered it from beginning to end. Donald also coached me on **how** to deliver the incredibly powerful presentation we developed. Some of the changes were subtle and others were dramatic. I learned that a series of small changes can lead to a dramatic increase in sales. I began to enjoy immediate sales increases.

At the same time, I was helped enormously by reading and re-reading Ken and Donald's best-selling book *Unlimited Selling Power*. In fact, I read and underlined it so many times that it fell apart and I had to buy a second copy—which is now itself almost worn out through overuse.

As my sales and income increased, I decided to hire several telemarketers to sell my books, tapes, and seminars on foreclosures. I hired Donald to write scripts for them and to train them in the mesmerizing sales techniques he and Ken Lloyd were becoming famous for. One of my telemarketers was a tall, slim young man named Eric Lofholm, and he also became one of Donald's star students. Eric went on to become the number one salesman for Tony Robbins and now heads his own highly successful training firm, SalesChampion.com. The last I heard, Eric was making more than $30,000 a month from the sales skills he learned.

From Donald's personal coaching and scripting work, I was able to raise my closing ratio from 2–3 percent to 10 percent, then 19 percent, and later to more than 25 percent. It was incredible to me that if I spoke to 100 people in a room, 20 or more of them would buy my books or tapes or would want to attend one of my advanced seminars. Many of my book and tape series cost between $295 and $795. Using the sales skills Donald helped me develop and internalize, I earned more than $10,000 on some days! Just as important to me, I was able to get my books, tapes, and information into the hands of people who used that knowledge to make tens of thousands to hundreds of thousands of dollars for themselves. It is amazing to me how effective these sales skills are.

Unlimited Opportunity

A few years later, one of Donald's other clients, Tony, decided to take early retirement from his business. I had watched Donald take this young man from living in a one bedroom apartment in Reno, Nevada, to owning a seminar and infomercial business in San Diego, California that brought in more than $10 million a year. Tony's business was educating people on a little known investment called government tax liens. Dr. Moine helped Tony develop a seminar on this topic and then write several books and a tape series on tax lien investing. Once revenues increased to a couple of million dollars a year, Donald helped Tony develop an infomercial that ran nationwide, packed Tony's seminars, and brought in more than $1 million a month.

I had known about tax liens for many years. In more than 30 states it is possible to buy tax liens on real estate properties when the owners do not pay their taxes. With the right knowledge it is possible to safely earn from 12 percent to, in some cases, more than 50 percent, on these tax lien investments.

When I heard that Tony was leaving the tax lien investing business, I decided to jump in. I developed my own series of books and tapes and hired Donald to help me develop a seminar. Donald used some very powerful techniques of psycholinguistics and persuasion in writing mailing pieces and advertisements to promote my tax lien investment programs. The rest is history.

Today I am living in a beautiful home on the ocean in Merritt Island, Florida. I am married to the woman of my dreams. I only go in to my office for a few hours a week. With my trusted employees, the office runs on autopilot. I've made several million dollars from sales of my comprehensive books, tapes, and seminars on tax lien investing. At one recent seminar I closed more than 30 percent of the audience using skills that Donald taught me. That day I made about $93,000. On another day I actually brought in more than $100,000 from selling my book and tape programs. More than $100,000 in one day!

Of course, my books and tapes are outstanding. I am a tax lien investor myself and know the field inside and out. I have hundreds of testimonials from around the country from people who are routinely making 14 percent, 18 percent, 24 percent, and even more per year from tax lien investing. The people who have bought my programs have made fortunes. However, as great as my books and tapes are, I would probably be selling very few copies had I not learned the powerful sales and persuasion techniques taught by Donald Moine and Ken Lloyd.

Just as important as the techniques, they developed in me a true sales success mindset. I am proud to be persuasive and I believe that sales and salespeople contribute greatly to our wonderful country.

I think you can now see and understand why I am such a raving fan of Dr. Moine and Dr. Lloyd. Their teachings and coaching have had a quantum impact not just on my income and net worth, but on the very quality of my life. I hope that you are able to benefit as much as I have benefited from *Unlimited Selling Power* and now, *Ultimate Selling Power.*

> —Ted Thomas
> The Tax Lien Authority
> Merritt Island, Florida

Introduction

In 1990, our book *Unlimited Selling Power* was published. The *Los Angeles Times*, *Success* magazine, and *Selling Power* magazine selected it as one of the top business books of the year. We gave numerous radio and television interviews across the United States, Canada, and Australia, and the book became a bible for salespeople all over the world.

A few years later, *Success* magazine selected *Unlimited Selling Power* as one of the top 10 sales books of all time, and then it was translated into several foreign languages. Nightingale Conant, the top audiotape company in the world, released a highly successful audio version of the book. Today, the book is in its ninth printing and is still a best-seller.

What makes *Unlimited Selling Power* so popular? Simply put, the book made readers more successful. It made them money. It showed them powerful methods of human communication that enabled them to close more sales with less effort. As the *Los Angeles Times* pointed out in its review, *Unlimited Selling Power* showed how salespeople could earn $10 in extra sales profits for every $1 spent on persuasion processes such as sales scripting. And scripting was just one of dozens of powerful techniques revealed in that book.

Readers from around the world have requested an updated version of that book. Some readers reported they had doubled or even tripled their incomes from techniques they had learned in the book. As you will learn from some of the case studies in this new book, some of our students have become millionaires and multi-millionaires from using these techniques. *Rather than write an update to our previous classic, we have decided to write an entirely new book.* Many of the techniques and sales strategies we wrote about in our previous book are timeless and they remain as powerful and effective today as the day the book was published. However, there have been powerful new developments in the sales field, and that is what we are sharing here in ***Ultimate Selling Power: How to Create and Enjoy a Multimillion Dollar Sales Career.***

We have attempted to keep the theory in this book to an absolute minimum. Instead, *we focus on what the best, most successful salespeople in the world are doing today.* While we make reference to salespeople and sales managers making hundreds of thousands to millions of dollars per year in personal income, we want to stress that the techniques and strategies we share with you are ones that any salesperson, *even an average salesperson*, can use to dramatically increase his or her income. Throughout this book, we write about techniques for increasing sales and making more money. As psychologists, we also want to point out that money is definitely not the most important thing in life. However, because it is *so easy* to make a great deal of money in sales if you have the right techniques, the right mindset, and great products or services, why not earn a hundred thousand to a million dollars or more per year in sales? If you don't need all that money, give some of it away to worthwhile causes or your favorite charities—but make it while you can.

We call the techniques in this book "**sales magic**" because they work almost like magic.

Our economy desperately needs these sales and marketing techniques now because sales are down in almost every industry.

Unless sales increase on a nationwide level, the United States is in danger of falling back into a recession. Based on the success we have had in dramatically increasing sales for individuals and national and international corporations, we know that the techniques and strategies in this book can significantly increase sales in dozens of industries all across our great nation.

The Real Psychology of Selling

Almost every book on sales has a chapter on the psychology of selling. The psychology of selling seems to be one of the most popular subjects in the world of sales and marketing. You may have noticed, however, that almost none of the books on the psychology of selling have been written by psychologists. As well-intentioned as some of those other books have been, they contain errors, falsehoods, and mistaken ideas that, in some cases, can actually harm sales performance. As psychologists who have specialized for more than 20 years in the fields of sales and marketing, we will clear up some of those dangerous misconceptions.

The psychology of sales is a complex field bridging key areas of psychology, sales, economics, marketing, and human behavior. Our goal is to take major insights and findings from the intersections of these disciplines and make them accessible to the 18 million Americans who make their livings every day from sales. The four major tools we use to accomplish this are linguistics, neuro-linguistic programming (NLP), expert modeling (the intensive study of the top experts in given fields) and, believe it or not, common sense. That last ingredient is necessary because we have found that without it, some people will fall in love with the tools (NLP, etc.) and will lose sight of the real goal of dramatically increasing sales. We hope that our use of the first three tools is invisible (or nearly invisible) and that in combination with common sense and lots of sales consulting experience, they yield at least one major insight, or "aha!" experience, every few pages. Throughout, we rely upon what is actually working in the real world rather than upon idealized situations, clichés, or generalizations.

We do not expect you to believe everything we share in this book. You will be exposed to some new ideas, new strategies, new ways of viewing the world, and new ways of doing things. All that we ask is that you keep an open mind and actually try out the mindsets, strategies, and techniques we share with you. Your experience will prove the power of these concepts and strategies that have made millions of dollars for some salespeople and hundreds of millions of dollars for different sales forces. Here are 10 years worth of the best strategies and success mindsets we have collected from the most powerful sales professionals in the world.

Persuasion for Professionals

As you read this book, you will notice that we also share with you case studies of professionals not normally considered "salespeople": lawyers, financial planners, accountants, negotiators, and others. It is our belief that many of these "nonsalespeople" can benefit just as much, if not even more, from learning the most powerful techniques of sales scripting, selling through the media, seminar selling, Unique Selling Propositions, and sales success mindsets. We have designed this book not just for salespeople but *for anyone who uses sales or persuasion skills in his or her work.*

You will notice that in many of our examples we write about "clients" and "customers."

Salespeople typically sell to people who become their customers and most professionals sell services to people who become their clients.

In industries where we have completed major consulting assignments, such as banking, those who buy products and services may be referred to as either customers or clients, or both! Whether you are in one camp or another, we would like you to understand our use of this terminology. We are not necessarily advocates of the term "customers" or "clients"—we **are** advocates of the completed sale. Most of all, as you will see, we are advocates and promoters of creating **customers for life** or **clients for life** (whichever you would rather have), and we have done our best to show you how to accomplish that.

Selling has changed in the 21st century. Hundreds of once mighty companies have each lost **billions** of dollars in market value because they could not sell their goods or services effectively. It is our goal to share powerful strategies that can help any company with an outstanding product or service sell successfully in today's highly competitive business world.

What is *Ultimate Selling Power?*

Ultimate Selling Power is not manipulation nor is it taking advantage of the customer. It is about creating a win-win relationship between the sales professional and the customer or client, and it is based on powerful persuasion techniques. Contrary to some of the "new age" philosophers, we do not believe it is bad to be persuasive. In fact, we believe that a lack of persuasion skills has seriously harmed thousands of American businesses and American consumers.

There is more to being persuasive than simply learning presentation and closing techniques. Our experience has shown us that salespeople can attend a seminar where they learn the most powerful persuasion techniques in the world, and they won't use them—unless they have the right mindset. For that reason, we begin *Ultimate Selling Power* with a chapter on the mindsets of sales millionaires, and throughout the book we share with you the views, values, and beliefs of sales champions as we explore the realms of high performance salesmanship. In our previous book, two of the most popular chapters were those on sales scripting. Here we add to that body of knowledge with some of our latest, most powerful scripting techniques and perhaps most importantly, we show **you** how to build the most powerful script book in your industry.

In future chapters, you will learn the lead generation techniques of sales superstars and how they network, use referrals, trade shows, and the Internet to create an unlimited supply of prospects. In the Chapter 5, you will learn how to create a unique selling proposition (USP) that will set you apart from all others in your field. You will then learn the mindset and the methods sales millionaires use in their presale warm-up. Chapter 7 will expose you to some new ideas on how to use the media to sell your products and services. We are not talking about paid advertising (although there is nothing wrong with that), but will instead show you how to get millions of dollars worth of free media publicity. Think you can't get on radio or television, or get an article or book published? Think again! We will show you how sales champions do it every day.

In Chapter 8, we will share with you the power of seminar selling. You will learn that selling to people in groups is one of the most effective and efficient means of selling ever created. We will show you how to minimize expenses, maximize sales, and leapfrog your competition with seminar selling. Next we cover dealing with challenging prospects and customers. In the real world, prospects, customers, and clients are frequently much more tough and demanding than those you hear about in sales training classes. We show you proven strategies for dealing with them and also provide you with exact scripts you can use.

Chapter 10 unleashes the power of customer relationship management (CRM). We show how you can use this incredible tool to learn more about your customers and clients than you ever thought possible, how you can use CRM to double or triple your efficiency, sell to more people with less effort, and provide higher quality service to them all. You may have thought that CRM was only for large corporate sales forces with million dollar budgets. We'll show you how a three- or four-person sales force with a budget of only a few hundred dollars each month can multiply its sales with CRM—without buying any software!

As you may have noticed, sales coaching is revolutionizing the world of sales and marketing. Just as all great athletes have coaches, many top sales professionals are now using coaches to develop and perfect world-class sales skills. For a number of years, our clients have been asking us to write a book on the new science of sales coaching. We have included a chapter on the state-of-the-art in the field. You will learn what sales coaching is all about, how it works, and how to find a coach who can help you acquire and master **any** set of sales skills you desire. In addition, you will acquire knowledge not available in any book, tape series, or seminar: how you can become a superstar sales coach, earn hundreds of thousands of dollars per year, and help your clients break sales records.

We hereby give you *Ultimate Selling Power*.

Donald Moine, Ph.D.
Palos Verdes, California
TheSalesDr@aol.com

Kenneth Lloyd, Ph.D.
Encino, California
LloydOnJob@aol.com

1

The Mindsets of Sales Millionaires

Several thousand books have been written on sales techniques and persuasion. You can buy books and listen to tapes that contain hundreds of sales techniques, opening techniques, presentation techniques, and closing techniques. With all of this available information, why then are so many salespeople struggling to meet their quotas? Why are so many companies struggling to sell enough products and services to make a profit?

A cynic or pessimist might say that the products and/or services are low quality, that they are unneeded, or that they are impossible to sell. We don't buy any of those excuses.

There are thousands of companies that go out of business despite having outstanding products and services.

Why do these companies fail? They do not have a sales force that can sell. You probably have known companies like that, may have worked for a company like that, or may have started a company like that!

It is no longer true that *if you build a better mousetrap, the world will beat a path to your door.* Today, if you build a better mousetrap, it is likely that several other companies will copy it within weeks or months.

You not only have to build a better mousetrap, you need a superior sales force to take over market share.

Some people say that the reason so many companies and salespeople are struggling is that their goods and services are not needed. We do not buy that explanation. Everywhere we look we see need. There are millions of homes that need painting, yards and gardens that need new grass, and millions of cars that need repairs, painting, or replacement. There are millions of businesses and families that need new, faster, more powerful computers and computer networks. We all need better, more delicious and more nutritious food and most of us could benefit from a new wardrobe, hairstyle, or makeover. We need more and better housing. We need to tear down old dilapidated office buildings and replace them with new, beautiful energy-efficient ones. We need newer, safer airplanes. We need better financial products and services. We need more and better professional services. Needs are everywhere. You could undoubtedly add many more items to this list.

The pessimists among us would say that all we need is shelter and some food and water to get by. While technically that may be true, such thinking that "we have all we need," holds back the growth and development of a society. The belief that "we don't need anymore," and "what we have is good enough," cripples the growth of a nation's economy and the growth of its people. We are not promoting mindless consumerism here, but by examining and working to fulfill our needs and wants, we can reduce human suffering, raise living standards, and promote happiness (there are no guarantees!). In the process of working hard to fulfill human needs and wants, millions of jobs have been created and millions more will be created to produce goods and services. However, it still takes great sales professionals to sell those goods and services.

There is much real-life evidence that the need for these products and services exists. We have consulted with more than 100 companies and have worked with and trained more than 10,000 salespeople around the world. In almost every company there are a few salespeople who sell more than all the rest. These individuals are selling the same products or services at the same prices as their fellow sales professionals. They are usually working with similar demographics and more or less equal territories. Yet some of these sales superstars sell millions or tens of millions of dollars worth of a product or service, while other salespeople sell little. In most companies, all salespeople receive the same training and learn the same sales techniques. Given all of these similarities, how are some salespeople able to become sales millionaires and help their companies gain market share, while so many other salespeople struggle just to make their minimum quota?

The success of sales superstars goes beyond having good products and services, knowledge of those products and services, and knowledge of sales techniques.

Sales millionaires literally see the world differently.

Sales millionaires have a different mindset. A mindset you can learn.

The Sales Millionaire's Mindset Placed Under a Microscope

Those of you who have read our earlier books or who have seen us speak at seminars and workshops know that we do a tremendous amount of sales coaching. We have been hired to coach not only struggling salespeople, but also sales income millionaires. A sales income millionaire is a sales superstar who is **not just a millionaire**, but rather, she earns more than $1 million **per year** from selling. Who hires us to coach these Olympians of the sales world? In those cases, we are not hired by sales managers or corporate executives, but by the sales superstars themselves. *Why do they hire us?* They want to get even better. They want to help more people and make more money—even if they just give the money away to charity.

Whether we are coaching a sales novice who is struggling to make quota or a sales income millionaire, we always examine the salesperson's mindset. In working with average salespeople, we ask, "Why are others able to sell more of the same product or service than this individual?" If our client is a sales superstar, we ask, *"What is your mindset when you are breaking sales records?"* We study that mindset, formalize all of its features and install it *permanently* in the sales superstar so that she can call it up and use it every day.

Whenever your sales performance is below
where you know it should be,
examine your mindset.

Don't just look at your product or service for an "explanation." Don't rush to blame a sales slump on price or some other factor outside yourself. Take responsibility. Empower yourself. Is **anyone** else selling more than you are selling given the same products, services, and prices? If so, what is the mindset of that individual? Learn all you can about that person's mindset, and internalize every detail of that mindset.

When you acquire the mindset of a sales millionaire, you will have tremendous energy to sell. You will have **real** enthusiasm, not phony, manufactured enthusiasm. With a powerful sales success mindset, you will love what you do. People will be drawn to you, your products, and your services. You will intuitively be able to persuasively describe all the benefits you, your products, and your services offer.

If you do not have the mindset of a sales superstar, your company can have outstanding products, services, and prices, and you still won't be able to sell very much. If you do not have this powerful mindset, you can read dozens of books on sales techniques and go to seminar after seminar and you will still never achieve the level of success you deserve to enjoy. Once you develop the sales success mindset, you will be well on your way to becoming a sales millionaire or multimillionaire.

Do Not Be Afraid to Be Persuasive

Many salespeople underestimate the difficulty of developing a sales-success mindset. They confuse a mindset with the simplistic positive thinking movement ("Every day, in every way, I am getting better and better."). Perhaps most ominously, they do not understand all the forces that conspire every day to destroy a positive attitude toward selling. "Sales" has become a four-letter word in many business environments today.

In many companies, no one wants to be perceived as a salesperson. We are handed thousands of business cards each year by salespeople who attend our seminars and workshops. Over the years, we have seen a flight away from business cards that contain the words "sales" or "sales representative" or "sales executive." Look at the business cards you receive or that are beamed into your Palm Pilot. You will see sales representatives using titles such as "customer service representative," "account executive," "customer satisfaction representative," "solutions specialist," "customer counselor," or any one of dozens of other vague, misleading, fuzzy, or disingenuous titles.

Recently, we asked a "client services coordinator" why her card did not identify her as a sales professional. She tried to explain that it is now "politically incorrect" to be a salesperson and that "no one wants to be a salesperson." Yet, her company wants her to sell. All she was hired to do was sell! Her business card says nothing about selling, her mindset is that "no one wants to be a salesperson," and she is expected to sell! Is it any wonder that the company that employs her is struggling, that its sales are down by more than 37 percent and that its stock has lost half of its value?

The sales success mindset is based first upon honesty.

Your business card does not have to identify you as a sales professional or a sales executive, but you must be honest with yourself that you are a sales professional. We have found that all sales millionaires know that they are sales professionals. This may seem like an obvious fact, but it is not so obvious today when millions of salespeople are walking around with business cards saying they are something else. Is it any wonder why so many salespeople are confused and suffer from low self-esteem?

The names, titles, and descriptions we give ourselves (and that we allow others to give us) are vitally important. To become a medical doctor, a person has to complete 12 years of schooling with outstanding grades, then apply to a top undergraduate university, work hard for four more years, get the best grades possible, and hope to get into medical school. At medical school, the student has to work harder than ever, compromise her social life, and give up all hope of holding down a job. Once she graduates, she may have to spend several more years doing internships and residencies. After completing this exhausting and arduous path, she will work long hours as a medical doctor to extend lives, improve the quality of her patients' lives, and to save lives.

For all of this studying, hard work, and dedication, many medical doctors used to earn several hundred thousand dollars per year. Nowadays, many doctors earn far less than $100,000 a year. Many well-known factors (HMOs, insurance companies, etc.) have contributed to this precipitous decline in the incomes earned by physicians. One factor that is seldom even mentioned is that, at many health maintenance organizations, medical doctors are no longer called "medical doctors" or "physicians." Instead, they are given titles such as "medical services provider." How can a mere medical services provider deserve an income of $350,000? If you are a mere "account services representative," how much could your services be worth—and how easily could you be replaced? Wouldn't you rather be a vice president of sales?

With pride comes power. In their quest to avoid "being a salesperson" at any cost, many people in sales have let their powers of persuasion atrophy. Others are not even developing skills in this area. After all, if you aren't a "salesperson" why do you need to be persuasive?

These salespeople are forgoing hundreds of thousands or millions of dollars in potential income due to their lack of persuasion skills. Many companies no longer even offer seminars on salesmanship or persuasion at their conventions or workshops. Executives at these firms wonder why their business has declined to the extent that it has. We have three words to share with them: **cause and effect**.

Recently we received a call from a financial consultant at one of the largest brokerage houses in the U.S. The caller was well-educated, intelligent, and offered his clients and prospects a wide range of outstanding financial products and services. However, he only had $3 million in assets under management. Charging the standard 1-percent fee on assets under management, this financial advisor was only earning $30,000 a year! When he told us this, we were appalled. His senior partner, his mentor and advisor, who has been in the business many years, has less than $7 million in assets under management and earns only $70,000 a year! How is this possible? Why are these intelligent, well-educated financial advisors earning so little when the public has such a great need for financial planning?

To put their level of success in perspective, many of the financial planners with whom we work earn $250,000 to more than $1 million a year. A number of them report that it is easy to earn several hundred thousand dollars a year if you know how to sell and market your services.

We asked the financial consultant to tell us how he describes his services to prospective clients. The cause for his lack of success was instantly apparent: he was bland and boring. We are talking plain vanilla. Milquetoast.

Beige. We asked him if he had ever heard a tape recording of the presentation he gave clients and he admitted he hadn't. He also admitted he seldom worked on improving his sales presentation to clients. He had two rationalizations for not working on his presentation: he was too busy "researching the market" and he didn't want to "come off as a salesman" (there's that old bugaboo again).

The Psychology of Sales Professionals

Many articles and books have been written on the psychology of selling and the psychology of consumers. Interestingly, few of them have been written by psychologists! Much ink has been spilled trying to explain why consumers buy a great deal of this product, but not so much of that product, and why they buy from this salesperson, but not from that salesperson. The area of expertise we have developed over the past 20 years focuses on the psychology of sales professionals. Why do otherwise intelligent salespeople and sales managers do the things they do that **limit** their success? What can be done to help salespeople who are struggling or who are in a slump?

There are several key factors that limit the success of many salespeople. Hint: It is usually not lack of product knowledge or laziness.

One of the prime factors limiting the success
of many salespeople is the lack of ability
to persuade another human being to take action.

Millions of salespeople have been brainwashed into believing that sales and persuasion are bad. If this belief system, and its devastating consequences, have affected you and your success, read on. We have a cure.

The Superstar's Mindset Toward Persuasion

Do you want to know how to more persuasively describe the many benefits of the products and services you offer? The first step, and **the most important step**, is to develop a healthy mindset toward persuasion and selling because if you don't, you will never use whatever sales and persuasion techniques you might know.

As mentioned, several thousand books have been written on sales and sales techniques. You probably have a few in your library, but *how often do you read them?* Do you ever use the techniques described? Why not? If you have been told, "You are not a salesperson, you are a client counselor," you have no need to read a sales book.

We act in accordance with the way we see ourselves to be. If your self-image is that you are a 200-pound person, you will always gravitate back toward 200 pounds, no matter how many diets you try. If you balloon up to 230 pounds, you will probably go back down to 200 pounds because that is your controlling self-image. If you drop to 160 pounds, you will probably regain about 40 pounds so that your actual weight matches the weight of your controlling self-image. Medical doctors who specialize in weight loss call this a "set point." If you want to drop down to 160 pounds and stay there, you must change your self-image set point to 160 pounds. You must thoroughly convince yourself that 160 pounds is your natural, normal weight. You must change the pictures you see in your mind's eye so that you always visualize yourself as a 160-pound person and you must change your self-talk. For example, when you are at 160 pounds, you should not say, "That's great! I managed to lose a whole 40 pounds!" Instead, you should say, "I am back at my **normal** weight of 160 pounds. This feels very natural and comfortable."

We always act as we see ourselves. People who see themselves as intelligent do the things that intelligent people do. People who see themselves as athletic do the things that athletic people do. It takes no effort. What takes effort is acting contrary to your self-image—and it usually ends in defeat.

As long as you see yourself as a "customer counselor" or a "client services representative" or a "customer satisfaction specialist," you will not engage in the behaviors sales millionaires engage in.

**If your self-image is that you are not a salesperson,
you will not engage in the sales behaviors
that can make you and your company highly successful.**

Perhaps you see yourself as an "advisor" rather than a salesperson. Maybe you forced yourself at some point to read a book on selling. Today you are probably not using the techniques you learned, or could have learned, from that book. Why not? There is probably a little voice in the back of your head saying, "That's a sales book. That's bad. I don't need it. I want to be an advisor, not a salesperson." Due to the brainwashing of millions of salespeople that "selling is bad," some do not read sales books, some don't go to sales seminars, or if they do, they don't internalize and use the sales techniques and strategies they should have learned.

Looking for the Root Causes

Psychologists are trained to look for the root cause, or etiology, of a problem. When you determine the true cause of a problem, whether it is medical, psychological, or performance related, you can arrive at a true and lasting solution. If you do not know the root cause of a problem, you will get tricked into trying every fad cure that comes along.

Is knowledge of sales and persuasion techniques inherently bad? Let's get beyond the superficial blather you hear at motivational seminars and take a deeper look. Misused, knowledge of sales and persuasion **can** be harmful. No doubt about it. Sales techniques can be misused. We will not argue that point. Dr. Moine has worked as an expert witness in a $140 million sales practices case that was settled for more than $40 million. We have told defense lawyers that we will never defend salespeople who use their powers of persuasion unethically. Do you engage in those unethical sales practices? We didn't think so.

Developing and using your powers of persuasion to sell outstanding products and services that people truly need is a highly virtuous act. Doing so not only helps strengthen American families and businesses, *it helps strengthen our national economy*. In **persuasively** describing to customers and clients what you do and the benefits your products and services offer, you lay the groundwork for a mutually beneficial long-term relationship.

Without persuasion and without sales, our economy will not advance. You should be proud of yourself if you can persuasively describe the benefits of your products and services. We have found that in business there is no one a chief executive or company president respects more than a top sales professional. Why? A company president knows that his or her company can develop the best products and services in the world, but if you don't have highly skilled sales professionals to make these products and services come alive in the minds of customers, the company could flounder, or even fail.

We could have started this book with listings and descriptions of several dozen powerful sales techniques, but it would not do many readers any good. Why not? Because deep down inside, many of you have a mindset that prevents you from being persuasive.

Some of you have a little voice inside your head that acts as a governor on your sales performance. Just when you are moving to a higher level of performance, the governor kicks in and shifts you back down. The little voice inside your head says, "Don't be a salesperson," and you shift back into describing product features, you talk about the weather or sports or do almost anything but engage in effective sales dialogue. Congratulations! You have avoided being a salesperson, you avoided selling any products or services—and you avoided helping someone who really needed your help. Is this something to be proud of?

The cure for what ails you and your sales is that you must first reprogram your attitude toward sales and persuasion. You must develop a healthy attitude and respect for persuasion skills. It sounds easier than it is. Once you have a healthy attitude toward persuasion, you will actually find it fun to work on perfecting your sales skills. Of course, you will also make a great deal more money and will have the opportunity to work with many more people who will want to become your customers or clients for life.

Without a healthy attitude toward sales, you will never develop the skills you need to become a sales millionaire. You will never do the work you need to do in order to perfect your sales scripts and your presentations. It is as simple and profound as that. We find it ironic that some of the most popular speakers on the business circuit today are those who exhort most strongly, "Don't be a salesperson, be a problem solver" (as if salespeople don't solve problems!). Or they will proclaim, "Don't be a salesperson, be an advisor" (as if salespeople have not been advisors all along). The irony is that these speakers, some who are paid $20,000 or more per speech, are themselves some of the biggest salespeople of all! They heavily plug their new books on how to not be a salesperson. They plug their $2,000 per person seminars on how not to be a salesperson. They sell their expensive audiotape, videotape, and CD programs on how not to be a salesperson. They are engaged in nonstop selling as they tell you not to be a salesperson—and millions of salespeople eat this stuff up. Then the participants at these programs wonder why their sales don't increase.

Let us look at the root cause of this problem. The truth is that many of these "anti-sales" programs do teach sales skills. They simply relabel the sales skills as "listening skills," "probing skills," or "conversational skills." Closing skills are relabeled as "agreement skills." We don't wish to be overly critical of these programs. While they do teach some sales skills, the damage that is done to the salesperson's self-image overshadows the benefit of the training. It is essentially dishonest and counterproductive to tell a salesperson, "Don't be a salesperson," and then expect that person to sell with energy, commitment, and enthusiasm. There is absolutely nothing wrong with being a sales professional. In fact, you should be proud of being a sales professional.

Pride in your profession is one of the cornerstones of greatness. Have you ever known a great miler who was ashamed to run the mile? Do you think great mountain climbers are told, "You are not mountain climbers"? Do you think that undefeated super-attorney Gerry Spence teaches lawyers that they should not be lawyers? Why, then, should millions of salespeople be told, "Don't be a salesperson"?

Whether you are a doctor, a lawyer, a financial advisor, an architect, a business executive, a politician, or a religious leader, you can benefit from sales skills, and you should be proud of your ability to persuade others. The point is that we all need to know how to sell and be persuasive. One of the greatest gifts you can give your children or your employees is the ability to persuade.

How to Sell Yourself on Selling

Given all the forces in society telling us that selling and salespeople are bad, how can you sell yourself on selling and develop a healthy mindset so that you can be a true sales professional and become a sales millionaire?

Start by selling yourself on your company's products and services. No company always has the best products and services at the lowest, rock-bottom prices. If they did, why would they need you? However, you **must** believe that your company does have a number of outstanding products and services that are being offered at a fair price. If you do not truly believe in the products and services your company offers, you will be conflicted in your sales efforts and will never be able to give 100 percent of yourself to selling. Your prospects and customers will sense your inner conflict and they will not buy much from you. Therefore, if you do not believe in the products and services your company offers, get a job with a company where you can get completely behind their offerings.

We have found that many sales millionaires have a **unique mindset** about what they offer. The way they see it is that they have a cure for a life-threatening illness and their prospects and customers have this illness. That is the way we feel about the sales training and sales consulting we offer. Our nation is suffering because businesses cannot sell the goods and services that are being produced. Companies are losing hundreds of billions of dollars each year because sales are not completed. We have a cure for this crippling business problem. With this kind of a mindset, it is easy to have genuine enthusiasm.

Place a high value on what you offer. *If you don't value it highly, how can anyone else?*

Remember, you have a cure for a life-threatening illness.

You have a right to be somewhat persuasive in promoting it. If you aren't persuasive, people won't believe you and won't take the medicine. If you aren't very persuasive, not many people will do business with you—no matter what you are offering.

Believing in the Value YOU
Bring to the Table

Some readers will say, "I don't have a cure for a life-threatening illness. I am just selling widgets." Don't be discouraged! There are people selling widgets who make hundreds of thousands of dollars each year, who have lots of loyal customers, a great family life, and who are able to retire as millionaires at an early age. But let's take a closer look at the "just selling widgets" mindset. First of all, from where did this mindset come? Remember that you were not born with it!

A number of years ago, we were consulting for a large steel company. A senior executive vice president actually told us that the sheet steel, cold pressed steel, rolled steel, and other forms of steel his company made were indistinguishable from the products of his competitors. He said, "They are all just commodities and everyone buys based on price." His attitude created a mindset in the company's salespeople that they were just selling the same steel as everyone else.

We interviewed and studied some of the top salespeople at this steel company. There actually were salespeople who were selling many times more than the average salesperson—and they had a vastly different mindset than the company executives and the average salespeople. Once we determined exactly how the top people sold as much as they did, we built a formal model of their expertise and helped the average salespeople acquire it.

We helped the other salespeople in this steel company develop a mindset that **they** were the value added. Through skillful scheduling, just-in-time delivery, financing options, and quality guarantees, they helped their customers solve their problems. It may sound crazy, but we also encouraged the salespeople to go bowling, golfing, fishing, and hunting with their customers. We encouraged them to live in the same neighborhoods as their customers, to go to the same PTA meetings and Kiwanis Club and Rotary Club meetings, and to go to church or temple with their customers. These are some of the keys to establishing long-term clients in the steel business. These are some of the secrets to bonding with customers in that industry. When there is a temporary price change in steel prices, your customers will stay with you.

Through this type of training and a change in the mindset of the salespeople (that **they** were the value added), we were able to help this company increase its sales and profits in a very challenging industry environment.

We do a tremendous amount of sales training and coaching in the financial services industries. We actually had the president of a major brokerage firm tell us, "Nowadays, all firms offer just about the same products and services at more or less equivalent prices." He is no longer president of that major brokerage firm.

Granted, in the brokerage industry, everyone has about the same products and everyone charges fairly similar prices and fees. A few years ago, Merrill Lynch and Charles Schwab were considered polar opposites. Merrill Lynch had hundreds of analysts on staff and offered a great deal of stock market research to its clients. Trades were done through live stockbrokers and were relatively expensive. Charles Schwab offered relatively little research and trades were done over the phone or via the Internet at very low fees. Today, both firms offer lots of research; trades via live brokers, telephone or over the Internet; and a similar wide range of product offerings.

If you are a stockbroker or financial planner, how can you get excited and passionate about what you are offering? If you can find the most appropriate and powerful products and services for a young family, if you can help them diversify their holdings, reduce risk, enhance returns, lower their taxes, avoid hidden fees, pay off the mortgage early, fund the kid's college education, and retire early and rich over 25 years, you can turn a $100,000 net worth family into a $5 million net worth family.

Through all of these solutions combined with a second-to-die life insurance policy and a Stretch IRA, some of our financial advisor clients have been able to turn $1 million net worth families into $20 million net worth families. How can you not get excited and passionate about that? How can you not be excited to sell that? It does not matter that almost all financial planners and stockbrokers now have access to the same products and services at about the same prices? YOU make the difference. YOU and your solutions are the all-important value-added, and for that your clients will happily pay you a great deal of money over time.

If a financial advisor can help families and individuals accomplish their goals, *they can accomplish miracles*. However, as great as these products, services, and solutions are, *people still must be sold on them*. Due to the unprecedented $6 trillion loss in the stock markets that has devastated the portfolios of millions of Americans, investor trust is hard to come by. Ironically, there has never been a greater need for sophisticated financial planning advice.

Those financial advisors who can proudly and persuasively describe the benefits they provide will make fortunes for themselves and their clients. We have worked with and coached a number of financial advisors who earn between $500,000 and more than $2 million a year from offering **the same** products and services at about **the same** prices and commissions as other advisors. The all-important difference is that they have a mindset that **empowers** them to more persuasively describe these benefits.

The same is true for every industry and profession in the U.S. If you have a mindset that enables you to confidently and persuasively describe the benefits you, your products, and services provide, you have a major advantage over all others in your field.

At our seminars, salespeople will ask us to recommend the perfect sales field or the world's greatest sales specialization. These are salespeople who are looking for the "low hanging fruit," the easiest sales, and the lay-downs. We have worked with salespeople who earn hundreds of thousands or more than one million dollars a year selling homes, advertising, automobiles, mortgages, annuities, office buildings, apartments, stocks and bonds, computers, software, financial planning, pension management services, military equipment, electrical components, legal services, medical equipment, consulting services, insurance, jewelry, commodities, personal jets, weapon systems to the military, satellite systems, and dozens of other products and services. There is no one perfect or "easy" field of sales specialization.

In every sales specialization, there are professionals who earn hundreds of thousands of dollars or more per year and there are those who are starving trying to sell the same products and services at about the same prices. Often, the difference between sales superstars and average salespeople does not come down to good looks, better education, more product knowledge, or even knowledge of more sales techniques. It comes down to mind-set. Those who are proud of what they sell, what they offer, and what they do are vastly more successful than all others in their industry. We would like you to join this elite and, in fact, we would like to broaden this elite.

Often, when a salesperson in a seminar asks us, "What is the perfect sales career or the perfect sales area in which to specialize?" we quote the song lyric, "Love the one you're with." We are not being flippant and we are not saying this simply to make your sales manager happy.

There is probably a powerful reason you are in the sales area in which you now specialize.

Think about it. Do you have a great knowledge of these products or services? Are any of these products related to a hobby, an avocation, a passion, or a lifelong interest? **Why** do you want to change sales fields? Remember that in **every** sales field, there are professionals who make a great deal of money and who have hundreds or thousands of happy and grateful customers and clients. Why not become one of the **top producers** *in your current sales specialization*? All it may take is a change in your mindset.

When you change your mindset, including how you see yourself, your profession, your company, and your products and services, you change your life. With a change in your mindset, your prospects, clients, and customers could see you as a trusted advisor or a savior. A change in your mindset may be the catalyst that enables everything else in your life to work properly. A change in your mindset may be the most critical ingredient in your ability to earn hundreds of thousands of dollars per year—or more.

With a sales superstar's mindset toward your company, products, services, solutions, and toward **yourself**, you may find you will achieve and enjoy all the success you desire right now in your current sales specialization. With this sales millionaire's success mindset, your clients and prospects will look at you differently. They will see you as a self-confident problem-solving professional.

But first you must be **proud** to sell the products, services, and solutions you and your company offer. And you must be **persuasive**. As great as your company's products and services are, they will not sell themselves. You must fully believe in yourself, in your company, in your products and services and in the value of selling. If not, why are you in this field—and why are you working for the company that employs you? If you do not believe in the core of your being in the value of your products and services, how can you possibly sell anyone else?

The Truth About the Process of Selling

Selling is a **process** between human beings, and it is ever-changing. Sales millionaires are excited about this fact. Because selling is an ever-changing process, you almost always have a second, third, or fourth chance to visit with the prospect again in order to close the sale.

As sales psychologists, we know that **persuasion is a transfer of conviction**. When one human being (the prospect) encounters another human being (the salesperson), the most convinced person is usually the

persuader. The less convinced person is usually the **persuadee**. How do most of these encounters end up for you?

When you first meet with a prospect, who is the most convinced person? If the prospect's conviction of, "I am not interested," is stronger than your conviction of, "I have an effective solution for you and your company," the prospect will not become your client. *You will both lose.* She will never get the needed solutions and you will not earn the commission or fee you deserve.

> Why doesn't every qualified prospect do business with you?
>
> Do they think your prices or fees are too high?
>
> Who is the most convinced?
>
> Who is the persuader and who is the persuadee?
>
> Do they think another company offers better products or better solutions?
>
> Who is the most convinced in their beliefs?
>
> Do they think you don't offer enough benefits or a good enough guarantee?

In our sales coaching work, we ask our clients to describe the benefits of the products, solutions, and services they offer. We usually do this by going over one or two initial prospect meetings they have recently conducted. Frequently, we go over sales calls in which the prospect did not become a customer or client. We go over **everything** the sales professional said and everything the prospect said. As we show the sales professional exactly how to turn these prospects into customers or clients (while at the same time being totally honest), we also deeply sell the sales professional on the benefits of his or her products and/or services.

We have found this to be the most powerful method of all in helping sales professionals build the mindset of a sales millionaire. In going over everything the sales professional says and does, her mindset becomes apparent. Rationalizations and excuses are revealed and can be reprogrammed. Asking the question, "Why doesn't everyone buy from you?"

exposes both the strengths and weaknesses of products and services and the inner workings of the salesperson's mindset.

Skill-Building Exercise

Take out a piece of paper and write down every reason why a prospect may not buy from you. Be totally honest with yourself as no one will see this except you (the ultimate beneficiary!). In addition to listing every weakness of your product or service, including price and delivery issues, honestly list any personal weaknesses or limitations you may have. Now, ask yourself: *How much of this is absolutely, totally true, and how much of this may be colored by my personal perceptions and my mindset?*

As the second step in this exercise, ask yourself, "How is it possible for some people at my company (or in my industry) to sell more than me?" Write down every answer and reason you can think of. Pay close attention to ways that people selling the **same** products or **same** services at the **same** price to the **same** group of customers can sell more than you. Because you cannot blame or excuse such performance differences on product, service, or price differentials, you will clearly see that the salesperson's mindset (and resulting behaviors) make most of the difference.

Now, as a final step in this exercise, do your best to identify the components of the sales superstar's mindset that enable her to sell more than you. How does this sales champion look at herself, her products, her services, and her prospects? Which components of this mindset can you adopt? Granted, this exercise is a lot of work. In fact, it may entail more analysis than many salespeople have ever engaged in when thinking about their sales careers. However, the results can justify all the hard work. From completing this exercise and doing all of the analysis, we have seen salespeople develop insights, a new mindset, and new behaviors that have led to their making tens of thousands to hundreds of thousands of dollars in extra income each year.

If you are a sales manager, do this exercise with your people. You can do it either as a group exercise or, even better, on an individual level with your people. In working with your people on an individual level, you will find they are more honest and revealing when there is more privacy. Collectively, you may be able to help your salespeople sell millions to tens of millions of dollars in additional products and services from taking them through this exercise.

The previous exercise is not just a theory to us. We know it is effective because we have used it with several hundred of our coaching clients to help them break out of sales slumps and set new sales records. We have taught it to sales managers who have used it to help their salespeople achieve record profits. Instead of teaching theories of persuasion or going over lists of sales techniques, a much better use of training and coaching time is to use actual prospects, customers, and clients in detailed, real-life analysis and teaching. Combining powerful persuasion skills with a deep conviction in the value of the salesperson's products and services gives the sales professional tremendous self-confidence and empowers him or her to convert the vast majority of prospects into customers and clients.

The Power of Invisible Selling

Why don't more salespeople study and use powerful persuasion techniques? Many are crippled by the fear of "looking like a salesperson." A solution that we have developed and that we teach in our seminars is what we call "Invisible Selling." You will find examples of it throughout this book and especially in the chapters on sales scripting and sales coaching.

The irony is that to build this type of deep relationship, you must use certain forms of persuasion! The irony is that to master Invisible Selling, you must believe in the power and the value of selling! You can't just "shoot from the hip" or "shoot from the lip." You can't just hope that you will "think of something to say" and that it will be "good enough." Those are the words of the rank amateur who wonders why he or she is not more successful.

There are many myths about persuasion and selling that may be hampering your success as a sales professional. Unfortunately, many of these myths are perpetuated by seminar leaders and public speakers who make the rounds on the lecture circuit. Whenever you hear a speaker tell you, "Don't be a salesperson, be a _____," a warning light should go on in your mind. What you are about to hear, no matter how "motivational," will contain slams against salespeople and may contain false beliefs that could hamper your ability to engage in effective sales behaviors in the future.

Examine any seminar or workshop you attend to determine if you are being inadvertently programmed with any of these career killing mindsets:

Salespeople are manipulators.

Salespeople are product pushers.

Selling is taking advantage of people.

Selling is lying.

Salespeople are dishonest.

Salespeople should not be trusted.

None of these are true. You don't need to be told that you should become "something better than a salesperson." Salespeople contribute mightily to our country. You need to be proud of being a sales professional and should be proud of your persuasion skills.

Persuasion has brought many benefits to mankind and has greatly sped up the evolution of modern societies. All great world religions were founded by human beings who were persuasive. All great military leaders are persuasive. At one point, people had to be persuaded to bathe more frequently. Thank goodness we had persuasive people to accomplish that task! Later, we had to be persuaded about the benefits of school and lengthy education. We had to be persuaded about the benefits of the scientific method. Our ancestors had to be persuaded about the benefits of the use of money, then of paper money, and then of a common currency. We had to be persuaded of the benefits of the telephone, the automobile, and the computer. Where would our society be today if we didn't have persuasive people to motivate us to change and grow?

As a persuasion professional, you are the heir of a distinguished lineage of people who have changed the course of human history. As a persuasion professional, you should be proud of your family tree composed of ancestors who created and popularized the world's great religions, motivated citizens to defend freedom and win wars, who promoted education and scientific advancement, and who contributed to the adoption of every major innovation and progressive development in our existence.

Our mindsets are revealed in everything we do and everything we say. To gain greater insight into your mindset, tape-record yourself making a presentation to a prospect. When you listen to the tape, you might be appalled at what you hear. That is perfectly fine. You have taken the first step (and the most important step) in growing and improving: you have learned what you need to improve! Write down what you say to prospects and clients. In the next chapter, you will learn how to rewrite it, dramatically improve it, practice it, and focus on the many benefits you, your products, and your services offer. You will learn how to make the benefits of whatever you sell come alive for the prospect.

Listen to the tape again and ask yourself how your mindset is affecting your self-confidence and your enthusiasm (enthusiasm is contagious!). Sales millionaires cultivate a mindset that empowers them to be totally honest, passionate, and sincere. Using the techniques you'll learn in the next few chapters, you will be able to develop a new, improved, and vastly more persuasive presentation and almost all of your prospects will be excited about becoming customers or clients.

The mindset of the sales millionaire requires that he or she continue working on and improving his or her sales presentation over time.

**Sales millionaires know that working on one's
presentation is a process,
not a one-time event.**

If you need help, ask a sales superstar within your company or industry, or your sales manager or a professional coach to assist you. Why should you do all of this work on your presentation and your mindset? *Because nothing else is going to help you become a sales millionaire or multimillionaire.*

It is the processes of continuing to examine one's mindset and one's belief systems and continuing to improve the work you do that can turn a $75,000 per year average salesperson into a $500,000 or more per year superstar. In this book, we will occasionally mention money and how much money you can make from being more persuasive. As psychologists, we know there are many things in life more important than money. We use it only as a point of reference and a way of keeping score. Just as many of us like to know the scores from a basketball game, or what Tiger Woods hit at Pebble Beach, or how a gymnast scored at the Olympics, or how much money a blockbuster movie grossed over the weekend, so do many people in sales like to look at the numbers they can put on the scorecard and in their bank balances.

In the process of developing the mindset of a sales millionaire, you will also find that you create many new customers, clients, and friends for life. In this chapter, we have introduced you to a few of the most powerful core mindsets of sales champions. In future chapters, we will show you how sales superstars look at lead generation, selling to so-called "difficult" customers, how they develop the most powerful persuasive presentations in their industry, and how they use the media to sell for them. You will learn not only the techniques and strategies they use, but also the mindsets they hold in each of these areas. Developing the mindsets of sales millionaires will help you become more persuasive and powerful throughout your life. In addition to gaining a rock solid self-confidence, you will find selling much less stressful because you will be focused on helping your prospects, customers, and clients solve problems. Developing the mindset of sales millionaires is a process that is truly win-win for you, your company, your family, and your customers and clients.

2

The Best Ways of Dealing With Concerns, Objections, and Resistances

All prospects, customers, and clients have concerns and objections. Every single one of them. Even the ones who say they will love you forever and will do business with you forever, no matter what. If you think your prospects, customers, and clients do not have objections and concerns, you are deceiving yourself and this deception does neither you nor them any good.

Think about any major customer or client you **lost** over the past few years. Why did you lose them? He had a question, concern, or objection you did not adequately address. In losing that customer or client, you may have lost thousands or tens of thousands of dollars a year in income, **and** the opportunity to help that person.

The concerns and objections of your prospects, customers, and clients may either be stated (overt) or unstated (covert), but they are *always* present. To deny this fact is to deny reality. Even the customer or client who you believe totally loves you, who will be with you forever, has concerns, un-answered questions, and objections about how things are going. The only question is:

How aware are you of these issues your prospects, customers, and clients are thinking about?

Recently, one of our coaching clients called us with a tone of panic in his voice. We have helped this person become a legend in his field. This sales superstar was shocked to learn that one of his top clients was moving her business to another firm. The client had been with him for a little more than 10 years. He thought that this client loved him and that he would have her business forever.

What happened? The client had some concerns he had not answered, or had not answered adequately. Compounding the problem and the challenge, his client did not voice her concerns. She wanted him to, in a sense, "read her mind." Unfortunately, the sales professional called her and said some things he should not have said. The client became defensive and ended the conversation abruptly. The sales professional was despondent because he was losing about $50,000 a year in income and also felt he was losing someone he had considered a friend.

When the sales professional called us, he said it would be "impossible" to win her back as a client. He said he could not match his competitor's lower fees and the competitor had somewhat different products. The first thing we worked on in our coaching session was changing the salesperson's mindset. If you believe something is impossible, it surely will be. The sales-person was skeptical about the power of sales scripting, but we then coached him on some changes in the words he could use to effectively win her back.

The sales pro did **not** change his products, services, or fees. We coached him on how to change *the words he used* to describe his products, services, and fees—and it made all the difference in the world. We then spent one hour with him the following day role-playing, rehearsing, and practicing the important meeting with his ex-client. From one hour of analysis and scripting and another hour of coaching and rehearsal, he was able to save a client that yielded him more than $50,000 a year in income. When he saw how a change in the words used (and the way you say those words) can turn an ex-client into a current mega-client, *he became a believer in the power of words.*

As this salesperson learned, **all** customers, clients, and prospects have concerns and objections—even the ones who claim they will be loyal to you forever. Assuming you have good (or great) products, services, and prices, if you know how to skillfully deal with these concerns, objections, and stalls, you will be able to create clients for life. This is a recipe for success decade after decade.

In this chapter, we will share with you some of the most powerful ways of dealing with prospect and customer objections, concerns, and resistances. You will learn that one of the most powerful strategies of all is to sometimes deal with objections or concerns *even before they are raised* by the prospect, customer, or client.

To create clients for life, you must know the most effective ways of dealing with the questions, concerns, and objections of your prospects and clients, whether **stated** or **unstated**. Remember, all of your clients and prospects have objections and concerns. Every single one of them.

The Incredible Power of Words

Just how powerful are words? We have known sales superstars working from their wheelchairs who earn hundreds of thousands of dollars per year from the power of their words. We have known salespeople who are more than 80 years old who make a huge amount of money from the power of their words.

Your words can set you free. The words you use can **guarantee** you a tremendous lifelong income that makes stock market returns look like a bad joke. Early in his career, Dr. Moine had the opportunity to work with Ben Feldman, the world's most successful life insurance salesman. Ben was a short, heavy-set man who spoke with a lisp. He lived in the small town of East Liverpool, Ohio. With all of these supposed limitations that would discourage or cripple most other salespeople, how was Ben Feldman able to outsell more than 900,000 life insurance agents from around the world? With the power of his words.

To put his accomplishments in perspective, Ben Feldman was able to outsell nearly 1 million other life insurance agents not just one year or two or three—but for decades. Decade after decade this short, heavy-set man with a lisp outsold every other insurance agent in the world. His success enabled him to give millions of dollars to charity. While he offered outstanding products and solutions at a great price, the **real secret** of Ben Feldman's success was in the words he used.

What is the best way of dealing with customer, client, and prospect objections and concerns? With words. With organized, persuasive words.

We know that this may seem obvious, but *it is not as easy as it seems.* **What** do you say? **How** do you say it? Therein rests one of the major keys to your success (or lack of success) as a sales professional.

Your products are what they are. Your service is what it is. Your prices are what they are. You cannot change any of those instantly. Maybe you cannot change them at all (if you work for a large company). What you can change **instantly** is what you say to your prospects and clients. And as you will see, **what** you say, and **how** you say it can make all the difference in the world.

Take out a Post-it note and write this down: *"My words can make me rich."* Place that piece of paper in your wallet or in your daytimer or on the back of your Palm Pilot. Look at it 10 times a day and repeat this truth as a mantra: "My words can make me rich."

Hemingway knew this. Steinbeck knew it. Stephen King knows it. John Grisham knows it. You need to know it. Your words can make you rich. Just as much as Hemingway, Steinbeck, King, and Grisham, **you are a word merchant**.

The great Oprah Winfrey knows it. Johnny Carson, Jay Leno, and David Letterman know it. Howard Stern and Rush Limbaugh know it. Each makes far more than $10 million each year. Rush's latest contract is for more than $250 million and Oprah now has a net worth of more than $900 million. They are all word merchants, just as you are.

Many of the highest paid people in our society are word merchants. In addition to the above, think of Dan Rather, Bryant Gumbel, Jane Pauley, Peter Jennings, Robin Williams, Barbara Walters, Bill O'Reilly, Jim Cramer, Dennis Miller, super-attorneys Gerry Spence, Johnny Cochran, and Gloria Allred. All of them, in so many diverse fields, have made their fortunes through the clout of words. As a sales professional, you are a member of this elite group that has the ability to influence and change human behavior through the power of words.

You can offer **exactly** the same products and services as another person in your company or in your field, but that other person could be *10 times more successful* than you are. *How is this possible?* He has better words to describe those products and services. You might have exactly the same prices as another sales professional within your company but he might be seven times more successful than you. Why? He uses better, more persuasive, more powerful, more impactive, more life-changing, more motivational words. Your words can make you rich—*if you have the right words*.

Do Not Be Intimidated by the Power of Words

Please do not misunderstand us. Do not think that because we have Ph.D.s that we are trying to be smart, proper, or precise. Our goals are: to help you sell more, to help you make more money, and to assist you in helping more prospects, customers, and clients. When we refer to the power of words, we are **not** referring to grammar (you can exhale now). We are not referring to spelling. We are not referring to syntax (whatever that is). We are definitely **not** referring to punctuation.

When we refer to the power of words, we are referring to the power of human communication. To the power of one honest, helpful human being looking into the eyes of another human being and explaining, in the most powerful, persuasive words possible, how you can help them solve a problem and/or enjoy a benefit. This has almost nothing to do with grammar, syntax, spelling, or punctuation. It has to do with moving people, with motivating people to take action, and with bonding with people.

Let us be direct:
If you are not a highly successful salesperson, it is most
likely because your words are not good enough.

You may need to reread that sentence several times before its full impact sinks in. Your products and services are probably good enough. We doubt that you are trying to sell bad products or low quality services. Your prices are probably within the ballpark: not too high and not too low. Remember that there are people who will gladly pay $4 for a small plastic bottle of water, who will fork over $300,000 for a car that gets them from point A to point B, or who will hand over $1 million for some shiny jewelry to hang around their neck. Price is not an obstacle if you can convince someone your product or service has "value." People are not rejecting you because of your products, services, or prices. Why, then, are they not becoming your customers and clients? They are rejecting you because your words are inferior. Forgive us for speaking the truth directly, but we must.

Your words may be weak, nonpersuasive, or boring at times; at other points, your presentation may be fantastic.

However, it is the weak points that turn prospects off and it is the weak points they remember.

It is the weak points in your presentation that prevent your prospects from becoming your customers and your clients.

A few years ago, we were hired by someone who is a genius. He wasn't just smart and hard-working, he was a certifiable genius. You may have known someone like this. You may be someone like this. This man was (and is) a giant in his field.

Unfortunately, he was barely able to make a living because he could not effectively communicate the benefits of his research and his services. His services were outstanding, but his words were not good enough. He had invested years of his life in research and perfecting his services when he would be been better off (and his clients would have been better off) if he had spent a little more time and energy on developing an effective presentation.

Let's face the truth. If you're not rich it is because your words are not rich. What else could it be? Are you offering low quality products or worthless services? No. (If you are, you should work for another company). Are you lazy? No. Are you uncaring toward your customers and clients? No. Then why don't you have more customers and clients? The words you use to describe your outstanding products and services are not persuasive enough.

Change your words and you can dramatically improve your business. Change your words and you can double or triple the amount of business you get. Keep offering the same high quality products and services you have always offered, but use higher quality words.

Change your words and you will change your life.

The Power of Organized Words

We have conducted a number of seminars for salespeople and professionals on the subject of psycholinguistics. As far as we know, we are the only psychologists in the U.S. teaching salespeople how to use psycholinguistics to communicate more effectively. We often start a seminar by asking the intriguing question, *"How many of you use scripts?"*

Out of an audience of 200 or 300 salespeople and sales managers, maybe five or six will raise their hands. The honest ones. The aware ones. Dr. Moine recently did a seminar for 47 financial planners and only one woman admitted she used scripts. It just so happened she was the most successful financial advisor in the room. Random chance? We don't think so. In fact, we know that her success was due to the high quality scripts (words) she used.

Then Dr. Moine shocked the rest of the audience by telling them, "**All** of you use scripts. Every single one of you. Your scripts are either **written down** and practiced or they are **unwritten**, but you **all** use scripts."

Then Dr. Moine added, "The only question is: How **good** are your scripts? How good are the organized words you use?" Some audience members stared in stunned disbelief, daring Donald to prove his hypothesis. It was easy for him to do so because he has science on his side. He did not present opinions. He presented scientific facts and at the conclusion of this seminar, he received a standing ovation. The following are strategies Dr. Moine presented at the seminar.

Linguistic scientists define a script as a collection of organized words. It is as simple and as profound as that. If you think before you talk, you are using a script. Because you are selecting and organizing words before you say them, you are using a script (an organized collection of words). The only question is:

How good is your script?

The problem is that many salespeople do a poor or merely adequate job of selecting and organizing the words they use, and that is why they only achieve ordinary results.

**Sales millionaires recommend the same products
and services you recommend,
but they use superior words.**

Logically, the only alternative to scripting (the use of organized words) is to use unorganized words. Linguists call the use of random, unorganized words **glossalalia**, or **word salad**. Have you ever heard yourself on audiotape? Have you ever wondered, "**Why** did I say that?" In those instances, you were speaking in glossalalia. When you speak in glossalalia, you miss sales and do not achieve the income you deserve to earn. High quality sales scripting, along with knowing how to say those words, empowers all of your presentations and can help you close significantly more sales.

You are already, consciously or subconsciously, selecting and organizing the words you use with prospects, customers, and clients. The problem is that the words you select and use are not nearly as effective as they need to be. You will now learn how to solve that problem and dramatically improve the quality of all of your sales communications.

Real-Life Examples

People love real-life examples. Even that most serious business newspaper, *The Wall Street Journal*, opens many of its articles with real-life stories. Why? They get people to read the article. Even if you are only skimming the front page stories at a newsstand, the dramatic real-life stories mentioned in the first few paragraphs of an article will pull you in and will make you buy the newspaper. *The Wall Street Journal* knows how to sell newspapers.

Let us share a few real-life stories about scripting with you. Did you call your spouse, boyfriend, or girlfriend today? What did you say to him or her? *The words you used determined the response you received.* Your words always have a significant impact on the person who hears them—whether you realize it or not.

At a recent seminar we conducted, we asked the audience members, "Did you call a significant other last night?" Almost everyone said they had. Some had called the person they were married to, or a boyfriend, a girlfriend, or a child. We then asked, upon calling your spouse, boyfriend, girlfriend, did you say, "What did you do today?" "Did you take out the trash?" "Did you feed the dog?" "Did you clean the cat box?" "Did you wash my car?" "Did you mow the lawn?" "Did you do the laundry?"

The audience laughed and it was a chuckle of recognition. We then asked, "What was the response you got?" Some audience members said their spouse seemed bothered by their questions. One man said his wife seemed resentful that he got to go to a nice resort location for a seminar while she had to stay home and feed the dog, take out the trash, and do the laundry (that is what he talked about in his phone conversation—that was his script with her).

We then posed the question: "What if, instead of the previous statements, you had said, 'Honey, I am attending a really great seminar with some smart and funny speakers. I am learning so many powerful communication techniques. When I get home, I am really going to increase my sales. I am going to make a lot of money and I am going to help a bunch of new customers. And in about one month, I'd like to take you on a trip for about a week or 10 days. Hawaii. Paris. San Francisco. Hong Kong. You name it. I love you so much. I miss you so much.'"

Then we asked, "If you had used the above words (scripts), would you have received a different response?" The audience members roared, laughed, and nodded their heads in agreement. One man said that if he spoke to his wife like (using the words we suggested) that she would cry tears of joy. Of course. You see, your words (your scripts) don't just determine what you get in sales—*your words determine what you get in life.* Your words (your scripts) determine not only how successful your business will be, they also determine how happy you will be in your marriage, in your relationship with your children, and in your life.

High quality words help create both high quality, very successful sales and a high quality, happy life.

Why Salespeople Deny They Use Scripts

In our seminars and workshops, we like to involve the audience members rather than lecture them, as so many other speakers do. If a workshop participant says, "I don't use scripts," we ask why. It usually comes down to a negative attitude toward scripts. A salesperson might say, "Scripts don't work," or "It is too hard to come up with a good script." We feel sorry for these salespeople because we know that they will never make a great deal of money until they change both their negative attitude and their scripts.

Imagine trying to teach dieting and exercise to a person who is absolutely convinced that dieting and exercise do not help a person lose weight (despite all the evidence to the contrary). It would be quite a challenge to help this person lose weight, but you still must teach the power of dieting and exercise because you know them to be true. In addition, if you can motivate this person to try a better diet and get more exercise, you can greatly help him. We feel the same away about sales scripting. Through our teaching and coaching in the area of sales scripting, we have been able to transform some struggling salespeople into sales millionaires.

**The bottom line is that a salesperson will not use
powerful scripting techniques as long as he or she has
negative attitudes towards scripting.**

In this chapter we will share the most important attitudes and mindsets that sales millionaires have toward working on **what they say** to clients. We will also share some of the most powerful scripting techniques we know and use.

Why, then, do some salespeople have a negative attitude toward scripts, and what can be done to change that attitude? At a recent seminar, one of the participants in the audience told the group that she disliked scripts because "bad salespeople use scripts." She was surprised when we agreed with her. Everyone, at one time or another, has been called during dinner by someone selling long-distance phone services. These salespeople don't listen, they use bad scripts, and they don't know how to deliver their scripts. In short, they do everything you do **not** do.

Please, do not confuse what you do with what the worst performers in the world do. Remember that all sales superstars use scripts (organized collections of words). If you ever had the opportunity to hear Ben Feldman, the world's greatest life insurance salesman, interact with clients, you would never recognize what he said as a "script." Like all great salespeople, his words sounded real, genuine, heartfelt, and totally sincere. When Ben spoke to a prospect, he or she might think it was the first time Ben ever spoke those particular words of wisdom. The prospect had no idea that Ben Feldman had analyzed, practiced, and perfected his scripts for hundreds of hours over the years. It was no accident that Ben Feldman earned millions of dollars per year and, for several decades, outsold every other insurance salesman in the world. If you were selling insurance, you were probably offering the same products and services that Ben Feldman offered. The only difference? Ben Feldman used better words.

The fact that some people mangle their scripts and misuse them should not dissuade you from practicing and perfecting your scripts. Some people drive dangerously. Are you going to give up driving? No. Of course not. Any skill or activity can be misused, overused, or misapplied. Do not let the misuses of others prevent you from utilizing the powerful sales magic of scripting.

Instead of thinking of those who misuse scripting, think of those who have perfected it.

Every great communicator uses scripts.

Every president of the United States used scripts and speeches (oral scripts) to guide our great country. Ronald Reagan, "the Great Communicator" used scripts on 3 x 5 cards. No matter what you personally think of Bill Clinton, he is regarded as one of the most powerful communicators to have occupied the Oval Office. He now commands $200,000 per speech and has more speaking invitations than he can handle. Great religious leaders throughout history have used scripts. Great parents use scripts. Top attorneys use scripts.

Be proud of using scripts. When you think about, and work on, the words you use, you join the pantheon of the greatest communicators the world has ever known. Welcome to the club. We think you will be very, very happy here.

Another reason some salespeople won't work on their scripts is that, deep down inside, they doubt how much difference it can make. We've had salespeople and professionals at seminars and workshops ask us, "How much difference can a few words make?" At a recent seminar, a struggling salesperson said, "I don't use scripts—I just shoot from the hip." We call it "shooting from the lip." This unsuccessful salesperson wondered how much difference a few words could make in his sales presentations.

How much difference can a few words make? Mark Twain once said, "The difference between the right word and the wrong word is the difference between lightning and a lightning bug." We are probably the only sales trainers on the speakers' circuit who quote Mark Twain. After we use this quote, we ask the audience, "Which would you rather be, lightning or the lightning bug? What would you rather have, the power of lightning or the power of a lightning bug? Your words can make all the difference."

Multiply the difference that one word can make by the difference that a few hundred words or a few thousand different words can make. In sales and marketing, we have seen that difference add up to hundreds of thousands of dollars in extra income for sales professionals who **upgrade** the words they use.

The third reason that salespeople give for not wanting to work on their scripts is that it is too difficult. In the next sections of this book we will share with you some powerful time-saving techniques we have developed for perfecting what you say (and how you say it).

The work is worth the effort. Tom Gau is one of the most successful financial planners in the world today and his time is worth at least $1,000 per hour. Why would he spend **several hundred hours** working on his scripts? Because his powerful scripts have enabled him to earn well over $10 million as a financial planner in just the previous few years. Dr. Moine is proud to say that he worked with Tom Gau on his script book.

We now spend a great deal of our time helping sales professionals convert prospects into customers, develop the most effective ways of dealing with objections and resistances, and close sales. We accomplish all of this by helping our clients develop the most powerful scripts in their industries. Sometimes this involves editing, rewriting, honing, and polishing scripts and substituting more powerful words and phrases for less effective ones. In many cases, the return on investment for effective sales scripts is 10 to 1, which is far better than any return you can get in the stock market or in real estate. In some cases, we have seen salespeople enjoy a 100 to 1 return on investment. Working on your scripts **does** involve some effort and some thinking, but the payoff can be tremendous. Your words can make you rich.

We have had the privilege of working with people identified as some of the top salespeople in the United States, Canada, and Australia, but we cannot think of any of them who are the world's greatest product knowledge experts. Someone else always seems to know more about the products or services than they do. If product knowledge is not the common denominator of their success, what is? Some are tall, some are short; some are skinny, some are heavy; some are young, some are old; some are well-educated and some are only high school graduates; some live in big cities and some live in small towns; some are handsome and some are plain.

> **As far as we can tell, the only common denominator among highly successful salespeople is that they are all persuasive.**

Every single one of them. They **all** know how to use language effectively.

In analyzing our more than 20 years experience as consultants, trainers, and coaches to salespeople and sales organizations, we realize that we have never met a highly successful salesperson who was not persuasive. However, we have met many unsuccessful salespeople who are not persuasive!

Do you belong to the camp of sales superstars who work hard to develop great sales presentations and great sales scripts **or** do you belong to the much larger group of salespeople who just hope that "something good" comes out of their mouths when they speak? The great news is that *you can change your camp affiliation*. By studying and improving the power of the words you use, you can double or triple your powers of persuasion and dramatically improve your income. You may not be able to control the price of your company's products or services (or what those products and services are), but you **can** control the words you use—and that is almost all you need to control to become a more successful sales professional.

Your words can give you the power to deal effectively with any objection or concern raised by any prospect, customer, or client. When you internalize this truth, you will know *you are totally in control of your sales career* and you will develop a deep level of true optimism that no one can ever take away. Your words can make you rich.

The Reality of Positive Thinking in Master Salesmanship

Sales is a field that is rife with **phony** positive thinking. You've seen it: the salesperson who claims he is going to "break every sales record in the books," yet he cannot articulate how. The salesperson who is so relentlessly cheerful you suspect that she has overdosed on candy and *Mary Poppins.* And yet there are sales superstars who engage in a very real form of positive thinking that is genuine, honest, and unshakable.

The mindset of sales millionaires who engage in this very real form of positive thinking is one that assumes that almost every qualified person they meet will become a customer or client. How can they possibly make this assumption? Not on blind faith, but because they know that they offer outstanding products and services, great prices, and, even more significantly, that *they have the best words of anyone in their industry.*

If you are down and depressed about your sales, it is probably because your words (your presentations to prospects and customers) are not good enough. If your words are not of the highest quality, you will lack success in turning prospects into customers and in getting more business from existing customers and clients. Chances are, your products and services are pretty good. Chances are, your products and services are fairly similar to those of your competitors. *They might even be quite a bit better.* However, no matter how outstanding your products or services, if your words (and your presentations) are not outstanding, *you will not enjoy the success you deserve.*

It is our goal to help you reach a higher level of success than you have previously attained—or than you have ever imagined you could attain. The quickest and most certain way we have ever found for accomplishing this is to *upgrade the quality and power of the words you use.* Many salespeople become obsessed about upgrading their computers every few years, or upgrading their cars or their wardrobes. That is all fine and good, but if you upgrade the quality of the words you use, all of your other goals will take care of themselves because you will be making more money.

Every salesperson you encounter will tell you that he believes in positive thinking; yet relatively few walk their talk.

To be able to engage in positive thinking,
you must first of all engage in positive actions.

"Positive thinking" without positive actions is merely a fantasy. You are in the same position as the person who tells you he has a financial plan for success only to discover that his "plan" is to win the lottery. Mere fantasies and daydreams (as enjoyable as they can be) do not constitute positive thinking, no matter how frequently you engage in them. Most importantly, you must back up your positive thinking with positive actions, such as working hard on improving what you say (your scripts) and how you say those words if you really plan to become as successful as you could be.

The Meat and Potatoes of Sales Scripting

As we were writing this section of the book, we submitted drafts via e-mail to sales millionaires around the country. A comment we heard more than once is that this section contains the "meat and potatoes." It is rich in content and technique. We normally share this material in a workshop or seminar setting where we combine it with powerful exercises to actually generate sales scripts for audience members. Because we are sharing these million-dollar scripting techniques in print, you will need to do the interactive part on your own. If you truly have a positive attitude, you will find the work to be fun and self-reinforcing (especially as you close many more sales with your new scripts). Your experience will demonstrate how specific word patterns can rapidly create new customer and client relationships and close sales. This is not material to be read in a passive manner! To get the most out of these techniques, take action and do the scripting exercises we recommend. You should enjoy doing the exercises and feel truly empowered by the results.

Steps in Building Powerful Scripts

You may not have any desire to learn how to write a script or screenplay for a Hollywood movie or for a best-selling novel, but you do need to know how to create powerful scripts that will turn your prospects into clients. As you know, we do a tremendous amount of sales and practice work with some of the top financial planners and stockbrokers in the U.S., Canada, and Australia. One of the top commentators in the financial planning world today is Bob Veres, who is one of our heroes. Bob has written eloquently about the many well-educated, kind, idealistic, big-hearted, highly skilled financial planners who are starving due to lack of business. He asks, "Why?" We know why. These financial advisors can't tell their story. They can't motivate prospects to become clients. *Their words are not good enough.* The same can be said for hundreds of thousands of professionals and salespeople in other fields.

Bob Veres's question leads us to the first strategy in building your mastermind sales script book:

1. Identify and write down every objection, stall, and resistance you encounter.

These are the roadblocks that prevent you from turning prospects into customers and clients. You must know how to best deal with these objections, stalls, and resistances (OSRs) or you will never become highly successful. The first step is to identify them. Here is the good news: they are limited in number. There may be only 12 reasons that prospects do not become your customers. More good news: no one has all 12 concerns! Mr. Smith only had two concerns that you did not successfully answer. Mrs. Jones had three different concerns. But you must identify **all** of these reasons that prospects do not become customers and that customers do not buy even more from you.

2. Organize the objections, stalls, and resistances you hear.

Do not list every different objection you hear on one page with little notes next to each one. You will never be able to find your best, most powerful responses if you have them all mixed up on one or two pages. We have helped hundreds of salespeople and dozens of companies around the country write scripts and come up with the best ways of handling objections, stalls, and resistances. One of the most common problems we have seen is **disorganization**. If your best words are disorganized and you cannot find them, what good are they? You must have immediate access to your best, most powerful compelling words and word pictures. Therefore, devote an **entire page** in your notebook or in your computer file to each objection, stall, or resistance. At the top of the page list the objection. For example, "My brother in law is in the business. Why should I buy from you?" Leave the rest of the page blank. Then, on the next page, list another objection at the top, such as, "Your products cost too much." Create 12 or 15 pages or as many as you need, with one page for handling **each** objection.

3. Start by writing down your best response to each objection.

For example, what is the very best thing you can say when a prospect says, "I'm happy with what I have"? Some salespeople will then say, "What do you like most about it?" If you use this response, write it down. This is a common response, but it is just one response. You need *many* additional responses. After you have written down your best response to each objection, write down your **second** best response, and then your **third** best, and so on.

We have found that many average salespeople have only two or three good responses to any objection, stall, or resistance. Sales millionaires literally have dozens of powerful responses to each and every objection they hear. They always have something compelling and fascinating to say that takes the power out of the objection. Write down *every* great response you can think of to each and every objection, stall, and resistance you hear. *You have now begun your mastermind sales script book!* This is a book that can truly make you rich, and can enable you to help many more customers and clients.

4. Generate additional quality responses.

Congratulations. You have now written down your best responses to the most difficult OSRs you hear. Now, you need to **add** to that list of responses. Why? Remember, your words can make you rich. If the quality and variety of your responses are more powerful and make more sense than the OSRs of your prospects, those people are very likely to become your customers and clients. In our seminars we like to say, *"Whoever has the best words wins. And remember that in using the best words, your prospect also wins because he or she gets to become your customer."*

5. Include responses for every personality type of prospect and client.

The words that work beautifully with one prospect may fall upon deaf ears with another. If you want prospects as clients, you must use different words. Don't expect your prospects to talk your language. Doing so is disrespectful and ineffective. *It is your job to talk their language*, to put whatever you are offering into words that *make the most sense to that individual prospect.*

Therefore, in your list of responses to each OSR, you will want a wide variety of responses. What will you say to a successful, hard-charging, highly dominant person who says, "I want to think about it?" Remember that *strong people respect strong people.* If you have a weak, wimpy response chances are that person will never see you again. You need responses for strong people, for analytic people (who like facts, charts, graphs, etc.), for low-key people, for people who need to be entertained, and *for every other personality type you are likely to encounter.* A response that works well for the analytic person may bore an expressive fun-loving person to death. An expressive sociable person needs a story response that imbeds the facts in a short, interesting "real-life" example. Use story scripts to turn these prospects into your customers.

It will take time to add to your mastermind script book. Be patient. Write down responses for different personality types as you think of those responses or as you hear them. Your book will get better and better over time. Many sales professionals have told us that their mastermind sales strategy book is the single most valuable book they own. This is one book that truly can make you wealthy. Most remarkable of all, you wrote it!

6. Brainstorm new responses to objections, stalls, and resistances.

It is difficult to come up with great new responses to OSRs, and this is the reason that so many salespeople use just a few responses over and over. The problem with using the same responses again and again is that this small range of responses limits the number of people you can reach and influence. In addition, it leads to salesperson burnout. You get tired of saying the same thing over and over again—especially when it is not working. You need to have as many great responses as you can possibly collect.

When you can't think of any new responses or when you have an especially important prospect meeting coming up, brainstorm new responses with an associate or your coach. Most importantly, *write those responses down*! If your coach thinks of or shares with you a powerful new approach, record it in your mastermind script book. Human memory is fallible.

If you don't write it down, it is highly probable that you will forget it within two weeks.

The next time you have a sales meeting with a fantastic prospect, you won't remember those great words and you will not obtain that person as a customer or client. If you do write down every great new response you hear, your collection of mastermind scripts will get better and better each week and it will become much easier for you to convert a large percentage of your prospects to customers and clients.

When brainstorming responses, do not be overly critical. The key task up front is to generate a large number of powerful new responses. *Keep an open mind.* A response that you might not like at first could later become one of your favorite (and most effective) responses. Give yourself a chance to warm up to different types of responses. Remember, you don't have to necessarily like each and every response. A response that you might not particularly like might be *exactly* what a certain prospect needs to hear to decide to give you and your company $100,000 or more in business.

7. Interview a sales or marketing superstar.

If you have the opportunity to spend time with, study, or interview a sales or marketing superstar in your industry, seize that opportunity! One of the reasons that we became successful on the seminar circuit is that we were not repeating the same old clichés that many of the other speakers had been using for years. Our sales consulting and coaching practices are based on studying and working with sales and marketing superstars. Donald even did his doctoral dissertation on sales superstars. At our seminars, instead of repeating something we read in a book, we share the exact words, phrases, and powerful language patterns that the top people in the field are using—and we explain **why** they work.

We have more than 2,000 books in our libraries, yet most of what we know about persuasion techniques, influence strategies, and closing techniques we learned from top producers rather than from books. We are sure your experience will be the same. When you interview a sales or marketing superstar in your industry, *pose the most difficult objections, stalls, and resistances you hear and ask that person what he would say to answer such OSRs.* Then, write down his best responses. By doing so, you will capture much of the persuasive power of these individuals and you will be able to **duplicate** much of their success. Face it, these people are probably offering the same products and services you offer, but they are using better words to communicate the benefits and to motivate prospects to become their customers and clients. Add their best responses to your mastermind sales script book and you will capture much of their sales magic.

Sometimes a top producer will deny he uses scripts. However, as you now know, any organized set of words is a script. If he denies that scripts are being used, that is fine. Just ask, *"What do you say when a prospect says…(pose your most hated objection)."* Listen to what the top producer says and you will hear some powerful **scripts**—even though the producer may not label them as such! The only time we have not been able to collect powerful scripts from an interview with a sales millionaire is when he was holding back. Sometimes highly successful people come up with words, phrases, word pictures, and descriptions that are so powerful they don't want to share these million-dollar word patterns with others. That is fine because there are always other great producers you can interview. And when you hear *their* best lines, phrases, and images, add them to your masterminds sales script book.

When a sales professional has the opportunity to spend time with a sales or marketing superstar, we find that many times they ask questions such as, "What are your favorite hobbies?" "Do you like to golf?" or, "What kind of car do you drive?" Who cares? Don't squander the opportunity by chatting with this sales superstar about trivia. Instead, make the most of your opportunity and find out **how** he handles the toughest objections any sales professional in your industry encounters, and capture those responses *for your future use.*

The sales superstar you meet at a conference or workshop might be earning $1 million a year and you might only be earning $100,000. Why would he agree to an interview with you? If you have different territories, you are not a competitive threat. Offer to take him out to the finest restaurant in town and make sure that **you** pay for the meal. The meal might cost you $200 but we guarantee that if you do a good job eliciting the superstar's best responses, you will learn verbal strategies that could earn you tens of thousands of dollars—or more. Talk about return on an investment!

We are lucky because we've been hired by top banks, savings and loans, medical equipment companies, automobile manufacturers, payroll services companies, headhunters (executive search), brokerage firms, and others to study their sales superstars, capture their scripts, and build verbal models that average producers can use to dramatically increase their sales effectiveness. We are paid very well to do this work because it produces rapid sales increases. Using the trade secrets and strategies we have shared with you in this chapter and in the next one, you can achieve the same results for yourself with the power of million dollar sales scripting. The scripts you collect and organize are truly insider secrets of the best in your industry.

8. Edit, hone, and polish your scripts.

Make every line effective. Make every line sing. It has been said that all great writing is rewriting. The same can be said for your sales scripts and presentations. *Writing sales scripts is like writing great advertising copy.* You need to look at *every* word and phrase. Get rid of lazy or ineffective words. When we are not doing seminars or giving speeches, we spend about half of every day working with salespeople around the country on their sales presentations. We didn't plan it that way, but that is what many of our coaching clients are most interested in because it produces the most profound sales increases.

Much of what we do is role-playing and conducting in-depth "sales autopsies." However, we examine **both** the unsuccessful sales and the **successful** ones. You can frequently learn as much from analyzing the successful sales as from analyzing the ones that didn't succeed. How, exactly, does this sales coaching process work? The salesperson tells us what his prospect or customer said and then what he said. We examine it, rescript it, and practice it. We go through every part of the sales presentation. This is what we call **"play-by-play" sales coaching** and it produces the most dramatic sales increases of any training or coaching program we have ever developed.

Why is it necessary to rescript sales presentations? We have learned over the years that a fair percentage of what salespeople say to prospects is unnecessary, nonpersuasive, or counterproductive. We cut out the unnecessary verbiage, and that saves the salesperson and the prospect a great deal of time. We then perfect the remaining parts of the sales presentation. Sometimes we add new material, new sales stories, or benefit statements to replace the weaker parts that were removed. We provide better, more powerful scripts that we have learned or developed over the years. Together with our clients we edit, hone, and polish the scripts to make them best fit the personality of the salesperson and the prospect or customer. This whole process can be hard work, which is why few salespeople or sales managers do it on their own. However, it can also be fun and empowering. No one ever forgets its very serious purpose: to turn a larger and larger percentage of your prospects into your customers and clients.

**Remember, your scripts and sales presentations
can never be too powerful
unless every single person you meet
becomes your customer or client.**

Continue to edit, hone, and polish your scripts until you can almost effortlessly turn a very high percentage of your prospects into customers and clients.

We hope you have enjoyed the techniques and strategies we have shared with you in this chapter. We normally spend several hours in a seminar or speech teaching and demonstrating these script collection, brainstorming, and script polishing strategies. To get the maximum benefit from these techniques, you will need to do some of the script collection and polishing work on your own or with your sales manager or coach. The techniques you have just learned have led to massive sales improvements and several billion dollars of new sales for our corporate and individual clients over the previous 20 years. If you use them, we know they will work for you, too.

In the next chapter we will share with you some additional strategies we have developed for rapidly building your own powerful sales strategies book and also for **using** your sales scripts. We will show you how to make your sales scripts **invisible** so that no one will ever know you have previously said those magical words. All they will know is, "I like this person." "He understands me." "I totally trust him." "What he says makes sense." "I like this product." "I like this service." "It fits my needs and my budget." "I want this." "I am going to buy this." Of course, this does not happen instantly, but it does take place over the course of your sales conversation *because of the power of the words you use.* Your powerful new words and new, massively improved sales presentations, along with your outstanding products and services, will rapidly enable you to become a sales millionaire or multimillionaire. Your words will make you rich.

3

How to Build a Multimillion Dollar Mastermind Sales Script Book

Answer: Be good enough to not need a script....

If you knew of a book that could help you make hundreds of thousands of dollars in extra income and bring in a large number of new clients, would you be interested in obtaining a copy? There is (or could be) such a book but the catch is that *you have to write it*. This is a book that contains your most persuasive words, word pictures, metaphors, explanations, and methods of handling questions and objections. This book is called a sales script book, or a marketing script book.

Sales script books have helped some salespeople make millions of dollars in extra income and have helped some companies make hundreds of millions of dollars in additional revenue. In the previous chapter, we shared with you seven techniques for beginning your mastermind sales script book. We call it a "mastermind" script book because it includes not only your best ideas, words, scripts, and word pictures, but also the most persuasive words of any top producers or sales superstars you are fortunate enough to interview. In this chapter, we will share with you some more advanced techniques for further strengthening your mastermind sales script book. If you implement these script book development strategies, the finished product will be the most powerful and effective marketing tool you own.

Advanced Script Book
Development Strategies

Some advanced script book development strategies we use in our corporate sales consulting and teach in our seminars and workshops on building mastermind sales script books include:

1. If someone does not become your customer or client, ask them why.

This is a shocking suggestion to many salespeople. It is even more shocking to professionals such as lawyers, CPAs, and financial planners who rely upon salesmanship to build their practices, but do not see themselves as "salespeople." When we make this suggestion at our seminars, often someone in the audience will say, "If I ask them why they did not become my customer or client, they will think I am desperate." Not true—**if** you know how to ask them properly.

We are currently working with a small firm on the East Coast that has just started its mastermind sales script book. This firm gets much of its business by doing sales seminars. We've helped this company dramatically improve their seminars and they are now attracting a large number of prospects. Their next challenge was how to get seminar attendees to come to their office. Due to some changes we made in the ending segments of the seminar, they are now able to get a high percentage of seminar attendees to come to their office for appointments. The final challenge once prospects come to the office is how to convert them into clients.

This company was built on seminar selling, yet we knew the seminars could be much more successful than they had been in the past. Sales is all about numbers, so let's take a closer look at the numbers this company was generating. Previously, they had mailed out about 6,000 seminar invitations to attract approximately 30 people to a given seminar. We changed the seminar invitation to make it more persuasive and to add urgency, and now our client is able to attract about 50 attendees for each seminar from mailing approximately 4,000 seminar invitations. Of course, you must also use good mailing lists to consistently pull prospects to your seminars month after month.

Previously, this company was getting about 20 percent of seminar attendees to come to their office for face-to-face appointments and they converted two or three people from each seminar into clients. Due to changes in the seminar scripts, they are now getting more than 50 percent of seminar attendees to visit the office for appointments. Our client has done a few seminars after which nearly 80 percent of all attendees wanted to come in for a face-to-face office appointment, which we call a "free, no obligation consultation." On average, our client is now turning more than 25 percent of those prospects who come in for an appointment into clients. For some seminars, their closing rate has been much higher. But we wanted even more success for our client.

From doing some research, we learned that most of the prospects who declined to become clients said they "wanted to think about it." We coached the owners of this company in how to use several different pieces of sales dialogue to further increase the number of prospects they can turn into clients.

One script that has worked very well is:

"I understand. Hopefully I can help you and your family in the future in the way I have been able to help so many other families. I want to apologize to you. I obviously did not do something right. I know if I had fully explained the many benefits of our services and if I had fully answered your questions, you would have wanted to become a client. What did I not explain as well as I should have? What do you have questions about?"

These are powerful words and so we coached our clients to, in most cases, say them softly and in a friendly tone of voice. The only exception is when dealing with highly dominant personalities because strength respects strength. In those cases, we showed them how to deliver the words in a more powerful tone.

By using the previous sales dialogue, we have shown our client how to get his prospects tell him **why** they didn't become his clients or **what** they want to think about. One prospect recently said, "You didn't explain your fee structure very well. I don't understand why you charge different rates for different services." Our client replied, "Oh. I didn't explain that? I'm sorry!" He went on to explain it and this prospect became a client.

Notice what happens in the dialogue. The sales professional starts first by using the words, "I understand." He does **not** challenge the prospect. He does not use high pressure. The rapport and trust that have been previously established are maintained and enhanced. Then the sales professional goes on to say, "Hopefully, I can help you and your family in the future in the way I have been able to help so many other families." The sales professional has an opportunity to say something positive about himself and to make use-benefit statements. The sales professional then apologizes. This is what is known as the **"one down" technique** in negotiating. All of the top negotiators and lawyers we have studied use this technique from time to time. Salespeople would benefit from learning it.

The one down technique is effective because you are apologizing and asking for help.

Americans like to help others.

Think about it. Whenever there is a tragedy anywhere in the world, Americans are the first to rush in and offer help. Give your prospect a chance to help you.

Another powerful variation of the sales dialogue is:

"I want to apologize. I obviously did not do something right, or you would have decided to become a customer. So that I do not make that mistake again, can you tell me what I did wrong? Can you help me?"

A very high percentage of prospects will help you. Why? Psychologically, you are down on one knee asking for help and they want to provide it. When they help you, by explaining what you did not cover very well, you are given another chance to explain. Once you explain or more fully answer their concern, a number of these prospects will become customers or clients. You have just answered their most pressing remaining objection or question. If they have any additional questions or objections, answer those and invite them to become customers or clients.

When your prospects tell you why they did not become customers or clients, you always win. You may learn **what** to say to turn them into customers or clients, or what you should cover in the next meeting to convert them into customers or clients. Or in some cases, they still will not buy from you. You *still* win because you will learn what you need to emphasize in meetings with **other** prospects—what you need to say and how you need to say it—to close those sales. Add these new scripts to your script book and it will get dramatically more powerful in a short period of time.

2. If you hear a new objection, it means it is time to write new scripts!

Most sales professionals hear the same 15 to 18 OSRs over and over. These objections are sometimes **overt** (the prospect says them out loud) and are sometimes **covert** (the prospect just thinks, "Your prices are too high!" but doesn't tell you). Once you get skilled at handling those 15 to 18 OSRs, you will be able to convert a high percentage of your prospects to customers or clients. Meeting with prospects then becomes much simpler and less stressful as you know that you have a persuasive presentation **and** great answers to all of the prospect's concerns and objections.

However, occasionally you will hear a new OSR. You will hear something not covered in your script book. *Do not be discouraged!* This simply means it is time to add a new section to your mastermind sales script book!

Usually you hear a new OSR when you are introducing a new product or service, or if there has been a major change in the market or the economy. For example, one of our clients is now offering a 1031 Tax-Free Exchange real estate product that enables his clients to sell a highly appreciated apartment building, office building, or piece of land and exchange it, totally tax deferred, into a grade A professionally managed property that produces more income and requires no work. This is a real estate solution many of his clients have been looking for and now he has it. The only problem is that he was not skilled at handling client concerns about this new product. We are creating a new section of his script book and are writing down the very best responses to the predictable questions clients have about this exciting new real estate product offer.

The 1990s were great boom years for our national economy. If you had a great product or service and if you possessed powerful sales skills, it sometimes seemed as if the sky was the limit. We helped many of our corporate and individual clients break sales records month after month and year after year during the 1990s. In the 1990s relatively few prospects brought up budget restraints, cutbacks, or limited funds as reasons for not buying. However, the new century has brought with it a mild recession. Money is tighter and is not as freely spent.

A couple of years ago, relatively few of your prospects and customers said, "We can't afford it. It is too expensive for us." Today, this may be a common concern. Or due to a change in your industry, or the national economy, or the stock market, you may be hearing a different new objection. *Whenever you hear a new objection, don't get upset.* Instead, adopt the mindset of sales millionaires and tell yourself, "That's interesting. Now I'm going to develop a new section of my mastermind sales script book and write down one or two dozen powerful responses to destroy that objection."

3. There should be NO objection you fear or dread.

When we first begin coaching a sales professional, one of the questions we ask is, "What are your most feared or dreaded objections or stalls?" Those are the OSRs that the salesperson needs to work on first. Those are the objections that are preventing the sales professional from turning even more prospects into customers and clients. Those are the first OSRs we help the sales professional overcome.

Why is it so important that you overcome your fear of OSRs?

Fear paralyzes.

A salesperson who is afraid of hearing an objection or of being rejected will not make as many sales calls as he should. We have been hired by a number of companies to figure out how many hours each week salespeople actually spend selling. In many cases, the number of hours spent selling is appallingly low. We have studied some sales forces and found that the average salesperson spends 11 hours per week selling. In others, salespeople spend an average of seven hours per week selling.

In almost no cases do we find that salespeople spend more than 20 hours per week directly selling. It almost seems that in some sales forces, salespeople will do anything except sell! They will reorganize their files, go to meetings with one another or the boss, spend hours writing letters or "doing research" on the Internet. Does this sound familiar? Look around your office and notice how many salespeople are there instead of out meeting with prospects and customers. And sales managers and company presidents wonder why their sales are so low! Your salespeople are spending relatively little time selling!

There are relatively few ironclad take-it-to-the-bank Laws of Sales Success. Here is one of the most powerful: Everything else being equal, the salesperson who spends the most time directly in front of (or on the phone with) prospects and customers makes the most sales. Period. Take two salespeople with equal products or equal services and equal prices and whoever spends more time calling on prospects and customers will sell the most. This law is so powerful that in some cases, the salesperson with weaker products or services **sells more** because he spends more time directly interacting with prospects and customers.

The mindset of sales millionaires is:
Nothing is more important than the time I spend
directly interacting with prospects and customers.

This is truly sacred time.

Given that nothing is more important for a salesperson than direct interaction with prospects, customers, and clients, why don't more salespeople spend a greater amount of time in these interactions? Because *selling can be stressful.* What makes selling stressful? All the objections and rejection you receive. We've had the opportunity to help some of our friends and colleagues get sales jobs where they had the potential to earn several hundred thousand dollars per year and they turned us down. Why? They didn't want to take the rejection.

What is the solution or cure for all of this rejection? You need to have great scripts and highly persuasive sales presentations. If you have more great answers than a prospect has questions, the stress goes out of the job and your self-confidence soars. You can hardly wait for the prospect to raise a particular objection because you know that you have not just one or two ways of dealing with it, but literally more than a dozen powerful ways of obliterating it! What is there to fear? **Nothing!** The net result is that your mastermind sales script book gives you the strength to make more sales calls with less effort. Each sales call takes less out of you because you are so exquisitely prepared.

However, it does take time and energy to build a mastermind sales script book. That is why some salespeople and sales managers don't create one. Instead, they stumble along hoping they will "think of something to say" when they are hit by a difficult objection ("I've heard your product breaks down a lot!"). These objections and the rejection they get sting them and, consequently, they make considerably fewer sales calls than they should. They suffer, their incomes suffer, and the entire company suffers from low sales. A powerful sales script book, along with training in how to deliver the scripts, can solve this problem and can make it easier and more enjoyable for the salespeople to spend more time out in the field selling.

The time you invest in building your sales script book is well worth it because we have never seen any other sales or marketing effort that pays off so well. However, given that it takes time to write this book, you need to realize that you cannot write the entire script book overnight. Some sales millionaires work on their scripts off and on for months—and all the while they are making more sales calls than the salespeople who are not writing a script book. We have known some sales millionaires, such as Ben Feldman, who worked on his script throughout his entire life.

We know a lot of shortcuts in writing scripts, but it still takes time to write and polish quality, highly persuasive scripts. For this reason, we suggest you *prioritize* what sections you should start on first. We strongly suggest you begin writing down, honing, polishing, and perfecting responses to your *most feared or hated objections*.

What do you say if a prospect says, "I have a brother-in-law in the business. I think I am going to place my $100,000 order with him"? What do you say when a prospect says, "I've heard your company is having some financial problems. Why are you laying off so many people?" What do you say when a prospect says, "Your prices are okay, but I have heard that your service is terrible"? What do you say if a prospect says, "I can do it myself"? What do you say if a prospect says, "I am totally happy with what I have now and I will never change"? Write down your very best responses to any of these objections you hear! Add to them. Hone and polish your responses. Then add even more powerful responses. Destroy these objections and you will never fear them again! Many prospects with these objections and concerns will become your customers and clients—if you have great responses to their questions and objections.

4. Conduct a formal data collection session.

When we do a **mastermind script book project** for a company, one of the first steps is **data collection**. While we do meet with and interview some sales superstars on an individual basis, we frequently start with a formal script book data collection session to speed up the development of powerful scripts. We often gather the top producers of the sales force and the sales managers for a day or two at a hotel or resort location where everyone can relax and focus on their work. We start by listing every major OSR the salespeople hear and then we all brainstorm and tape-record the responses. It is absolutely amazing what happens at some of these script data collection sessions!

At one recent script data collection seminar, we listed all of the most hated objections the sales force heard. At the top of the list was the objection, "Your price is too high." In fact, this company did have some of the highest prices in their industry. After listing all the objections, we told the participants we would be going down the list generating the most powerful responses we could think of for handling each one. We asked the seminar participants, "What is the best response you can think of to the objection, 'Your price is too high.'" One salesperson replied, "There is no response. Our price is too high. We are the highest in the industry. Once the company lowers its prices, we will be able to sell more." We sat in stunned disbelief. Later we learned that this salesperson was one of the least successful in the room.

We coaxed some of the other participants to share some of their best responses to this hated objection, and then we added a few more of our favorites. Soon we had more than a dozen ways of handling this objection. Salespeople brainstormed and recalled powerful responses from years past. The list got longer. Even the first salesperson who spoke up, who said there was "no response" to this objection, got excited. He realized there were more than a dozen ways of handling it. When we got up to about 17 or 18 different responses, the salespeople and sales managers ran out of ideas. Then we brought in a few techniques for handling price objections that were used in other industries. These methods were virtually unknown in their industry and the audience members found them exciting and empowering.

We went through a similar process with all of the other objections and generated dozens of responses. The transcript for the two-day data collection session was more than 80 pages in length! Over the coming weeks, we met with some sales superstars and sales managers individually to hone and polish the scripts to make them as powerful as possible. We also did a great deal of editing and rewriting on our own and compared the scripts with the scripts of other top sales forces with which we have worked. The net result is that the finished scripts have resulted in tens of millions of dollars in additional sales beyond their projections of what was possible. Some of those who were the most skeptical of sales scripting became the biggest fans and advocates as their incomes increased dramatically from the use of the scripts.

If you want to get off to a **fast start** in building your mastermind sales script book, we highly recommend group data collection sessions with your top salespeople and sales managers. If you have a small sales force, you should include everyone in the group data collection sessions. Hold them at a relaxed environment—hotel or golf course or resort—where you can really concentrate on generating and capturing the very best responses to your most difficult objections. To get the most out of this, you don't want to be interrupted by phone calls, office mail, and other distractions. Then take the scripts you have collected and organize, polish, edit, and add to them over the following weeks and months to increase your sales by millions or tens of millions of dollars.

5. The power of bringing up objections first.

**The ultimate test of your self-confidence as a
sales professional is that you will get to the point where
you will bring up the objection or concern first.**

Instead of waiting for your prospect to eventually ask you about your prices or fees, you can self-confidently say, "If I were in your position, I would want to know about our prices and fees. We are very proud of how we have been able to keep our prices low while offering the highest quality products and services in the industry. Let me show you how we accomplish that...."

Why do you want to bring up the objection first? By doing so, you take almost all of the power out of it. Your prospect might have thought that he would save the objection until the very end of the sales call and then use it on you. Why? The prospect might have remembered that he was able to discourage the last salesperson by using this objection. When you bring the objection up first, you show you have absolutely no fear of it and in fact, you use the prospect's objection as a reason **why** he should buy your products or services! Suddenly, the prospect loses interest in the objection.

If you have a great script, don't be surprised if your prospect says, "Well, that is not really a concern of mine. I am more interested in...." At that point, he is likely to bring up any remaining objections or concerns. Often, some of the first objections raised are smokescreen objections that are used just to discourage you or to test your self-confidence. Once you use powerful scripts to disarm these objections, you can focus your prospect on his real concerns. And you can use your other great scripts to handle those concerns and close the sale!

Here is another great way of bringing up a common objection. Let's say that you work for a relatively new company in your industry. If your company has only been around for a few years, a common objection might be, "I want to go with a more established company." To anticipate and disarm that objection, you can say, "I know what you are probably thinking. You are probably thinking that our company is relatively new and that you might want to go with a more established company. Is that right?" Your prospect might have an astonished look on his face. He might even say, "You read my mind!" The fact that you brought up this objection first shows that you are not afraid of it.

You then share with the prospect a number of powerful advantages your company has over more established companies. You don't have the overhead, bloated payrolls and pension expenses of those old companies. The first benefit is that you can keep your costs much lower and your clients save money. The second benefit is that you are not married to the old technology and old methods that the older companies in your field are stuck with. The third benefit is that your clients get the latest, most efficient and powerful technology and the latest designs. You can think of several other powerful benefits to add, but the most effective way of handling that objection is to bring it up first.

By bringing up certain objections first, you will then have a rapt client who will be impressed by your self-confidence and who will listen closely to your every word. Your chances of closing that sale multiply exponentially. It all starts with the words you use. High quality words, combined with the mindset of a sales millionaire, empower you to break sales records.

Perhaps the saddest thing we see in business today is the tremendous waste of money on sales and marketing efforts that produce meager or nonexistent returns. For example, a company may spend millions of dollars or tens of millions of dollars on advertising that generates little or no business. The company may spend millions of dollars to hire salespeople, equip them with $3,000 laptop computers and send them out in $30,000 leased cars to make sales presentations. After this expenditure of tens or hundreds of millions of dollars, the salespeople still don't know what to say and they can't handle the objections, stalls, and resistances they hear.

As proof, look at the stock of hundreds of companies where the sales force cannot sell the products the company produces. Many of these companies have lost hundreds of millions of dollars or billions of dollars in market value because sales have either dropped or have not met earlier projections. We see the same situation, on a smaller scale, in the marketing of professional services. A professional (lawyer, CPA, financial planner, etc.) spends a great deal of money to put on a seminar, attracts a number of participants, gets some of those to his office for appointments, and then converts very few to clients. Everyone loses because the professional becomes discouraged and the prospects do not get the help they need. Why does this happen? In many cases, the professional or the salesperson does answer every question and concern the prospect asks, but does not answer it effectively or persuasively. In other cases, there is another problem: the professional or salesperson does not answer the prospect's **unasked** questions and concerns.

These are the prospects who conclude a sales meeting saying they "want to think about it" because the sales professional did not address these unasked questions! Why would a prospect **not** ask certain questions? They might be afraid of offending you. They might be afraid of seeming ignorant. "How does that _____ work? I didn't understand it." They might not even consciously know what to ask!

How can you solve the challenge posed by unasked questions? By asking yourself the questions first! Let's face it. If you have been in your field of selling or in your profession for several years, you probably know most of the concerns and objections your prospects will have. These objections and concerns are **highly predictable**. If a prospect does not ask certain questions or raise certain objections, *don't assume that he doesn't care or isn't worried about those issues.* He might be very concerned but does not want to hurt your feelings or seem ignorant by asking.

> **Therefore, if a prospect is not asking the most important questions that should be raised, ask them yourself.**

Look at your prospect's face. Frequently, when you ask these questions and then answer them, you will see a sign of relief. Your prospect's body language will communicate, "Yes, that is exactly what I was thinking or worrying about. Thank you for bringing it up." Then, address those questions with your most persuasive, truthful, powerful, informative, educational answers. You are well on your way to converting this prospect into a customer or client. After leaving that meeting, he will have nothing left to think about because you will have answered all of his asked and unasked questions, persuasively described the benefits of your products and services, and made a friend and customer in the process.

6. Do not read from your mastermind sales script book.

It is one thing to have a collection of the most powerful sales scripts in your industry and it is another thing to know how to best use them. We usually suggest that you do not read from your sales script book. There are a few exceptions, primarily in telemarketing and tele-prospecting. However, even in those cases, we usually suggest that you slightly paraphrase the scripts. To get the most out of your scripts, it is essential that your delivery be genuine and authentic.

Ronald Regan was considered one of the greatest public speakers of our time. His nickname was "The Great Communicator." He put his scripts on index cards and few people were aware that he used them. Later in his career, he read from a TelePrompTer, and again, few people were aware that he was reading because his delivery was so natural and genuine. Have Ronald Regan be your role model (even if you are not a Republican!) in how to use your scripts. Have the scripts disappear in actual usage.

Pausing occasionally while reading brief parts of your script over the phone will allow you to accomplish this. We have even coached some of our clients to slightly stammer or seemingly stumble over a few words to make the delivery even more natural sounding. Remember that the words are so incredibly powerful (if you have created your scripts properly), that they will still close the sale. That is one of the great ironies of sales scripting: even if you intentionally "mess up" the words of a powerful script, they are still likely to be many times more powerful than what the average salespersons says!

Obviously, in face-to-face selling, when a prospect or client hits you with an objection or difficult question, you can't say, "Wait a minute, let me look that up in my script book!" However, there are ways of reviewing for a client or prospect meeting that will make you so totally prepared and self-confident that you won't need to look anything up in your script book. Best of all, these methods of preparation take only a few minutes once you have a powerful script book.

Before you have a face-to-face meeting with a prospect, customer, or client, go over everything you know about that individual and his needs. What are his most likely objections? Your mastermind sales script book might have 21 sections divided by index tabs for each of the 21 OSRs you encounter in your sales work. Remember, however, that most prospects and customers only have three or four major objections that prevent them from buying. Of course, these three or four objections can be different for each prospect, and that is why you need all 21 sections in your mastermind sales script book.

Spend five or 10 minutes reviewing for your face-to-face sales meeting. When you have identified the three or four objections this particular prospect is most likely to bring up, go over those sections in your script book. Look at your favorite responses. Look at the responses that have closed sales for you and for the superstars of your company in the past. Because you have reviewed these responses previously, you should almost be able to memorize them with just a few minutes of review. This 10 minutes of review of the most powerful sales scripts for handling these objections could be the most valuable 10 minutes of your day! Now, put your script book away and meet with your prospect, customer, or client.

When he raises the objections or concerns you knew would be raised, you will have the most powerful responses in your industry on the tip of your tongue. You will be supremely self-confident because you know that your answers are more powerful than his questions or objections. You can deliver those responses in a totally natural, relaxed tone of voice. Your prospect will not know that you have prepared for this meeting to the degree that you have. All he will know is that they trust you, they like you, what you say makes sense, the benefits of your products and services excite them, and they want to do business with you. Like Ronald Regan, you have made your scripts disappear. Assuming you have quality products or services offered at a fair price, by using the best scripts in the industry, you are very likely to close that sale.

The Limitations of Outsourcing:

Many of our corporate clients and professional clients now outsource almost everything. Did you know that some of the biggest shoe companies in the world now hire outsiders to design their shoes and then hire overseas companies to manufacture them? All that these billion dollar shoe companies do is market the shoes. Many billion dollar computer and high-tech companies do not manufacture their products. They "just" sell them, and yet they make much more money than the subcontractors who do the manufacturing. Many wineries do not grow their own grapes. They buy the grapes from others, make the wine, and sell it. Prestige beer companies do not make their own beer, they "just" market it. Did you know that many stock brokers and financial planners do not select stocks or make investment choices? Some of our clients in this field who make more than $1 million a year in personal income outsource all investment selections. They concentrate on client acquisition.

Most companies today outsource the design and maintenance of their Website and all computer-related work. They outsource tax preparation and other tax work. They outsource legal services. They outsource all of their advertising work. Outsource, outsource, outsource, outsource. Why do it yourself if you can hire an expert to do it better, faster, and less expensively?

What is the one thing you cannot outsource? Your ability to be persuasive. Many of the most successful companies in the U.S. focus on customer or client acquisition and client relationship management (CRM). They then find the very best experts, suppliers, and consultants to handle everything else. This simplifies their business and allows them to sell more, service more customers, and make more money.

Many salespeople and professionals are good at setting goals. Salespeople and sales managers have goals for everything: number of prospect calls; number of sales calls; closing ratios; conversion ratios; number of "be-backs"; reduced numbers of returns and canceled sales; number of sales per day, week, month and year; cross sales ratios; etc. Yet one of the greatest ironies of all is that few salespeople set goals in the one area that can make **the most difference** in their lives: their ability to be persuasive! Adding to this irony is the fact that you cannot outsource your ability to be persuasive. Even if you outsource everything else, you still must meet with and speak to prospects, customers, and clients.

We now wish to encourage you to set real goals to add your best, most persuasive words, word pictures, metaphors, explanations, and objection handling techniques to your sales script book.

7. Have at least 20 responses to every major objection.

What goals do you think about every day? One of our clients, Sean Higgins, sells a very sophisticated and expensive technical analysis computer software program that has enabled him to earn about 78 percent net return so far in the 2002 year. We recently worked with Sean and his partner, sales superstar Steven Clements, on the sales presentations they gave at the Money Show in Las Vegas. Whatever your sales or investment goals are, we hope you achieve them.

One of your primary goals **must** be to convince your prospects, customers, and clients of the benefits of your products and services. Your products and services could have more benefits at a lower cost than any others in your industry, *but this will be meaningless unless*:

A. Your prospects are excited about these benefits.

B. Your prospects really believe you and your company can deliver these benefits.

C. Your prospects have an urgency to buy your products and/or services.

Unless you fulfill these three criteria, you will be unsuccessful in turning prospects into customers or clients *due to a lack of persuasion skills*. Your great products, services, and low prices will be of little value if you cannot turn prospects into clients.

This is exactly the situation hundreds of American companies are now facing. They have great products and services, but the salespeople are not persuasive enough to sell them. As a consequence, the companies are losing money, losing market share, are having to lay off hundreds or thousands of employees, and their stock prices are collapsing.

Therefore, in addition to having all of your return on investment goals, sales activity goals, measurement goals, etc., you must have a goal of becoming more persuasive. *Becoming more persuasive is the secret ingredient that makes it possible to achieve all of your other goals.* Becoming highly persuasive is the **catalyst** that makes all of the other ingredients work.

In our seminars and workshops, we put this into concrete terms by telling audience members they need to have **a minimum** of 20 great responses to every OSR they encounter as sales professionals. Sometimes audience members look at us aghast. We almost always have someone ask, "**How** can you possibly have 20 different responses to the statement, 'I want to think about it?'" Someone else will ask, "**Why** would you want to have 20 different responses to any objection, stall, or resistance?"

When addressing the first question, we suggest that you write down every great response you can think of to a given objection, stall, or resistance. Then, look at your list of responses tomorrow (or even tonight). You will probably remember two or three more great responses from years past. These may be some of the best, most powerful responses of all!

Then ask your most trusted friends and colleagues in the business what they say when they hear that objection, stall, or resistance. If this person is in a different city or is not a competitor, he might feel comfortable sharing his most powerful words, word pictures, metaphors, etc. Write these words down because they can literally make you rich! At this point, you might have 10 responses to a given difficult objection or stall.

When you read a book on sales or marketing, write down any great lines of sales reasoning, sales metaphors, or responses you learn. *Don't just underline them!* You may never look at that book again. Often, we will read an entire book on sales or persuasion and only find seven to 10 sentences that make fantastic sales scripts. When you find such precious words, write them down in your mastermind sales script book—the one selling tool you may use, at least for a few minutes, each and every day.

From doing all of the previously stated work, you may now have 15 powerful responses to an objection, stall, or resistance that previously prevented prospects from becoming your customers or clients. *Keep working at it.* We know it is hard work, but it is also fun. Remember that being persuasive is the one professional activity that you cannot delegate or outsource! And remember your **goal** of having at least 20 great responses to every OSR you hear. We have worked with sales superstars such as Tom Gau (one of the most successful financial planners in the U.S.) and with $100 billion pension fund companies, such as Frank Russell, and they both have **more than 30 written responses** to any objection or stall they might encounter. It is no accident they are so successful!

If you want to be highly successful, do what highly successful people do.

The second question we most frequently hear in our seminars on Sales Persuasion is, "**Why** would you want to have at least 20 different responses to any given objection?" After all, most salespeople only have two or three canned responses they use over and over to handle a given question or objection. One of the principal reasons you need 20 different responses is that the response or answer that works well with one person may fall flat on its face with another. When it comes to sales scripts, one size definitely does **not** fit all of your prospects or customers. You need vastly different words for your prospects and customers with different personality types, for different educational levels, and for different backgrounds, needs, and interests.

You also want to have a wide choice of responses to keep **yourself** from getting bored. It can get tiresome to say the same thing over and over in answering the common questions and objections that prospects raise. You can end up feeling like (and sounding like) a human tape recorder. A wide range of responses solves this problem and helps prevent you from becoming burned out. Finally, you want to have a wide variety of responses because some of your competitors do. Your competitor's products and services may not match yours in quality or price, but if he has more persuasive words, he is going to win over more prospects and sell more than you.

It is not enough to just keep up on technological changes in your field, PowerPoint presentations, Palm Pilots, and industry publications. *You must also keep up on advances in professional persuasion.* The words that may have worked for you in past years may not be very effective today in converting prospects into customers and clients. The good news is that you can learn and master the best, most powerful and persuasive forms of master salesmanship in the world today. It is not a matter of being "born with" these skills. Using the strategies we have shared with you in Chapters 2 and 3, you can literally double or triple your powers of persuasion—if you practice and use these skills.

8. Tape-record yourself making presentations.

In our seminars, we ask the audience members, "Have you heard yourself on tape?" "Does your voice sound the way you thought it was going to sound?" Most of the seminar participants admit their voices sound different than they had expected. We then ask audience members, "When was the last time you heard yourself on tape?" Many admit they have not heard themselves on tape **in years**. That is truly unfortunate because those people (and maybe you) are missing one of the greatest growth opportunities of all.

Because we have given so many seminars, we have heard ourselves on tape (and seen ourselves on video) many times. We always learn something new. For example, over a period of several years, Dr. Moine was hired by H.D. Vest to speak at several of their national conferences. In delivering his seminars, Dr. Moine trained several thousand CPAs in trust-building techniques and in sales scripting. H.D. Vest told Donald that audiotapes of his seminar outsold those of almost all the other speakers they had hired. Donald listened to the tapes and figured out what he was saying to this audience that made his seminars so powerful and popular. He then used what he learned to further improve and perfect the seminars he delivered to other companies.

You can learn a great deal about both your **strengths** and your **weaknesses** by listening to audiotapes of your interactions with prospects and customers. Because so much of what a person says is intuitive, *you are not consciously aware* of what parts are good (persuasive) and what parts are bad (boring, bland, trivial) in your sales presentations. Listening to an audiotape dramatically develops your **conscious awareness** of what you are saying and **how** you are saying it.

A performance coach will tell you that *you cannot (and will not) change anything until you are consciously aware of it*. When you become aware of a stain on your shirt, you will change that shirt. When you become aware of that dent on your car, you will have that dent fixed. When a baseball player becomes aware of the fact he is holding the bat incorrectly, he will work on changing that.

> **Therefore, if you are serious about developing money-making persuasion skills (the one skill you cannot delegate), it is essential that you vastly increase your conscious awareness of what you are saying and how you are saying it.**

You will develop this increased awareness most rapidly by listening to audiotapes of yourself interacting with prospects and clients.

A few years ago, we were working with a wonderful sales professional who was struggling to become more successful. She had been in her professional field for more than 10 years but was still only moderately successful. She had tried all sorts of mailing programs, coaches, brochures, sales referral programs, lead programs, motivational seminars, etc. and nothing had helped her build her sales to the desired level. More recently, she had spent a great deal of money on "Internet based marketing," to no avail. In fact, a number of prospects accused her of sending spam and requested that she never send them an e-mail marketing pitch again.

She was referred by one of our existing clients (a sales superstar in that industry) and we began coaching her. We asked her to tape-record some of her interactions with prospects and clients, and then we listened to the tapes. Although she had a vast knowledge of the products and services in her industry, when listening to the tapes, she realized she was sharing that knowledge in a manner that was boring and uninspiring. In answering questions prospects raised, she learned that she had a habit of saying, "Uh, yeah…yeah, yeah, yeah, yeah…" and then she would answer the question. Her answers were quite good, but because of the way she began her answers, some prospects lost interest. She also had a tendency to speak in generalizations and seldom used stories, metaphors, or real-life examples. These may seem like small points, but in their totality, they added up to a sales presentation that lacked effectiveness. Prospects said they "liked her" and "learned a lot from her," but few became her clients.

She also had many outstanding parts of her sales presentation and we were quick to point those out and to reinforce her for those skills. Through weekly sessions and through coaching her sales presentations, we cut out her bad habits and the weak parts of her sales presentation, further strengthened the best parts of her presentation, added stories and concrete examples, added urgency to take action, gave her **dozens** of great new scripts and power phrases, and doubled her persuasiveness and self-confidence. Why do we say "doubled her persuasiveness"? Because we helped her double her income in a six month period of time.

What makes this even more remarkable is that she continued to sell the same products and services to the same group of prospects in her area. The dramatic growth in her sales skills and her income all **started** by having her listen to audiotapes of her interactions with prospects and clients.

We strongly suggest that every salesperson who wants to increase his or her powers of persuasion listen to tapes of their interactions with prospects and customers. We guarantee that you will gain tremendous insights from listening to these tapes. You will no longer have to guess what you have to say differently. You will now **know** exactly what you must change in your presentations.

These techniques on scripting and powerful sales presentations have helped many salespeople and sales managers become sales millionaires. Some of our clients make more than $1 million a year in personal income from their powers of persuasion. These are "just" salespeople or marketers, they are not CEOs or company presidents, but they are paid all this money because they bring in so much business to the company. There are many more sales scripting techniques, sales data collection techniques, script analysis techniques, script enhancement techniques, and implementation techniques than we have the space to share with you here. Some of these are trade secrets that our clients have forbid us to share with the general public. After all, if a company, through hard work, has developed certain persuasion techniques that enable its sales force to bring in hundreds of millions of dollars in extra sales per year, it is important to protect the confidentiality of those sales scripts.

If you use the sales scripting techniques explained thus far, we know they will work for you. By definition, they have to work because mastermind sales scripts are the most effective word patterns of the top sales superstars within a company or an industry. The problem is that most salespeople and sales managers do not know how to collect great sales scripts, organize them, and perfect and enhance them to break sales records. You now have the tools and hopefully have the motivation to do some of the hardest sales work you have ever done, but also some of the only sales work that is virtually guaranteed to make you a sales millionaire or multimillionaire.

A Billion Dollar Success Story

Throughout the past 20 years, we have had the privilege of working with some of the finest companies in the U.S. and some of the top salespeople and sales managers in the development of record-breaking mastermind sales scripts. We've also given many seminars and workshops on sales scripting and the psycholinguistics of effective sales presentations. Many of you have written us letters or e-mails to share the great success you have enjoyed because you wrote down and practiced your most persuasive words. We enjoy these letters and e-mails, but one we received recently leads us to a final point we must make in this chapter.

A highly educated sales manager with an MBA in finance sent us an e-mail asking for assistance in increasing his company's sales. They had spent millions of dollars in advertising and had little to show for it. Additional millions were spent to hire a sales force. The company had outstanding products and good prices. The sales manager had created dozens of spreadsheets with sales projections, pro formas, and growth targets. None of the projections had been met. The sales manager was in danger of losing his job and the company's very survival was threatened because sales were so low. He had read a feature article we had been hired to write on sales scripting and decided to call us. However, he started out his telephone call by informing us that sales scripting would not work in his industry because they did "big ticket" selling.

A common misconception that prevents some salespeople and sales managers from working on developing more persuasive presentations or better ways of handling objections is the mistaken notion that scripts are not for big ticket selling. Some doctors, lawyers, accountants, and financial planners think that sales scripts won't work in their fields. *Please don't let this mistaken belief prevent you from becoming more persuasive.*

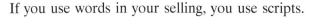

If you use words in your selling, you use scripts.

**If you make those words (scripts) more persuasive,
you will sell more.**

Period. No ifs, ands, or buts. No matter what you sell, more powerful presentations will help you sell more.

**The bigger or more important the prospect or client,
the more essential it is that you do
the finest job possible in making your presentation.**

Disagree?
New Markets
Uber in '09?

As just one example, a number of years ago, Dr. Moine was hired by the Frank Russell Company to work with an elite group of their top advisors and representatives. The Frank Russell Company manages billions of dollars in pension assets and retirement accounts for major companies around the world. Believe it or not, pension management services have to be sold—and the sales professionals in that industry are paid very well.

Dr. Moine worked together with the Frank Russell sales team and identified **every** possible reason a company or pension fund might not want to work with the Frank Russell Company. Then they brainstormed ideas and identified the very best, most persuasive responses to these objections. Some of these data collection sessions were held at the Frank Russell headquarters and others were held at hotels and resorts. It was Donald's job to write all of these mastermind scripts down, to cut out the fat, add more powerful persuasive scripts from his previous work with other companies, and interview other top performers within the company and add their best ideas.

When Donald started this mastermind script book project, the Frank Russell Company had tens of billions of dollars under management. A few years later, they had tens of billions of dollars in **additional** assets under management. Tony Whatley, the senior vice president of the Frank Russell Company who brought Donald in, said that the sales scripts that were developed and taught to the Frank Russell marketing professionals helped to bring in some of those additional billions of dollars in assets under management. The Frank Russell Company always had great products and services. The persuasive scripts and powerful presentations we developed together just made those outstanding products and services easier to sell.

Is this an isolated case? Certainly. Based on its size, it is also a rare case. It is not often that you can get a sales increase of that magnitude. However, it is not the only billion dollar sales scripting project in which we have been involved. At Home Federal Bank, we studied the best mortgage originators and salespeople in their system and wrote a mastermind sales script book that led to the sale of more than $1 billion in new mortgages. We even got Olympic athlete Bruce Jenner to appear in a 20-minute videotape to introduce some of the scripts (that was an exciting project!). We have worked with medical equipment superstars at Toshiba Medical and helped them write scripts that resulted in record-breaking sales of up to $1 million in ultra-sound, X-ray, CT, and MRI scanners. We wrote scripts for AT&T that helped their salespeople sell telephone switches that cost hundreds of thousands of dollars each.

Sales scripts and powerful sales presentations are not just for selling low cost items or low cost services. The bigger the ticket of the product or service you sell, the more important it is that every one of your sales presentations be as powerful as possible. As you now know, your words **will** make you rich—if you have the right words and know how to deliver them for maximum impact.

4

You Take the Lead

Leads are the lifeblood of the sales professional. Leads become prospects who become customers and clients. All salespeople, even the very best, need many leads. Sales millionaires generate many more leads than average salespeople do. It is as simple and as profound as that.

There's no point in having the best sales skills in the world if you don't have any prospects. That's merely the sales equivalent of being all dressed up with nowhere to go.

Some salespeople complain that there are not enough leads available. In fact, there are billions of leads in the world. How can we say that? The world is populated with more than 6 billion human beings. We all have many needs and wants. Each of us is a lead for many types of clothing, food, computers, office supplies, automobiles, financial products and services, housing, home furnishings, personal care products, books and educational programs, music, television shows, films, entertainment, medicine, health care, and dozens of other product and service categories. When you look at the wide variety of product and service choices within each category; the almost insatiable human needs, desires, and interests; and multiply all that times the 6 billion inhabitants of planet Earth, you will see that there truly are hundreds of billions of sales leads. Remember this and you should never again feel depressed about a paucity of leads.

It is almost impossible for a sales professional to have too many **high quality** leads within her own field of specialization. Take all the first rate leads you can get. However, there is much more to the issue of leads than simply gathering as many names as possible and then hitting the Internet, the phones, the fax, or the road to make your presentations. There are actually two key steps in which sales millionaires engage in this crucial first step in the sales process. First, they devote tremendous effort to **generating** as many **quality** leads as possible, and second, but just as important, they use great discipline in **qualifying** and **managing** these leads.

Looking for Leads

Some salespeople ask the question: "When is the best time to be looking for leads?" The answer is twofold: **Right now** and **all the time**.

No matter how successful you are, don't put off lead generation for some later date. By then it might be too late. One of your competitors might have just made a presentation and a sale to a prospect who could have generated hundreds of thousands of dollars of business for you. Had you called, e-mailed, or faxed this person a week ago, she might be your client or customer **today**.

> **The mindset you want to cultivate is one that places a premium on contacting as many high quality prospects as you can as soon as you can.**

The law of numbers and probabilities will contribute greatly to making you a sales millionaire.

There is another powerful reason you do not want to put off looking for leads until you need them. If you wait until you "need" leads, you will be too hungry for them and maybe even a little desperate for the business. You will not be as **selective** or as **discerning** as you should be. You may very well end up doing business with accounts that are smaller or less desirable than the accounts you should be working with.

Waiting until you "need" leads is like going shopping on an empty stomach. *Everything in the grocery store looks good to a hungry person.* When you get to the checkout counter, you find a whole bunch of junk food you wouldn't normally buy in your basket. *Had you shopped on a full stomach, almost none of that would have ended up in your shopping cart.* You would have been more selective and would have a shopping cart full of food that would not lead to liposuction and a coronary bypass.

Don't wait until you need leads to look for them. Get as many high quality leads as you can **now**—while your business is good or great. While your mind is clear. While you are not driven by hunger. By generating leads now, before you really need them, you will be able to find and attract the best prospects in your industry.

Sales millionaires seek prospects all of the time—they even look for leads during the sale itself.

For example, when the sale has been completed, you will hear good salespeople ask the customer if she knows anyone else who could use their products or services. Sales superstars often ask for, and receive, those leads *even before a sale has been consummated!* Here is an example of how one of the top sales and marketing minds in the U.S. accomplishes this.

> Tom Gau, MBA, CFP, CPA is one of the most successful financial planners in the world today. Tom is not just a millionaire, he makes millions of dollars each year in income by helping his clients slash their taxes and increase their investment returns. In his very first meeting with a new client (before anything has been sold), Tom will say, "I am paid in two ways. One is a very small money management fee. The other is that when I do an outstanding job for my clients, they tell their friends about me. If I do a truly outstanding job for you, is there any reason you would not want a few of your friends or relatives to know about the benefits I offer?"

What can a person say? Because they want the best for their friends and relatives, they have to recommend Tom Gau. Tom has told us that his average client gives him five or six high quality referrals during the next few months. Even more remarkable is that Tom Gau's powerful lead generation strategy costs him virtually nothing. He simply tells clients in the very first meeting that **he expects leads** when he does a great job. Clients are happy to supply those leads. It is not by accident that Tom Gau built his assets under management to nearly $500 million.

Present Company Included

In addition to being a great source of leads, your present customers and clients are also some of your best leads. After all, your customers are not only customers, they are prospects as well. By maintaining regular, high-quality contact with them; monitoring what is going on in their company, their industry, and their lives; making special efforts to understand their needs and letting them know about new products and services you and your company offer, you will be in an excellent position to generate additional sales. You may have various products or upgrades that they need, and with a solid relationship already in place, why should they go to anyone else?

It is much easier for prospects to buy from salespeople who are already providing them with first-rate products, service, and support. This means YOU! With this established trust, responsiveness, and reliability already in place, you are at the finish line while your competition hasn't even started the race. Your best prospects are your existing customers and clients.

When was the last time you contacted your best clients and customers? We have been hired by a number of companies to do "sales autopsies" to determine what caused sales to die (and to figure out how to bring the dead or near dead back to life) and to figure out what caused customers to leave. In many cases, we found that regular customers and clients stopped buying when they were not regularly contacted by their sales professional. Ken Unger, a sales millionaire who was the top performer for more than one decade for the highly respected real estate investment firm of Boston Capital, refers to the process of constantly keeping in touch with clients as providing them with "sales vitamins." We agree completely.

Action Step

Go through your client and customer list **right now** and determine your last date of contact for each person on that list. Contact frequency varies by industry. In some cases, clients and customers need to be contacted once a week or even more frequently. In other industries and professions, you may be able to get away with quarterly contact. If you have any neglected client or customer contacts, get to them NOW! Remember, everything else being equal, if you are the sales professional who makes the most contacts, and the most friendly and helpful contacts with clients and customers, you will become the sales professional of choice in your industry or profession.

Referrals Get Results

Referrals are among the most powerful and effective sources of leads. They make every cold call much warmer, and they give you a running start in building trust with the prospect. In fact, a strong referral from a respected person has the power to turn a cold call into *an almost closed sale.*

Sales millionaires know that they are surrounded by referral sources. We are all swimming in a sea full of wonderful referrals, just waiting to be asked. Do them a favor. Ask them.

As noted above, your customers and clients are an outstanding source of referrals. However, some salespeople feel reluctant to ask their customers for leads, fearing that they may look unprofessional or needy. There is **no reason whatsoever** for this type of apprehension. Satisfied customers not only enjoy being able to help salespeople who have provided outstanding products and service, but they actually **take pride** in referring highly successful professionals to their friends and colleagues.

If you are seeing one of the top medical specialists in your city or town, aren't you proud to refer her to a friend? If you are represented by one of the top lawyers in your city, aren't you proud to refer a friend or business associate to this legal expert? *Your clients and customers feel the same way about referring people to you!* Doing so not only validates their decision to go with you in the first place, but also gives them a feeling of "pride of ownership" in having the opportunity to work with you. Beyond referrals from your current group of customers and clients, there are several other territories in which you can do some serious mining for sales gold.

Use Your Network to Net Leads

You have a tremendous source of leads just waiting for you. These veins of gold are hidden in your **network**. This network not only includes everyone you deal with in the context of your work, whether directly or indirectly, but also the qualified people whom you have met in **all** other activities in your life, such as through friends, clubs, associations, hobbies, classes, conferences, civic and community work, school groups, and social events. By stopping and looking **closely** and **objectively** at the vast range of people whom you know in this wide range of contexts, you can identify some of your greatest leads—those with the most potential to do business with YOU.

These are the people who know **you** and trust **you**, and most of them know at least one individual or company who could truly use what you are selling. You just need to say the word. *Ask and you shall receive.* Here is a powerful example of how one of Donald's coaching clients uses his network in a very low-key professional way.

Michael V. is one of the most successful stockbrokers in Southern California. He is also a generous patron to several charities (he began giving to these charities before he had much money). He gives one charity about $10,000 a year. Until recently, he never got any leads or business from this charity. In fact, that wasn't his goal in becoming involved with the charity. However, he knew that many of the other professionals involved with the charity did have the need for a great stockbroker and financial planner. Yet Mike never spoke about his financial advisory services due to his concern that people might think he was "needy" or "unprofessional." Actually, quite the opposite was true. Michael V. did not need more clients, but hundreds of investors in Pasadena, California, *desperately needed the guidance and wisdom Michael V. offered.*

Dr. Moine coached Mike in how to use some powerful but indirect verbal language patterns at certain social events sponsored by this charity. The last three years (2000, 2001, and 2002) have been devastating in the stock market to a number of investors and many people have lost 40 percent or more of the value of their portfolios. As people at these gatherings talked about their losses, Mike only used a few words Donald shared with him.

As he listened to these tales of woe, Michael would say, "You're kidding." Donald also coached Michael V. on the uses of certain powerful forms of body language. Sometimes, as he heard about all these stock market losses, with a slightly surprised and concerned look on this face, Mike would say, "You're pulling my leg, aren't you?"

That's all he says. Just a few words. The right words, with the right expression. Like Clint Eastwood or Al Pacino. People see the surprise on Mike's face and hear the concern in his voice. They subconsciously understand on a very deep visceral level that Mike has not been taking any losses in the stock market. There is little need for him to say anything more to turn this casual conversationalist into an excited prospect.

If the prospect goes on to say, "Well, haven't you lost a lot of money in the stock market? Everyone has." Mike just smiles and says, "No, actually my investors have done quite well. We haven't gotten rich over the past couple of years, but we have beaten all of the averages. We diversified and went into bond funds and a few stock sectors that were performing well. We've added to our net worth over the past few years." That is all Mike says. Just a few words. It takes less than one minute to say. Some of the people Mike has been meeting at these charity gatherings practically beg him to manage their million dollar plus portfolios.

The point is that Mike does not give $10,000 a year to the charity to get leads. He believes in the charity. He wants to do good and to help a worthwhile cause. However, when he is at these events, he does meet a number of high net worth people who desperately need his services. By using just a few carefully selected words that Dr. Moine supplied him with, Mike has brought in tens of millions of dollars in new assets under management. Mike's networking, which only takes a few hours a week, is now generating almost all the business he can handle.

Go to the Source

As in all matters of business, you need to exercise your good business judgment when assessing the referrals that others give you. It is essential that a lead be more than the prospect's name and company, lest you end up in a situation where you call a lead, use the name of the individual who referred you, only to hear something like, "Who was that again? Oh, I'm not sure but I think I met him once at a bar a few years ago." You find yourself embarrassed to have even called this lead.

In psychology, this issue is known as **source credibility**. For you to have a successful referral, the individual who is referring you must be perceived as both **credible** and **trusted** by the prospect. Without source credibility, you are finished before you even start.

To get a better understanding of the impact of source credibility, suppose a medical doctor proclaimed that his studies, funded by a prominent medical center, found that a high-fat diet can actually, in some cases, be good for the human heart. Such a finding may cause many people to do some serious rethinking because he is at a prestigious medical center.

Now take the exact same doctor, with the same study and the same findings, but remove the funding from the prominent medical center and replace it with funding from the International Whaling Lobby, which has proclaimed for years that whale blubber is the best thing in the world for one's heart. Suddenly, the significance and meaning of the physician's findings drop to zero, and so does the physician's ability to generate leads. That is exactly what happens to you if the individual referring you lacks credibility or is perceived as biased by the prospect.

Fortunately, there are a number of steps you can take to prevent this type of problem. First, you should take a careful look at the individual who gives you the lead. If this individual is successful, high-achieving, and well-accomplished in her career, the chances of a productive and credible referral increase dramatically. Put time and energy into this lead because it is likely you will be well-rewarded.

Researchers have found that successful people tend to know other successful people and spend a significant amount of time with them.

As you build your network, this is a very important fact to keep in mind. A network that is brimming with successful people also tends to be brimming with first-rate referral sources. And further, if you have a good number of successful people in your network, your chances of bringing in other successful individuals increase significantly. Sales millionaires invariably have many highly successful people in their network—even before they are millionaires! If you want to be first-rate in sales, you must cultivate and nurture relationships with highly successful people.

Second, if you are satisfied with the credibility of the individual giving you the referral, you should **still** try to learn as much as possible not only about the relationship between the referring individual and the lead, but also about the needs of the individual to whom you are being referred. If you hear the referral source fumbling and stumbling when you ask her for such information, you are setting the stage to fumble and stumble yourself when you make the call.

To prevent this from happening, before you make that call, do as much research as you can on the prospect, his or her industry, needs, and interests.

"But My Company Provides Me With Leads"

It's great if your company provides you with leads, but *sales super-stars are not prone to waiting for the company to hand them anything.* Certainly you want to do your very best with these company leads, but to join the ranks of sales millionaires, you will need to step out of the mold and *generate a great deal of leads of your own* as well. By doing so, you will see a real spike in earnings, recognition, and your personal sense of self-worth and achievement.

Besides, anything can happen to those company leads. What if the flow suddenly stops—where will you be then? Don't get hooked on company leads, but instead make sure you can generate quality leads on your own. Also, do not accept company leads uncritically. Ask a few questions. **Why** were you given these leads? Maybe they weren't very good. Maybe someone else didn't want them.

Unless you are the number one producer at your company, there is a good chance you are not getting the best leads.

Therefore, you must do all you can to generate high quality leads on your own. The salespeople who survive and thrive in **any** field and **any** economy are the ones who have built a solid bank of leads on their own and who are willing to continue to work hard to generate leads in the future.

Trade Show Tactics

Trade shows are bigger now than ever before. Billions of dollars are spent every year on trade shows. Why? Trade shows are one of the most efficient methods in existence of meeting, greeting, and telling your story to a huge number of qualified prospects in a short period of time.

Many sales millionaires have built or dramatically leveraged their success at trade shows. These industry gatherings offer excellent opportunities to significantly expand their network, visibility, and sales. You can **multiply** your success at trade shows by attending several of the panel discussions, meeting industry movers and shakers and, even better, by being on some of the panels. *Become a featured expert.* You must have the right mindset to do so, you must see yourself as an expert. Someone has to be an expert on these panels. Why not you? You will be **amazed** at the number of leads you generate.

Our clients have hired us to work at a number of trade shows teaching what we call **Boothmanship Salesmanship**. At one large medical equipment trade show, we helped our client get one of their salespeople on a panel. The other panelists were medical doctors. Our guy sold very expensive CT scanners and MRI (magnetic resonance imaging) machines.

Our salesman talked about how to install these $500,000 machines and how to shield the walls with lead to prevent the giant magnets from moving cars that might be parked on the other side of a wall. He told the story of one huge MRI machine that was improperly installed in a small building outside a hospital. When it was turned on for the first time, the giant magnets drew a car parked outside up against the building's wall. It was a very dramatic image! Our salesman was the hit of the panel. A number of attendees came up to speak with him afterward and he generated leads that resulted in several million dollars worth of sales of high-end medical diagnostic equipment.

During the trade show itself, you need to do more than just hang around the company booth (which is what many salespeople do). Be sure to work the entire trade show floor (you will be amazed at how many leads you can pick up at other people's booths!), never eat alone, and collect as many **high quality** names, numbers, and cards as possible. Don't just collect cards and names for the sake of collecting them.

Prequalify to make sure these people are genuinely interested in your products or services.

We have seen hundreds of companies use a fishbowl to collect cards at their trade show booth. A sign next to the fish bowl will say, "Drop your business card in here for a chance at winning a free trip to Hawaii!" Sure, you will get a lot of cards, but how many of those entering the contest are really interested in your products and services and how many of them just want a shot at the free trip to Hawaii?

At the height of the Internet mania, Dr. Moine was hired to teach Boothmanship Salesmanship at a major high-technology trade show. One of the companies exhibiting at this show was giving away a $100,000 Porsche

911 Turbo Carrera. Did their giant fishbowl collect a lot a business cards? You bet. The problem? Probably very few of those submitting their business card had any interest in the company or its products or services. They just wanted the Porsche! Most of the leads probably weren't even worth the time to follow up on.

Million Dollar Trade Show Strategy

**If you are going to use the fishbowl-and-a-prize strategy
for capturing leads at trade shows,
make sure your prize is something connected
to your company.**

Something that will prequalify the individual as a person genuinely interested in your company's products or services. The prize might be a free $1,000 package of your company's software. Or an all-expense paid trip to your company's headquarters and a tour of your operations. Or a free half-day consultation with two of your company's top consultants. You get the picture. By offering such a prize, you will actually capture leads of people who are **sincerely interested** in the products and services of your company. You will have leads that can produce hundreds of thousands to millions of dollars in additional sales.

Let each sincerely interested prospect know that you will be contacting them in the coming week or weeks. And then actually contact them. The proper use of trade shows can put you on the superhighway to becoming a sales millionaire or multimillionaire.

Generating Leads With a Hospitality Room

Think your budget will not allow you to buy a booth at a trade show? Think again. At some of the smaller trade shows, we have seen booths available for as little as $1,000. How many leads and how much business do you need to obtain to justify a $1,000 investment?

If your budget is limited and you still want to generate a number of high quality leads at a trade show, consider setting up a hospitality room. You can rent a room at a nearby hotel (preferably within walking distance), and host a meal or a cocktail hour. Invite the best prospects you meet at the trade show to your hospitality room.

An ideal time for a hospitality event is 4 to 6 p.m. By then, many people are tired of walking the trade show floors. They want a little break. You've met these people by walking the trade show floor yourself. When you meet fellow attendees who are interested in your company's products and services, give them an invitation to a cocktail hour meeting in your hospitality room. The invitation can be preprinted or something as simple as a note on the back of your business card. Be sure to include the exact address of the hotel, the room number, and the date and time of the reception.

Hospitality rooms are one of the most powerful trade show strategies of all. Why?

Because you have the prospects' undivided attention when they are in your hospitality room.

You don't have to worry about loud music coming from a nearby booth, or overly aggressive salespeople in the booth next to yours trying to attract the attention of your prospects. You have a captive audience nibbling on your food, drinking your drinks, and listening to your presentation. What could be better?

Once you have tried it, you will be amazed at how effective (and inexpensive) the hospitality room strategy is. Picture this: Prospects have been trudging for miles up and down trade show isles all day and you invite them for a cold beer, glass of Merlot, or orange juice and some appetizers to be served at 4:00 at the Marriott across the street. You'll have a rapt audience of 30 or so people, relaxing and listening to you tell your story.

Frequently, you can rent a meeting room at a local hotel for just a few hundred dollars. Some of our clients have been able to get a room free of charge because they have agreed to buy a few hundred dollars worth of food and drinks. Remember, you are just using this room for about two hours—the sweet spot of the trade show day—from 4 to 6 p.m. You don't want to interfere with anyone's plans for the evening. Some of our clients have spent about $500 on hosting a hospitality room that has generated dozens of highly qualified leads and tens of thousands of dollars worth of sales. *Some of them accomplished all of this at a trade show at which they did not even rent a booth!* Try it. This is one of the most powerful low-cost lead generation strategies in existence.

"But Trade Shows Don't Work in Our Business"

Occasionally clients will tell us, "Trade shows don't work in our business." Don't tell that to the salespeople and professionals in your industry who are making millions of dollars at trade shows!

Sales millionaires become millionaires because they always keep an open mind toward new business opportunities.

One of our clients will be exhibiting, for the first time, at a trade show to be held in Las Vegas. The total cost of the booth, transportation to the show, and hotel rooms for a few of their people comes to less than $20,000. How long will they have to wait to earn back their investment? *They already have.* Their salespeople are so excited about this new opportunity that they've been telling all their clients and prospects about it. Clients and prospects are seeing their business in a whole new light. Before even exhibiting at the trade show, sales have risen more than $70,000 beyond projections.

The above company is in a high-technology manufacturing field and they were totally convinced that "Trade shows do not work in our field." Their experience has taught them otherwise.

Recently, another client of ours exhibited their software for the first time at a different trade show. Sales superstars Steven Clements and Sean Higgins rented a small booth to display and demonstrate a highly sophisticated $5,000 software program that has helped them earn more than 78 percent per year over the past few years that have devastated most other stock investors. The combination of superior investment technology and outstanding salesmanship helped Steve and Sean set sales records. In addition, they walked away with dozens of leads who will become clients over the next few months.

Also at the same show was a friend of ours, Jeffrey Cohen, who manages a hedge fund for wealthy investors and who has designed a software program that helps investors make money whether their stock picks go up, stay flat, or even decline a little. Jeff consummated valuable sales and generated leads he never would have been able to obtain with his exhibiting at this trade show.

What if you still believe trade shows won't work for your business? Try exhibiting at **conventions** and **workshops**—anywhere you have a gathering of a large number of highly qualified prospects. Some of our clients have made tens of thousands of dollars in sales and have generated a huge number of leads by having a simple **table** set up in a hallway at a major conference. We've also used this technique ourselves with great success. For example, Dr. Moine was recently hired to deliver a speech to a large group of accountants who also do financial planning. His office manager was allowed to set up a table in the hallway outside the ballroom where Donald was speaking. Donald's office manager sold a number of copies of his books and also picked up business cards and contact information from several people who later became Donald's coaching clients. Exhibiting at trade shows and conventions is not just a theory to us. We know how powerful these techniques are because we use them ourselves. We walk our talk.

Fishing for Leads on the Internet

Another powerful source of leads today is the Internet. There are a growing numbers of sites that promise tremendous numbers of leads for users, with claims even stretching into the millions. *Do you really need a million leads?* What would you do with them? Could you even handle them? Such assertions need to be taken with a large grain of salt, but nonetheless, searching for leads on the Internet can be effective.

Be especially cautious in dealing with sites that promote mass e-mail marketing. These "lead generating businesses" will tell you that they have, for example, 9 million people who have opted in and have asked to receive their marketing pieces. Don't believe it! No matter what they tell you, most of these companies are selling and/or delivering spam, the equivalent of unsolicited junk mail on the Internet. Stay away from these firms if you wish to preserve your reputation and standing in the business community.

However, there are some sites on the Internet that provide forums for salespeople and sales managers to interact with each other. Some of these sites can help salespeople further build their networks and referral sources. In addition to the hundreds of industry-specific sites (plastics, chemicals, automobiles, agriculture, health care, financial services, etc.), we highly recommend *SellingPower.com*. SellingPower is the premier site for serious sales professionals all across the U.S. and Canada. It seems that almost every week they add some incredible new feature or benefit to their Website. This powerful resource is available free of charge, so bookmark *SellingPower.com* today and add it to your list of favorite sites.

Another one of our favorite Internet resource sites is *Hoovers.com.* Let's say you have an idea that a large company might be interested in one of your company's products or services. If the company is publicly traded, just go to *Hoovers.co*m and enter its stock symbol. In the flash of an eye, you will see on your screen full contact information, addresses, phone numbers, fax numbers, and a description of the business. You will also have instant access to the names of top corporate executives. All of this is free. For a small additional fee, you can access a tremendous amount of even more detailed information and the names, addresses, and contact information of additional executives. You may be able to make hundreds of thousands of dollars in additional income from information and leads you acquire from *Hoovers.com.*

Ad Hoc Steps to Add Referrals

As you step into the Ultimate Selling Power mode of thinking, you will discover many additional creative steps to help build your referral base and generate leads.

For example, one way to stand out from the crowd and gain instant respect is to write some articles for your industry journal or magazine, or even for the local newspaper. These types of articles do wonders to demonstrate your expertise, professionalism, and problem-solving skills. In addition, they get you and your ideas literally into the hands of the people to whom you wish to sell. Such articles make excellent calling cards when contacting prospects, and they make very impressive leave-behinds as well. This strategy is so powerful that we cover it in detail in Chapter 7. By writing articles for publications or Websites, you are using the power of the media to make yourself famous and to generate leads.

You can also build your network by increasing your involvement in community activities, such as by playing a more active role in youth sports, shelters, religious organizations, and various civic and business organizations. This is a way of doing good and doing well. Remember the example of Mike (earlier in this chapter) who had a low-key way of letting people in his elite charity know about all the help he could provide with their investments.

Yet another successful salesperson found that the section of the freeway that he adopted has been a remarkable source of publicity, name recognition, goodwill, and referrals. Have you ever considered adopting a section of a freeway? The credit you receive on the sign by the side of the freeway could be seen by hundreds of thousands of people each week—at no or low cost to you.

The only limit to your ability to generate leads is your own imagination. If you want to be perceived as outstanding, remember that the word **outstanding** implies that you **stand out** from all the others. Do something to stand out from others in a positive way and the leads will come to you.

What to Do With Those Leads

It is not uncommon to find more emphasis being placed on gathering leads than on managing them. This is similar (and just as unproductive) as the farmer who focuses on planting seeds, but has little interest in watering, weeding, or fertilizing his crops. If you don't do the additional work, you won't have much to harvest.

Just as the farmer needs to plant, water, weed, fertilize, **and harvest** her crops, you need to actively work and **manage** your leads to turn your prospects into customers and clients.

Traditional Lead Management

For many salespeople, lead management is a random process. As one salesperson recently told us in response to a question on this matter, "I file the leads that I get, but frankly, it is not always easy to find them later." Many salespeople are happy if they can simply locate their leads in whatever system they may be using. "Yep, they are here," the salesperson says, pointing to a big stack of business cards. "And as soon as I can find the time, I am going to call all these people." Putting off lead follow-up until later is a big mistake.

Just like uranium, **leads have a half-life**. As time goes by, leads rapidly lose their strength and value. If you met someone at a convention or trade show one month ago and promised to call him, he might barely remember you today. If you wait two or three months, he either won't remember you or will think negatively of you for waiting so long to contact him.

Salespeople typically mismanage leads in two different ways. Some leads are lost, misplaced, misfiled, or buried. Are the leads from that last trade show in the shoebox on the top shelf or in the fourth drawer of the filing cabinet in the other office? Who knows? Secondly, the value of leads is lost due to the *lack of significant relevant information attached to them.*

For example, if a salesperson is able to find the lead, he or she may not recognize the individual or much about the company, its history or potential, and, as a result, may then let the lead slide. With an up-to-date lead management system, that salesperson not only would have been able to find the lead faster, but also would have known far more about the individual and the company. Armed with such information, the salesperson would then have been able to make a contact decision based on facts rather than on a faulty memory or thin air.

The solution? Right after you meet someone and get her business card, rank the individual as a potential client. If you think she is likely to give your company a great deal of highly profitable business, give that person a 10. If you think she might not give you any business, write a "1" on the card (or, throw it out!). As you do further research on the person and the company, you can change the ranking. Then write down exactly what the prospect is most interested in. If she wants the XRB Model 75, write that down! Next, write down any of the prospect's concerns such as price, reliability, financing options, trade-ins, etc. Write all of this down while it is still fresh in your mind.

If you use a Palm Pilot, Blackberry, laptop computer, or any other device, store all this information there and—as a back up—transfer it to your desktop as soon as possible. We had a client a few years ago who lost more than $50,000 worth of sales and dozens of leads from a major trade show because his PDA got damaged on an airline flight. Don't let that happen to you!

If your time to follow up on clients is limited, start with the 10s. Don't tell yourself, "I will get to that **whole** stack next week." If you do, you will never get to it! Sales millionaires are ruthless about managing their time. *They will always call their best prospects immediately.* As their time permits, they will move down the list. Calling or e-mailing your best prospects takes them away from all of the other salespeople who are procrastinating—and it maximizes your chances for success.

The real problem of "lead management systems" that many salespeople use is that they are not systems at all. So-called "systems" that we have seen salespeople use include scraps of paper, random lists carried around in briefcases, hundreds of leads residing in a Palm Pilot (and seldom, if ever, called), cumbersome software programs, and bulging files filling up cabinets and collecting dust on bookshelves. A true system is not based so much on the storage medium (paper, computer, Palm Pilot, etc.) but is based on the **discipline** to use the collected information. **Whatever** system you use, make sure that you engage in *rapid and courteous follow-up* on all high quality leads and you will be well on your way to becoming a sales millionaire.

Two Leading Types of Errors

Having a lead management system that is little more than a randomly organized laundry list actually illustrates the sales version of the two main types of errors described in statistics, namely **type one** and **type two** errors. From the sales standpoint, a type one error means rejecting, overlooking, or in any other way disposing of solid leads. Obviously, this is a costly error, and in many cases, the salesperson is not even consciously aware of how it happened. She planned to follow up and had the best intentions in the world. But it didn't happen or did not happen promptly enough, and someone else got the sale. When this type one error is repeated again and again over the course of a year, a company can lose millions of dollars in sales.

The type two error means spending a good deal of time pursuing inappropriate or low potential leads. This error can be just as costly as not following up on your high potential leads. Why do so many salespeople pursue low potential leads? Because of the fear of rejection. High potential leads are usually highly successful people. They may be senior executives or business owners who control large budgets and have the ability to almost instantly say yes or no. To communicate on their level, you must be polished and professional. Their standards are higher and they can be judgmental of you and your sales presentation. This is a fact of life. However, these A+ level prospects can make you rich because they have the ability to place much bigger orders. Due to a fear of rejection, many salespeople avoid or procrastinate on calling on these high level leads.

The low level leads tend to be friendly and approachable. They have lots of time to "chitchat" with you. If your presentation is a little disorganized, that's okay (as long as you are buying them lunch!). They are not as likely to judge you. The door is always open to another meeting, because their time is not very valuable. Because they are so friendly, agreeable, and nonthreatening, salespeople call on them again and again. The problem is that even if they like your products or services, they will probably have to ask a higher-up for permission to buy. And there you are, back to dealing with a higher-level, more judgmental executive.

To solve this problem and save massive amounts of time, *call on the highest level leads first and concentrate your energies on these people.* They are the only ones who can help you break through your quota and make you a sales millionaire. If you need help in calling on high level executives or decision-makers, work with your sales manager or a sales coach who can help build your self-esteem. The bottom line is that you will never have the career you deserve if you procrastinate in calling on A+ prospects. *Get over it and start enjoying the success you deserve.*

With a truly functional lead management system, whether high-tech or low-tech, the salesperson is able to **almost instantly** access and analyze every lead, and then make a rational business decision regarding the sales priorities, best sales strategies, timing, and sales goals for each one. The salesperson will then immediately call on the highest potential leads and work diligently on turning them from prospects into customers and clients. This is the sales process that turns average salespeople into sales millionaires.

Leads That Are Not Misleading

For leads to be truly useful, they should be accessible and include full information on the prospect (company or individual), including the key players, company history, buying influences, relevant company data and product developments, budgets, account status, ROI figures, and more. Without knowing the **who**, **what**, and **why** of the lead, it is very difficult for the salesperson to know **what** to sell and **how** to sell.

This does not mean that you need to use a high-tech CRM (customer relationship management) system. However, the movement is definitely toward CRM, and today there are many easy-to-use and cost-effective CRM applications that can dramatically help you manage your leads. Read magazines such as *Selling Power* to learn about the latest CRM systems, features, benefits, and costs.

What You Want to See in CRM

If you are thinking about using CRM in your lead generation and management, there are several key components you should insist upon. The system should easily and quickly access your new and existing leads. You should be able to simply and rapidly enter data, and the screens should be easy to read (some CRM screens are so busy they almost give you a headache!). Your CRM program should provide you with updated customer information on a 24-7 basis so that everything is current even if you want to log on Sunday morning at 3 a.m.

The information in your CRM system should include the leads' status, source, ordering history, rates of return, and closure rates, and the system should provide you with customization that fits your company, your industry, and products and services you sell. It should have the ability to network with other sales professionals at your company if you do any team selling or sharing of leads. It should also have the ability to network with key suppliers or partners outside your company. It should store your proposals and all of your other important sales and marketing documents. It should store all of your sales scripts and sales presentations. If it does all of these things and more, and is easy to use, a sophisticated CRM system can help make you a lead generation, lead management, and sales genius!

5

How to Develop and Use Your Unique Selling Proposition

There are more than 15 million salespeople in the United States. If you add to that the number of lawyers, financial planners, accountants, consultants, medical doctors, stock brokers, chiropractors, psychologists, architects, pension fund managers, and other professionals who must know how to sell their services, the number swells to more than 23 million. *Why should anyone buy from you?*

In this chapter we will show you how to develop and use a powerful Unique Selling Proposition (USP) that will distinguish you from all others in your field in your geographical area. In some cases, you will be able to *distinguish yourself from everyone else in your field in the country.* In other cases, you will learn that all you need to be able to do is to distinguish yourself from your competitors within a five-mile radius! The outcome is the same: you will become a sales millionaire or multi-millionaire.

Why is having a Unique Selling Proposition so important? If prospects think you are "just like every other salesperson or professional," how can you expect to get their business? Even if you do get their business, how **loyal** will they be to you?

There are also **personal** benefits to having a Unique Selling Proposition. A USP reminds **you** of how special you are. We have found that a powerful USP builds strong self-esteem in the salesperson or professional. When you know in your heart how special you are, it makes it easier to sell.

You can actually have **several** Unique Selling Propositions. We are now developing advertisements for financial planners, stockbrokers, and other professionals that contain several Unique Selling Propositions, along with a photograph of the professional and a personal statement from him. These advertisements are incredibly effective for our clients. Plus, you can combine these Unique Selling Propositions into an "**elevator speech.**" Our colleague and friend Mark Magnacca has convinced us that *every salesperson in the U.S. should have an elevator speech*: a brief talk you can share if you ever find yourself on an elevator with someone who asks, "What do you do?" A combination of several USPs can serve as the centerpiece of an elevator speech that will leave a **strong positive impression** on anyone you meet, not just in an elevator, but in a line at the airport, at the hardware store, at a soccer game, or in any one of hundreds of other social or business situations.

Developing Your Unique Selling Proposition

What makes you unique? What makes you stand out? What distinguishes you from other salespeople in your geographical area? You should base your Unique Selling Proposition on these special traits, characteristics, or accomplishments. You might think these characteristics or traits are ordinary, but in the eyes of a prospect or client, they can make you stand out from all of the others in your field.

Take this challenge. Imagine that you are selling a kitchen cleanser. It scours, it cleans, it has all the usual ingredients. Your company is doing okay, getting by, but is not nearly as successful as it could be. What could you possibly do to raise your public profile? How in the world could you get the public to remember and look for your brand of kitchen cleanser?

First, look at your **ingredients**. If you find your cleanser has all the same ingredients as every other kitchen cleanser on the block, is this a cause for despair? NO. Ask yourself this question: *Have my competitors made the* *best use of each and every one of their ingredients?* Of course, the answer is no. Therein lies your entry. Therein you will find your Unique Selling Proposition.

What have your competitors overlooked or taken advantage of? No matter how mundane the ingredients, features, or benefits of the cleanser may seem to you, they could be very special to some potential buyers. Let us illustrate.

Imagine that many years ago you were a senior executive with Ajax, a moderately successful kitchen cleanser with many more successful competitors. What could you possibly say that might convince more people to buy your product? How could you ever come up with a Unique Selling Proposition that might interest millions of Americans?

First, you analyze your product and its ingredients. To your dismay, you find that it has more or less the same ingredients as many others' cleansers, in just slightly different proportions and colors. What can you do? Why don't you take a closer look at those ingredients? What are they? How are they used? What exactly do they do?

One of the prime ingredients in your cleanser, as in almost all cleansers, is ammonia. Big deal. Ho hum. Everyone has it. So what? How can you use ammonia in a Unique Selling Proposition? Ask yourself this question: *Has anyone else made use of this ingredient or component in a USP?* If not, you may just have found the keys to Fort Knox, as Ajax did.

Ammonia is one of the most common substances on the face of the earth. How could Ajax possibly use it in a Unique Selling Proposition? How could Ajax make it seem special? To develop a USP based on a cleanser containing ammonia seemed to be an impossible task. Therefore, Ajax executives looked at every other component of their cleanser to come up with something more unique or compelling than "ammonia." They came up empty-handed.

Returning to the ammonia theme, they brainstormed ideas. Finally, one of the advertising executives thought of "activated ammonia." The other executives looked at him with a blank face. Activated ammonia? "Yes," he said, "Ajax contains **activated** ammonia."

What is activated ammonia? None of the executives knew. No one knew. It seems like all ammonia should be active in some sense. They discarded the idea but then returned to it again and again when searches for another USP were fruitless. Finally, almost out of desperation, they decided to use "Ajax contains activated ammonia" as their Unique Selling Proposition.

The public was intrigued. **Activated** ammonia grabbed their attention. Sales began to increase. The company started using "Ajax contains activated ammonia," in their newspaper, magazine, and television ads. Long considered an "also-ran" in the kitchen cleanser field, Ajax gained significant market share and bumped off other cleansers to become one of the most popular cleansers in the U.S.

This did not go unnoticed by other kitchen cleansers. Previously, no one had featured "ammonia" in their advertisements because almost all cleansers had it. Now that they saw the power of Ajax's new ad, other cleansers began stating on their labels, "Contains ammonia," but it was too late. Ajax now **owned** the ammonia concept in the minds of millions of American consumers. When people heard that other cleansers also contained ammonia, they said, "Ah, they are just copying Ajax!" The other cleansers now touting ammonia were seen as me-toos or also-rans. Through its Unique Selling Proposition, Ajax now owned almost all the mental real estate having to do with "ammonia" and "activated ammonia."

Think about the significance of these findings for your company and the products and services you sell. There are many lessons to be learned from the Ajax case study. First, a powerful Unique Selling Proposition can help you capture the attention and the business of millions of people. Second, the feature or benefit of your Unique Selling Proposition does not itself have to be that unique, *if you describe it in a unique way*. Third, and perhaps most important of all, if you are **the first** to capitalize on a particular Unique Selling Proposition (as Ajax did with "activated ammonia"), you can **own** that concept in the minds of customers and clients for years to come.

How Long Should Your USP Be?

A USP can be as short as a few words or can be several paragraphs long. A USP does not have to be long to be good.

In most cases, the shorter the better.

When Donald began his professional career after receiving his Ph.D., he had "Sales Psychologist" printed on his business cards. At that time, he didn't even know what a USP was, and yet he developed one that brought him wide recognition as a speaker and business consultant. At hundreds of seminars for major corporations, he was introduced as "the sales doctor."

Why don't more salespeople have USPs? In many cases, they don't know what a USP is and in others they don't know how to develop one. We've also met salespeople who were afraid to develop a USP because they thought it might trap them in a certain field. This is a worry you needn't have. *You can change your USP.* In the early 1990s, Donald changed his USP to "Sales and Marketing Psychologist," because he was doing a great deal of work in designing advertising and marketing pieces and brochures.

Just as Donald has changed his USP, *you can change yours*. Change is in order if you have outgrown your old USP or if you are developing a new specialty (especially one that could make you famous or, at least, highly memorable). Best of all, when you change your USP, you usually don't have to get any kind of governmental or regulatory approval. However, use your common sense in this area. For example, if you are a stockbroker or investment advisor, don't come up with a USP such as, "World's Greatest Stock Picker." You just might have the Securities and Exchange Commission come knocking on your door!

A Skill-Building Exercise

In helping salespeople around the country develop powerful USPs, we ask, "Why should someone buy from you?" "What makes you or your company's products or services unique or special?" Right now, as a skill-building exercise, we suggest you take out a piece of paper and write down **five reasons** you deserve to be the **sales professional of choice** for any prospect upon whom you call. Be honest, as you are doing this exercise solely for your own benefit.

The five factors you have just listed contain the heart of your Unique Selling Proposition. In fact, just one factor alone can be powerful enough to be the centerpiece of your USP. Remember how Ajax took over market share nationwide with the relatively simple yet very powerful USP that "Ajax contains activated ammonia."

Professionals can benefit from Unique Selling Propositions just as salespeople do. The following examples will illustrate how professionals around the U.S. are building their businesses by developing powerful USPs.

One of our clients is a brilliant financial planner in Prescott, Arizona. While Will Hepburn does comprehensive financial planning, his Unique Selling Proposition is a form of active mutual fund management he calls *The Super Sector System* (now trademarked). Using a sophisticated model based on moving average convergence and divergence, momentum, money flows, and other measures, he knows when to move into and out of certain sectors of the market, or when to move to cash. How has he done? Over the past two years he has outperformed the S&P 500 benchmark by more than 25 percent annually. We are now encouraging him to make his powerful investment service available to other financial advisors around the country.

In the middle 1990s, Donald worked with an insurance specialist in Florida and helped her develop and promote a powerful USP. Leslie concentrated on finding the best life insurance policies in the country to help protect high net worth families from the devastating effects of estate taxes. The Unique Selling Proposition Donald developed for Leslie is *Advisor to Some of America's Wealthiest Families*, and we ran this USP underneath her photo in seminar advertisements across Florida. All over Palm Beach, Naples, Marco Island, and Tampa, high net worth people referred to Leslie as "an advisor to some of American's wealthiest families." *We wonder where they got that idea?*

Donald also developed the following USP for her seminars: *Learn How to Slash Your Estate Taxes by Up to 90%*. We ran this headline in two-inch type in newspapers serving high net worth communities all over Florida. Combined with powerful benefit statements later in the advertisement, this headline drew hundreds of affluent people to Leslie's seminars. How effective were these two USPs? For many years Leslie earned more than $750,000 annually while only working about six months of the year. She was able to concentrate on doing the kind of work she most wanted to do: helping families preserve their wealth and slash their estate taxes. She took the other six months of the year off.

Jack Perry is one of the top professionals in the country in a highly competitive field known as financial wholesaling. Dr. Moine originally met Jack in the late 1980s when Jack was the chief executive officer of United Resources, one of the top annuity companies in the United States. At United Resources, Donald worked with Jack Perry and other top company executives to hire, train, and develop an elite level team of annuity salespeople.

They wrote comprehensive sales script books, filmed educational videos, and delivered sales seminars to hundreds of the company's salespeople around the country, and in the process they broke every sales record at United Resources.

During this time, Jack Perry became known as *the Knowledge Broker*. Whenever he found a great new idea or strategy, *Jack shared that knowledge* with his people. After the sale of United Resources to a multibillion dollar insurance company, Jack turned his attention to Perry-Morris Leasing, a multimillion dollar equipment leasing company of which he was co-founder and co-owner. His USP of being "the Knowledge Broker," followed him to Perry-Morris Leasing. He again retained Dr. Moine's services to train that sales staff, and develop sales scripts and powerful presentations. Together with Jeff Perry, they built annual sales to more than $100 million.

Now, 10 years later, as a senior executive for one of the top annuity and mutual fund companies in the U.S., Jack is still known as "the Knowledge Broker." His Unique Selling Proposition has served him well for 15 years in diverse industries. Jack Perry shows that sometimes an individual can develop a USP that is so timeless and so flexible, it can serve that professional even when he makes major changes across industries.

What if Your Services Are Not That Unique?

We know that many of you are now saying, "The products and services I offer are not that unique. How can **I** develop a USP?" The truth is that many sales professionals do offer similar products and services. Many of our clients, in fact, offer similar products and services, and yet they have been able to develop Unique Selling Propositions that help them stand out from the crowd. Here are some effective strategies.

1. Develop a Unique Name

Many of the salespeople we coach sell a wide range of products in a field crowded with similar products. Likewise, many of the professionals we work with are offering services and products similar to those of their competitors. For example, one of the most common specializations for financial planners is to work with seniors, retirees, or those about to retire.

How to stand out? Develop **and trademark** a very appealing, unique name. This can be a name for your business or a name or title you give yourself. Two of our clients in Redondo Beach, California, developed and trademarked the name *Retirement Protection Group*. Who doesn't want their retirement to be protected? We've coached Christina Jesperson and Tom Gray to mention their company name, Retirement Protection Group, over and over in their seminars and now it is on the lips of hundreds of retired people in the surrounding beach communities. It is also in large gold letters on the outside of the building they own in Redondo Beach.

Another one of our clients in Phoenix, Arizona, developed and trademarked the term *Retired Planning*. When Robert Zakian does his seminars, he explains what other financial advisors do and then he explains what makes his Retired Planning so unique. Retired Planning is something people remember and respond to, and Bob's business, AIM Financial Group, has grown very nicely over the past two years and now has two offices.

We are encouraging both of these clients to license their USPs to financial advisors in other states; thus the need for trademark protection. The above financial planners do not have unique specializations or unique backgrounds. However, they have somewhat unique names that they have done an outstanding job of promoting. They are now enjoying the rewards of having their USPs uppermost in the minds of retirees in their areas. Besides helping you build your practice, a powerful USP can be another income stream or **profit center** for your business if you license it to others in your field who are in different geographical regions or who are noncompetitive with you.

2. You Make the Difference

If the products and prices are about the same, what makes the difference? *You do.* The presidents of some of the companies for whom we have consulted have told us that their company's products are about the same as those of the competition. For example, a number of years ago, we did some sales training seminars for one of the largest steel companies in the U.S. The president told Dr. Moine that while they were very proud of the quality of their steel, it was just about identical to the steel sold by their competitors. He also said their prices were very similar. When the products are similar and the prices are similar, what makes the difference?

The individual sales professional: YOU.

Sometimes salespeople complain that their company's products are not the very best in the industry. At other times they complain that their company's products are not the lowest priced. Some salespeople even complain that their company does not have both the lowest prices and the highest quality. We believe salespeople should not make these complaints. Why? Think about it. If a given company always had the highest quality and the lowest prices (and, thank goodness, no company does), why would they need you? They could just put highly persuasive ads in newspapers, magazines, and on the Internet proving they have the highest quality and the lowest prices and they could fire all of their salespeople. Think about that the next time you find yourself complaining about the issues mentioned here. The fact that your company does not always have the highest quality and the lowest prices means that they need you!

Instead of focusing all of your attention on your company's products, services, or prices, ask yourself, "What makes **me** unique?" What special value do I bring to my clients and customers? In many sales situations, the extra value delivered by the sales professional overshadows and supercedes all product and price differences.

Just as your fingerprints are unique, so are many of your other traits, characteristics, and accomplishments. In the 1990s, Donald worked with a wonderful financial planner in Colorado Springs, Colorado named Dr. Bill McCord. Bill's doctorate in education distinguished him from all other financial planners in his area. People who thought other financial planners were product pushers saw Dr. Bill McCord as a teacher and educator. Donald and Bill McCord wrote a book, *Better Than Gold: An Investor's Guide to Swiss Annuities* (Regnery Press, 1998). The book showed how to purchase and use Swiss annuities, which are widely considered to be among the safest, most lawsuit-proof, IRS-proof investments in the world, and this book became a second USP for Dr. McCord. Although now out of print, the book has become a collector's item and sometimes commands more than $100 a copy on the Internet. The book continues to bring fame, name recognition, and international respect to Dr. Bill McCord, one of the top Certified Financial Planners in Colorado.

For just one moment, forget about your products, services, and prices. What makes **you** unique? Is your educational background at all unique? We have worked with salespeople who also have law degrees. Depending upon what is being sold, this can be a powerful advantage in convincing prospects to become clients. We have worked with salespeople who are also certified public accountants and we can use their educational background in helping clients analyze purchases and save money. One CPA client of ours who became a highly successful salesperson developed the USP of *Financial Solutions Specialist.* Who would not want to work with someone who was a specialist in Financial Solutions? We have worked with salespeople who have doctorate degrees in math and science and have helped them develop powerful USPs that create an unforgettable positive impression in the minds of customers and clients.

One of Dr. Moine's friends and clients is Phil Kavesh, Esquire. Phil has developed one of the largest estate planning law practices in California, with more than 10,000 clients (he has so many clients he has had to hire a number of other top lawyers to serve them!). In addition to having a law degree, Phil has a master's degree in tax and is a Certified Financial Planner. A Unique Selling Proposition Donald developed for Phil is *Immortality Planning* (now trademarked). While other estate lawyers can plan your estate, figure your taxes, etc. (yawn), Phil can show you how to use your estate to achieve **immortality** and build a **legacy** that will stand the test of time. Who would you rather work with, a mere estate planner, or someone who can grant you immortality? Now do you understand the power of a Unique Selling Proposition?

But What if I Am Really, Really Ordinary?

Occasionally we get the refreshingly honest client who says, "No one can develop a USP for me. I am truly, outstandingly ordinary." We love these clients.

Hey, we are all ordinary. The authors of this book are so ordinary it would curl your hair. We are both married, with children. We eat high-fiber cereal, read the local newspaper, and like to jog and work out. Man, are we boring. Call 9-1-1. Our hobbies are nothing unusual and when we are not doing seminars, consulting, or coaching, we like to travel and spend time with our family and friends. What is our point?

Being as ordinary as we are in most respects, we have achieved a fairly high level of success in a highly competitive field. We've consulted with some of the top corporations in the U.S. and several foreign countries. We've been an advisor and coach to some of the top salespeople and professionals across the country. How have we been able to do that? We have leveraged our USPs to become known nationwide in several key areas over the past 20 years. For example, in the mid-1980s, Donald wanted to become known as a professional speaker. The USP he used at that time was "Sales Speaker." When he got to the point that he was being booked five days a week to give speeches, he backed off on that USP and started using the USP of "Sales and Marketing Psychologist" and built a nationwide practice in that area. Ken Lloyd has become nationally famous as "The Organizational Behavior Consultant," and has consulted with numerous chief executive officers, presidents, and other top corporate executives.

In many ways, your task is easier than ours. In our business, we need to become known nationally. Most salespeople only need to become well-known and trusted by a limited number of customers and clients in a relatively small geographical area to achieve a high level of success. We advocate the use of Unique Selling Propositions because we know they have helped us dramatically build our own businesses and because we have seen the tremendous positive impact that USPs have had on the careers of our clients. We know that a great USP can help you achieve high level success in sales, no matter how ordinary or average you might think you are.

**Remember, when the products are similar
and the prices are similar (as they often are),
it is the uniqueness of the sales professional
that makes the difference.**

A powerful USP helps you develop and capitalize on that uniqueness so that your prospects, customers, and clients will never forget you.

**Another great tip for developing a USP is to review all
of your accomplishments.**

What are you most proud of? What have you helped your clients do? Maybe you have helped some of your clients enjoy record profits. That could be part of your USP. Maybe you have helped some of your customers or clients save thousands or millions of dollars. Use that in your USP. If you are a travel agent, think of all the people you have helped plan and enjoy "the vacation of a lifetime." You helped them and their family members create and enjoy experiences and memories they will never forget. That can be part of your USP. If you are a plastic surgeon, you have helped people rediscover their beauty and have raised their self-esteem to new heights. If you are a builder, you have created homes that have nurtured and strengthened American families. No matter what you sell, look at all the **benefits** you have provided your clients. Within those benefits, you can find powerful Unique Selling Propositions.

It does not matter that other people in your field might have the same accomplishments.

If you are the first to capture those accomplishments in a USP, you will own those accomplishments.

We have recently learned that back in the 1920s, there were a few Ph.D. psychologists in the U.S. who were helping major corporations with sales psychology. However, they **never** created a USP around sales psychology. Instead, they were known as "Industrial Psychologists." In the 1980s we created the USP of "Sales Psychologists" and it became **our international brand** through our seminars, speeches, books, and tapes. Now that there are a few other psychologists joining the field (and we welcome them!), they are seen as copycats.

We want these other sales psychologists to become famous and to enjoy great success, as there is a tremendous need for sales psychology consulting that we cannot fulfill. Based on our own experience, we know that if you create a Unique Selling Proposition in your field, you have a good chance of **owning** that identity for many years to come. No matter how "average" you might think you are, we guarantee that you have some accomplishments that could be the centerpiece of a stunningly effective USP.

Once you have a great USP, use it throughout all of your sales literature, on your business card, in your screen name, and in the name of your Website. Burn this Unique Selling Proposition into the minds of your clients and you will own it. You may not have a $100 million advertising budget like Pepsi, Coke, IBM, or dozens of other companies, but through **the power of repetition**, you can create and own what advertisers call an M-space (mental space) in the minds of your prospects, customers, and clients around the world.

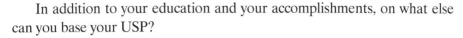

In addition to your education and your accomplishments, on what else can you base your USP?

Take a look at your values.

Your dedication to your clients and customers, your attention to detail and/or your caring attitude could form the basis of your Unique Selling Proposition. Service, dedication, and attitude are extremely important to clients and customers. You may not have control over the products or services your company offers or its prices; however, you have a great deal of control over the **level of service you provide** and almost total control over your **attitude**. Perhaps no other salesperson in your industry or in your area can match the level of service you provide. You **own** these benefits. Make the most of them in your Unique Selling Proposition.

Mistakes to Avoid in Your USP

Sometimes sales professionals and companies hire us to review their brochures, newspaper and magazine advertisements, Websites, and promotional packages. In the past few years, we have often been told that the salesperson's or the company's "brand" is the USP and the "brand" is conveyed via the entire brochure, advertisement, or Website. If you haven't noticed, "branding" has recently become one of the favorite buzzwords in sales and marketing.

Invariably, the mailing pieces and brochures we are hired to analyze have dazzling graphics, beautiful typesetting, and outstanding production quality. The problem is that the actual content is often appallingly bad. Sometimes it feels as if you are looking at a big shiny car with lots of chrome, fat oversized tires, and a big horn, but when you raise the hood, there is no engine. There is nothing to make these pieces go or to motivate the reader.

We never blame our clients because they seldom write much of these brochures or advertisements. Inevitably, these promotional pieces have been developed by an expensive advertising agency. We've seen individual salespeople spend thousands of dollars on advertisements and promotional pieces that are doomed to failure. We've seen companies spend $100,000 or more on fancy "branding" brochures and glossy advertisements that get them absolutely no business.

Take a look at the full-page advertisements in the *Wall Street Journal*, the finest business newspaper in the world. You might see a full-page picture of someone posing as an engineer. In small type at the bottom of the page you might find some boring, easily forgettable information about a network server. You might see another large ad for a mutual fund company touting its "Big Cap Value Fund." No problem, except that the ad is almost indistinguishable from those of its competitors. As you see page after page of these meaningless or ineffective advertisements, you wonder why a company would pay more than $100,000 a day to run such advertising.

Even more remarkable is the fact that many of these ads run day after day, costing millions of dollars per year. The same ads appear in many different magazines and newspapers, running the total to hundreds of millions of dollars per year. You might have spent five seconds glancing at the ad when you first saw it. After that, you turned the page as quickly as possible when you came across this fluff. Most stunning of all is that a number of these ads are being run and paid for by companies that are losing tens of millions to hundreds of millions of dollars per year (just look up the stock prices of the companies running the ads!). Don't they have a better use for their corporate funds?

We are great believers in advertising, but we only believe in effective advertising. Mindless advertising, just to say you are advertising, is a waste of corporate funds and is a form of management malpractice. Unless you are a corporate executive, you may not have any control over the type of advertising your company runs or the messages in the ads. However, if you are a marketing executive or if you own your own company, you **do** control your advertising and marketing.

Take a hard, critical look at the advertising and brochures you use. Take an objective look at those of your competitors. What is really working? Why do people buy products or services in your field? What can you do to stand out and to grab attention in a crowded marketplace? What Unique Selling Propositions are you using? What USPs could you use?

Not all USPs are good. For example, let's say you are selling industrial chemicals. You might come up with a USP calling yourself, "The industrial chemical salesman who likes to play tennis." It is probably unique because no other industrial chemical salesman is likely to have ever put this brand

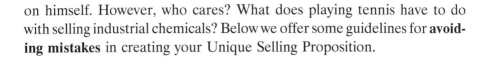

on himself. However, who cares? What does playing tennis have to do with selling industrial chemicals? Below we offer some guidelines for **avoiding mistakes** in creating your Unique Selling Proposition.

Mistake #1

The first mistake to avoid in developing a powerful USP is to **avoid fluff**. As we mentioned earlier in this chapter, in most respects, the authors of this book are thoroughly average. We don't think many of our clients have anything more than a passing interest in our hobbies, recreational interests, musical tastes, or culinary preferences. Do yours? Our clients hire us to do a job—to help them rapidly increase sales and profits—and we work as hard as we can to help our clients break sales records and make massive amounts of money. *Why do your clients hire you?* **That** should be the **centerpiece** of your Unique Selling Proposition.

We are not against brochures or advertising. Quite the contrary—we are big fans of it. We hope the *Wall Street Journal* and every magazine and newspaper in America runs even more ads. We'd love to see dozens of additional ads in newspapers and magazines because that means commerce is working and people are excited about buying goods and services. We've helped many of our clients rewrite bland "branding" brochures or "image" advertising to turn them into effective marketing pieces. Granted, the job is not easy and we do not have instant solutions. Frequently it takes a lot of hard work by our clients and ourselves to perfect the message. But the net result—more sales and more profits—is worth the effort.

Take a fresh look at your advertising and promotional pieces. Can you even find the Unique Selling Proposition? What makes you or your company stand out? Use the ideas contained in this chapter to revamp your brochure or advertisements. Make sure you concentrate on the reasons **why** people actually buy from you and your brochure or advertising will become many times more effective.

Mistake #2

The second mistake many salespeople and executives make in developing a Unique Selling Proposition is **ignoring their specialization.** Are your company's products or services **dominant** in one segment of the market?

Let readers know that. Do certain types of people or professionals really love your products or services? Share that news—not everyone knows that about you, your products, and your services.

If you or your company have a true specialty, you might really hit the Comstock Lode with the right USP. If you are the equivalent of a brain surgeon in your field, don't describe your services as if you are a general practitioner. That's a big mistake.

To give you some idea of the power of specialization, Donald recently wrote an article for a high-tech Website on the subject of protecting the value of company stock. In the article, Donald mentioned two Salomon Smith Barney brokers who became known for their work in the area of employee stock options. Working out of Atlanta, Georgia (not Silicon Valley), these two brokers built a **$2 billion** book of business that generated fees estimated at nearly $30 million a year. You read that right. That is not a misprint. Nearly $30 million a year. The average stockbroker at Salomon Smith Barney earns about $150,000 a year by being a generalist. These two brokers brought in nearly **$30 million a year** by becoming known as experts in one area: employee stock options. After the company's cut, it is estimated that each broker brought home nearly $10 million a year in personal income.

Skill-Building Exercise

Before you read any further, think for a moment about your sales practice or your business. Analyze the source of the majority of your profits. In many businesses or sales fields, 80 percent of the profits come from 20 percent of the products or services being sold. *What if you became known as the expert in this 20 percent area?* What if you developed a powerful Unique Selling Proposition that reinforced your image as the expert in these lucrative areas? Think of how much more you could sell in this most profitable area of your business. In your field, you could become the equivalent of the two brokers who earned $10 million a year at Salomon Smith Barney. Once you have identified these most lucrative areas of sales for your business or profession, come up with one or two USPs to distinguish yourself from all of your competitors in those specializations.

Avoiding Clichés in Your Unique Selling Proposition

One of our hobbies, as you might have guessed, is to read and study advertisements. It can be a frustrating hobby because, unfortunately, many advertisements have no Unique Selling Propositions at all. Others have words that the writers of the ads might consider USPs but, due to overuse, the words are really little more than clichés.

Banks, insurance companies, and lawyers are three of the worst offenders in terms of overusing these marketing clichés. Carefully study the advertisements for banks and insurance companies and notice how many times you see hollow words such as "**strength**," "**integrity**" and "**personalized service**." Frequently these words are placed in big bold letters directly underneath the name of the bank or insurance company, as in

Main Street Bank
STRONG. TRUSTWORTHY. LOYAL.

Consider this scenario. An individual reads such an ad and says to his spouse, "Oh, look honey. This bank is trustworthy. You said we should have a trustworthy bank. Maybe we should bank there." Has this scenario ever taken place in all of recorded human history? Never! Why, then, do banks and insurance companies continue to run such ads?

There is absolutely nothing wrong with words such as "strong," "trustworthy," "loyal," and "honest." In fact, these words can be powerfully persuasive in other contexts. The problem is that they are so overused that they have become clichés in certain fields. When words become so overused in a given profession, they cannot be considered a Unique Selling Proposition. They cannot even be considered effective.

Even worse than overused words are hackneyed clichés. Recently, we were analyzing some television ads running in Los Angeles. A large automobile insurance company had just unveiled its new television ad campaign. We are not making this up: their Unique Selling Proposition was, "*You've had the rest, now have the best.*" How many times have you heard that old worn-out expression? Would hearing that cliché get you to pick up the phone and call that insurance company for a quote on your auto insurance? We didn't think so.

Do not get the impression that a Unique Selling Proposition has to use fancy or unusual words to be effective. Quite the contrary. Some of the best USPs are composed of simple words that are powerfully organized. Some of these USPs are so powerful that they live on for years or even decades. When you hear the words, *The Ultimate Driving Machine*, you probably immediately think of BMW. Because we do not drive BMWs and have no connection to their advertising agency, we are objective and unbiased in praising their USP. How many other automobile USPs can you think of? What is the USP for Mercedes, Chrysler, Buick, Mazda or for Toyota? BMW has been rapidly gaining market share over the past several years. Do you now see the power of a great USP?

As you work on developing and perfecting your USP, avoid clichés and **focus on simple, powerfully arranged words**. Study the best Unique Selling Propositions you find and you'll be able to generate even more ideas on how to develop and polish your USP.

Tips for the Salesperson Who Has No Credentials

In some sales fields, many salespeople have advanced degrees or special certificates. In the high-tech computer, Internet, information technologies, and medical product fields, many salespeople have engineering degrees. The real estate field has many professional designations beyond becoming a Realtor and the insurance field also has a large number of specialty certificates, such as the CLU, which can be earned. We are sometimes contacted by salespeople, financial planners, and others who are either not college graduates or who have no credentials or minimal credentials. They will ask us how they can develop a Unique Selling Proposition given their lack of credentials and lack of education.

For example, a financial planner recently called us, told us his background was "weak," and wanted help in developing a Unique Selling Proposition. As we interviewed him, we learned that he had finished nearly 80 percent of his undergraduate degree before he dropped out. His lack of a college degree had always bothered him. We told him that, if at all possible, he should try to finish up his college degree through taking evening courses, weekend courses, or courses on the Internet.

**While formal education is not a necessity in all fields,
it is often considered by the public as one of the
basic components of competency.**

We also told him to look into picking up one or two professional credentials. *These credentials can sometimes be earned in as little as a week or two or formal instruction.* For example, did you know that you can take a one week course, take a test, and become a stock broker? It is that easy! It does **not** mean you are a good stockbroker, but it does mean you will have your license. American society respects experts and credentials. Gather up these credentials (and really study the material!) and use them to your advantage.

Do not let your temporary lack of credentials stop you from developing a Unique Selling Proposition. You need, and can benefit from, a powerful USP **right now**. The financial planner who called us was discouraged by his lack of a college degree and credentials. He was a skilled planner with a number of highly satisfied clients, but he wondered if he could ever make it to the big leagues given that he lacked much formal education and credentials. As we were working with him on his USP, we shared with him a case study that he found fascinating. It is the story of a person with even fewer credentials who, for a number of years, was one of the most prominent voices in the financial advice field in the U.S.: **Charles Givens**.

In the early 1990s, Donald had the opportunity to work with Charles Givens and a number of his seminar leaders. As far as we know, Chuck was not a college graduate and had no licenses or credentials. He wrote several books that could be classified as "financial advice 101." There was nothing revolutionary in the books, yet they were fairly well-written and had some interesting case studies. Despite his rather ordinary background, when Donald worked with Charles Givens and his seminar instructors, *Forbes* magazine estimated Charles Givens's net worth at more than $200 million. How is it possible for a college dropout with no credentials to enter a highly competitive field such as the financial advice business and become a multimillionaire? Chuck had a powerful USP to which hundreds of thousands of Americans responded.

Charles Givens' Unique Selling Proposition was *Wealth Without Risk*. It was also the title of his *New York Times* number one best-selling book. Chuck wrote other books, but they didn't do nearly as well. Why? He strayed from his Unique Selling Proposition. When he later returned to his USP and penned a book called *More Wealth Without Risk*, he again hit the national best-sellers list.

When Dr. Moine worked with Charles Givens and his team, Charles was so busy and so successful he didn't have much time to give seminars anymore. In fact, to meet Donald, he flew back from Europe on his private jet to his headquarters in Orlando, Florida where Donald was delivering an advanced sales training seminar. Donald's job was to train more than 40 of Charles Givens's speakers who conducted workshops around the U.S. every weekend. Chuck made most of his fortune (millions of dollars every month) by selling educational books and tapes and by offering financial education seminars around the country. He did not sell investments.

We are convinced that his powerful Unique Selling Proposition is one of the reasons Chuck Givens achieved such a phenomenal level of financial success. To his credit, he also presented financial planning concepts in a way that most Americans found interesting and useful. If Chuck Givens, with his limited background, could achieve all that he achieved with the help of his USP, imagine what a powerful Unique Selling Proposition can do for you.

Once you have developed your Unique Selling Proposition, **leverage it** and **promote it** in advertising, on your Website, in articles, and in the media and you will have a major business-building advantage over the vast majority of other salespeople and professionals in your area.

6

The Pre-Sale Warm-up

A neophyte salesperson who came to us for some coaching related a tale of woe regarding one of her ventures into the field. She was very excited about getting an appointment with what appeared to be a promising lead, and she could hardly wait to meet with him. She was ready to enthusiastically deliver a fantastic presentation and hopefully sell him a management training and development program.

She entered the meeting with a great deal of product knowledge plus all the enthusiasm in the world, having read numerous times that it is important to project a positive attitude. Unfortunately, if all that a salesperson brings to the presentation is product knowledge and enthusiasm, the situation can turn negative rather quickly. As her presentation moved along, the prospect began peppering her with questions about her understanding of his company, its products, services, corporate culture, style, and objectives.

The salesperson knew all about the features and benefits of her company's products, but painfully little about the prospect, his company, and their products and services. Then came the second toughest question that she was to hear from this prospect, "How can you meet our needs if you don't know anything about us?" She fumbled for an answer and came up with a partial save by saying that one of the reasons for her visit was to learn about his company.

Then she was hit by the toughest question of all: "We are a major clothing manufacturer. Everyone knows us. We are in hundreds of stores all over America. How can you come in here wearing an outfit that flaunts the label of a competitor of one of our divisions?" After a subtle but perceptible flinch, she started to respond by saying, "I didn't think that this would present a problem because…uh…uh…." All her prospect heard was, "I didn't think." And he did not think of buying from her.

This type of woeful story is replayed day in and day out in the world of sales, and it rarely has a happy ending. Fortunately, with state-of-the-art advanced planning, you can make sure that you never find yourself in that position.

Mind Over Matters

The first step to take in the sales planning process is a **mental** step, starting with the language you use. Some salespeople describe the initial sales preparation process with terms such as **sales presentation planning** or **prospect interview**. The problem starts with the specific label you use. The psychological message you are giving yourself if you use the above words is that the objective is merely a well-planned presentation or an interview with a prospect. What sales millionaires focus on right from the outset is successfully closing the sale.

Now let's examine the powerful language used by Jerry Frank, who served as the president of IMA Incorporated, a highly successful marketing consulting firm based in Phoenix, Arizona. At IMA, this activity falls under the heading of **pre-client contact**. Notice that from the outset, there is a strong **built-in belief** that the targeted individual or organization **is** going to become a client.

This type of language builds a powerful sense of **confidence** and a winning attitude among all of the players who are involved in the sales process. As they plan the presentation, the underlying message is that they believe in themselves and in their ability to turn prospects into clients by providing **exactly** what is needed. This sense of confidence not only helps them do a thorough job in the preparation stage, but also in the presentation itself and in closing the sale.

What You Expect Is What You Get

An important part of the mental game of pre-client contact is your set of expectations.

Psychological research has established that expectations profoundly influence outcomes.

For example, if a salesperson expects to have problems in a sales presentation and believes that he or she will most likely walk away without a sale, the odds for failure increase **exponentially**. You need to **inoculate yourself** against these types of self-defeating beliefs.

Our expectations have a subtle, yet visible and measurable, impact on our speech, body language, vocabulary, intonation, and overall demeanor. *These cues are consciously or unconsciously picked up by clients and customers*, and our clients and customers react in highly predictable ways.

At the same time, if you have **positive expectations** when meeting with customers or prospective clients, *these will also be perceived* and can profoundly influence their attitudes, enthusiasm, and suggestibility.

During the **pre-sale stage** (notice that this assumes a sale), if you sense negative expectations about **any** aspect of the forthcoming meeting with a customer or potential client, you should stop **immediately** and try to *locate the source of this negativity*. Then immediately reprogram yourself to get rid of this attitude that can kill sales. It sounds easier than it is, but by doing some more serious thinking at this stage, you will find that your sales closing ratio will soar to higher levels than you have ever achieved in the past.

Perhaps you have doubts about some of the features or benefits of your company's products or services. Perhaps you have a fear of rejection or a fear of failure. Maybe you have stage fright: are you presenting in front of people whom you think might judge you harshly? Share these concerns with the person you trust most. Don't keep them bottled up inside. Share your feelings and fears with your spouse, your best friend, your sales manager, your sales coach, your boss, or someone else you can trust **implicitly**.

Get With the Programming

One very successful salesperson at one of our entertainment client companies focuses on **sending himself** personal messages during the planning process. He consciously programs himself to remove certain negative words and expressions from his vocabulary, such as *can't, could not, should not, will not, won't, should have done, failure*, and *quit*. And on the positive side, the two words that have become his constantly repeated mantra are: **listen** and **solve**.

Rather than focusing on everything he wants to say about how great his company is and how great he is, he focuses on *listening* to his prospects and clients. **Whatever** problems or challenges he hears, he focuses on **solving** them. This approach has made him a sales multimillionaire and has brought great benefits to his clients. Try this approach. It works. We use it ourselves in being totally focused on listening to our clients and then becoming totally obsessed with helping them solve all of their sales and marketing problems.

Napoleon said, "Men are ruled with words." Just as people rule each other with words, *we rule ourselves with words*. What words are you ruling yourself with?

> **And as the marketing pros on Madison Avenue clearly understand, the more a message is repeated, the more it is internalized and believed.**

It may be unfair, but if a message is repeated enough times, it has a strong chance of being perceived as **reality**. Once you comprehend this, you can begin understanding both the positive and negative consequences. When a salesperson continues to use negative words ("I am not doing well," "The prospect doesn't like me," etc.), it is just a matter of time before he or she believes these words and then acts accordingly.

> **To get rid of negative results, first get rid of negative words.**

As another example, Medo Eldin, a very successful manager of promotions for PennySaver Media, approaches the planning stage and the presentation with one key word in mind: **possibilities**. As he studies prospects before his meetings, and then again during the meetings, he is constantly looking for *all the possible new ways to meet the prospect's needs*. As a result, you'll see Medo nodding his head frequently at every stage of the process, even when he hears supposedly "negative" comments from a prospect. He is always in agreement with the prospect. He listens, responds, and **educates**. And in the response and education, he turns almost all of his prospects into clients and helps them improve their sales.

Check Out the Company: Is It One You Want to Keep?

Today's sales millionaires understand that **the more they know** about the potential customer's company or organization, the greater the likelihood of sales success. This type of deep understanding helps in two important ways.

First, by understanding a company's history, products, services, current developments, successes, problems, challenges, and objectives, it is far easier for a salesperson to identify the key needs and some of the ways in which his or her company's products or services can meet them. During the actual presentation and discussion, this makes for a far more meaningful dialogue between the sales professional and the prospect, **and** increased likelihood of **accurately** identifying the **real** needs and the ways **your** products and services can meet them.

Second, by having a high level understanding of a client's or customer's organization, the salesperson is able to quickly build trust, credibility, and respect. The prospect will immediately detect that his or her company is important to the salesperson, and the salesperson is more likely to be regarded as a thorough, organized, and committed professional dedicated to helping the company meet its objectives.

Importantly, this type of knowledge cuts both ways. There will be times when a sales professional studies a potential client and determines that the prospect is *not worth the pursuit*. In our sales consulting, sales coaching, and public speaking work, we have sometimes had to make this difficult decision ourselves. After all, there are clients and customers who are a joy to work with, who are intelligent, positive, honest, and who pay their bills on time. These are the prospects, clients, and customers **you** should devote your life to serving. You must have standards. If prospects do not meet your standards, let someone else serve them.

Some salespeople allow their pride get in the way. They want to close 100 percent or nearly 100 percent of all their prospects. *In being promiscuous instead of selective, they pay a heavy price.* They end up taking on clients and customers they should not be doing business with. Careful analysis during the pre-client contact stage will help you not only determine the kind of presentation to make, but also whether you should make a presentation **at all.**

Sources of Company Information

There are several ways for you to gather key information that will help you develop a winning sales strategy for any lead. First, check with your sales manager and fellow sales associates. Perhaps they have sold to the company before, or they have had other direct or indirect dealings with the company that can be very helpful to you. *Don't reinvent the wheel.* Instead, use the sales intelligence they have already acquired.

Second, you can gather an abundance of information on just about every company on the Internet. Your first stop on this virtual visit to a prospect should be at her company's Website, if the company has one. When you get there, be sure to check out the key people who are running the organization, the company news, and the products and services. Study the history of the company. Pay special attention to the "About Us" section of the Website.

**As you thoroughly go over their Website,
read between the lines to look for challenges
they may be facing.**

Some of their challenges represent problems you and your company can solve.

In visiting the Websites of prospective clients, one of our sales millionaire clients makes a point of clicking on the "Careers" button if the site has one. He is obviously not looking for a job with the company, but he finds this information to be extremely helpful.

**If a company is doing a good deal of hiring,
that can be an important indicator of its current
financial condition and its prospects for the future.**

In addition, this salesperson likes to see what jobs the company is trying to fill, as they too can be informative indicators of the company's *future* direction.

Look also at the Website's "News" and "Press Release" sections. If the company is hiring nine ceramics engineers and you are working in electrical engineering components, you may find better prospects elsewhere. However, refer the ceramics salespeople at your company to this prospect.

These Websites often have the company's mission statement, and this can be particularly valuable reading.

Mission statements can give you a deep insight into what the company is truly trying to be and achieve.

Most companies put a great deal of thought into their mission statements, as the mission statements become their brand and identity. Only a very foolish CEO would post a mission statement she had not thought about and worked on for a great deal of time. Essentially, the mission statement is a public declaration of "This is who we are, this is what we believe in, and this is what we are trying to achieve." Use it to help your customer and to sell even more of your products and services.

We have held multiple-day seminars with some of our corporate clients at remote mountain locations, beach lodges, golf courses, and other locations where there are minimal distractions in order to help them define and perfect their mission statements. *Companies are judged by their mission statements.* Carefully study any mission statements you find on the Websites of your prospects. These statements will give you a deep insight into the needs, values, and interests of the company.

As a sales professional, you can review this information and look for specific ways that your products and services can help the company and the executives you are calling upon achieve their mission.

Many successful salespeople take notes on these mission statements and then include a few words and phrases from these mission statements in their presentations. The **wording** these sales millionaires use strikes a familiar chord with the executives (because it is a part of their mission statement), helps to demonstrate that the salesperson has a deep understanding of the company, and rapidly accelerates the trust-building process.

In addition to accessing company Websites, you can also use powerful search engines, such as *google.com* or *yahoo.com* to gather an abundance of information, data, and opinions on just about any company. You may be amazed at what you can learn with a few clicks of the mouse. Powerful information that would previously have taken weeks or longer to collect is now available almost instantaneously over the World Wide Web. Use it!

You can also find important financial information on a good number of these companies by going to some of the more business-oriented sites, such as *WSJ.com*, *morningstar.com*, *businessweek.com*, and the Dunn and Bradstreet site that is particularly helpful for salespeople, *sbs.dnb.com*. Some of these sites charge a fee to look up an archived article in which you are interested. Pay it if the site or particular articles on the site can help you do an outstanding presentation or close the sale. Remember that business publications are tax-deductible expenses. We have found that by paying $29 to $99 a year to some sites we have been able to acquire information that has helped us make thousands of times that amount of money. By selecting and using the proper sites, you might have the same experience.

In addition to all of the online information available at your fingertips, remember to regularly read newspapers, magazines, industry journals, and newsletters to keep current on the latest developments and the movers and shakers in your industry. Those people are your prime prospects and the more knowledge you have about them, the more power you possess.

Check Out the People

Just as it is important to gain insight into the company or organization where you **will** be selling (note the positive expectation), it is equally important for you to understand as much as possible about the individual or individuals who will be doing the actual buying.

The more you understand your prospect's needs, values, objectives, and buying behaviors, the more you can tailor your presentation and greatly accelerate the sales process and your sales success.

The first step in learning about your prospect is to check with your manager and coworkers to see if any of them have had prior dealings with this individual, or if they have gathered information about him or her from reliable sources. You can also use your own network to see if anyone in your wider circle of contacts has had any dealings with this individual.

It is also worthwhile to check back with whoever referred you to the prospect in the first place. Presumably this referral source has some degree of familiarity with the prospect, and as a result, is worth contacting again right before you go on the call. If the referring individual starts to hem and haw when describing the prospect, at the very least you will know not to play the referral card too heavily during the actual presentation.

Assuming that the company has a Website, you may also be able to find some information about your prospect on the site. Some companies even include biographical summaries or work histories of some of their key employees. If you don't see the individual listed, enter her name on the site's search engine. By doing so, you may be taken to some fascinating pieces of information about this person and her current projects that you would not otherwise have been able to find.

Carefully study the individual's **work history** and **education**—that can give you a real tip-off as to the best way to approach her. Did she start off working in the mailroom and slowly work her way up to senior vice president? Or did she join the company with an MBA from Wharton and start off as a vice president? Is the individual you are calling on the daughter of the founder? Sales millionaires customize their presentations based upon the personalities, needs, interests, and backgrounds of those they are calling upon.

As you learn about this individual's background, you may find some **areas of commonality**, such as schooling, hobbies, or technical interests. These types of mutually shared pursuits, common experiences, and shared beliefs can help build a feeling of familiarity and rapport with the prospect, and can rapidly speed up the trust building process.

Pay particular attention to hobbies and recreational interests. Most people in business work fairly hard. Between the demands of business and family, many people have little free time left over.

What they choose to do during that free time says a
great deal about who they are.

In our seminars, we say, *"Hobbies reveal the true person."* What a person does during their precious free time is very revealing. Many people even daydream about their hobbies and recreational interests. Remember that every hobby and recreational pursuit has its own **vocabulary**. If you use a few words from the vocabulary of that hobby or recreational activity in your presentation, your prospect will find whatever you have to say much more interesting.

We work with a very successful Hollywood screenwriter who still goes on sales calls to pitch his stories and ideas to various producers. This is a very meticulous screenwriter. For example, in producing his scripts, he does extensive research to make sure that every detail about an obscure city where the story takes place is accurate down to the cobblestones in the street.

And he does the same meticulous research before he meets with a producer. This screenwriter talks to his agent, attorney, and fellow writers to see who knows this producer best and who may have worked with him. He asks every question he can think of regarding this producer's standards, personality, meetings, and style, such as whether he prefers a brief pitch or the whole enchilada, how he reacts to humor, where he is parked on the political horizon, his personal likes and dislikes, and what his hot buttons might be.

This screenwriter looks for people who have worked with the producer not only to find out what makes the producer tick, *but also to have some names to mention during the presentation*. By casually dropping some of the right names, he builds credibility and lets the producer see that they are both running with the same successful crowd. In this way, the unspoken message to the producer is that, "We have a lot in common. You and I are alike in many ways and you can trust me."

This screenwriter also uses the Internet to gather even more data about the producer. He'll go to the search engines, enter the producer's name, and see what comes up. Learning about the kinds of movies the producer has made in the past gives this screenwriter a plethora of subjects to talk about with the producer. The screenwriter, who is truly a sales master during these meetings, also learns everything he can about the quality of production and **the financial backers** of the producer. This wealth of information gives him a highly accurate measure of the producer's heat and his ranking in the highly competitive Hollywood food chain.

There are many skilled writers in Hollywood. You can find a number of them in line at the State of California Unemployment Office or waiting on your table at a hip bistro in Hollywood, Century City, or Santa Monica. While many of these skilled writers produce great scripts, they have to work as waiters or waitresses because *they don't know how to sell their great writing!* Gathering these powerful forms of intelligence, our client combines his skills as a screenwriter with his skills *as a sales professional* to earn a handsome living in this glamorous but cut-throat field.

An Important Lesson From Hollywood

One of the most important pieces of information that a writer can have in any pitch meeting is the **one-liner** for her story. This is a highly polished sentence or two that captures the essence of the story and why it is so inherently compelling. If a writer needs more than a minute to give the one-liner, then it's a case of the writer not being ready, the story not being polished, or both.

This is a great lesson for sales professionals, sales millionaires, and millionaires in training.

> **They know the one-liner for the goods and services
> that they are selling, and they have it
> perfectly honed to make an indelible positive impression
> in the minds of their clients or customers.**

This calls for practice and more practice until the delivery is natural, comfortable, flawless, and compelling.

Beyond the confines of Hollywood, these summaries are now being referred to as **elevator pitches**. Imagine you meet a well-dressed successful person on a brief ride in an elevator in a high-rise building. After the usual pleasantries, the person asks you, "What do you do?" You have just a moment to explain what your work is all about and the benefits you offer. What do you say that leaves a lasting positive impression? That is your elevator pitch. Sadly, most salespeople do not have one. They do not have a powerful, brief interest-creating message they can deliver on an elevator or anywhere that time is of the essence.

One of our clients is MoneyTours, developers of online personal finance education programs. If you were on an elevator with one of the sales representatives of MoneyTours and asked her, "What does MoneyTours do?" you would be told, "MoneyTours is an online educational service that enables companies to provide their employees with a full range of personal finance information on their 401(k) plans, paying for college, retiring early, and much more. It is company branded, customized, and guaranteed to reduce employee stress and employer cost." This two-sentence elevator pitch has enabled MoneyTours to stand out and succeed in a highly competitive field.

Action Step

What is your elevator pitch? If you don't have one, start outlining your elevator pitch right now. If you do have one, work on improving it. Remember, an elevator pitch can never be too powerful.

Sometimes salespeople confuse elevators pitches for Unique Selling Propositions. A Unique Selling Proposition shows how you, your company, and/or products and services are unique. An elevator pitch does not necessarily focus on uniqueness, but instead presents, in one or two sentences, a highly persuasive, concise description of the benefits you and your products and services offer.

The Time to Qualify

Think of your pre-sales plan as a **treasure map**. The more details you have, the greater your likelihood of finding the treasure. Best of all, this treasure will benefit both you and your prospect. When the prospect becomes your client or customer, you both win. You, of course, get the sale. Your prospect gets to enjoy the many benefits of your products and services.

Remember that details are what make maps useful.

As you put together your pre-sales plan for a prospective customer or client, **continuously** qualify your prospect. With each additional piece of data that you gather, ask yourself, "Is this a good (poor, fair, or excellent) prospect for me?" "Should I be calling on this individual?" "How likely are they to buy from me?" "How likely are they to place a **large** order with me?" "What kinds of benefits can I deliver?"

Coaching Tip

You will find it very helpful to keep running tabs on your ratings of each client, giving them a grade of A, B, C, D, or F, or a numerical rating from one (excellent) to 10 (not worth your effort). It is important to remember that all prospects are **not** created equal, and one of the major skills of sales superstars is their ability to **consistently** and **accurately** distinguish between poor prospects and excellent ones. *Sales millionaires do everything they can to spend the majority of their time in front of excellent prospects.* By doing so, they are able to work fewer but much more productive hours.

One of our sales millionaire clients sells life insurance to companies as a corporate benefit they can offer employees. This top producer has wonderful shorthand for qualifying prospects. First he gathers as much relevant data as possible on the corporate executive and the company. Sometimes that is as far as things go, especially if he finds that there are problems with the company, such as dubious business practices, questionable ethics, or a dire financial condition.

If the company passes the initial screening test, this sales superstar then asks himself three powerful questions about the prospect, the answers to which determine whether his next step is to contact the prospect, move the prospect down on the list, or eliminate the prospect altogether. Those three questions are:

> *Can this person buy?* The objective of this question is to determine whether the individual has the responsibility, authority, budget, and overall ability to make a buying decision.

> It is a tremendous waste of time, energy, and resources to spend time with a person who cannot make the buying decision unless she is a gatekeeper who must be sold prior to getting to the real decision-maker.

> *Will this person buy?* Even if the prospect has the ability and power to make a buying decision, perhaps she is one of those notorious fence-sitters who loves to look at everything happening on both sides of the fence, but never makes a decision to move.

Some people's favorite decision is to make no decision at all. For others, there is a real fear of making a purchase, a reaction that typically comes from a deeper fear of failure. Rather than dealing with nondecision-makers, some sales pros will downgrade these prospects to a C or a D, and move on to better prospects. Other top salespeople will call on these individuals but will recognize them as the challenges they are and will use appropriate tactics and scripts.

Will this prospect buy from me? The prospect may indeed have all the ability in the world to buy the product or service and may have proven that he is a decision-maker who does in fact make buying decisions. However, that does not mean that he will buy from **you.** Perhaps there are existing contracts, agreements, or relationships that prevent this individual from even considering a purchase from you. For example, in your pre-sales research you might have discovered that this corporate executive buys all company life insurance from his brother's insurance agency. How likely are you to take the business from his brother? Not very. Or perhaps the prospect needs the product or service in a time frame that is impossible for your company to meet. Thus, he can and will buy the product, but unless you can perform a miracle within your own company, this prospect is not going to buy from you. In both of the above cases, it makes sense to move on to other prospects with whom you have a much higher probability of making a sale.

Importantly, the sooner you get the answers to the previous three questions, the better. The information you gather in answering the questions will enable you to spend less time with the wrong prospects and more time with the right ones.

Speaking of Questions

Another one of our clients uses what he calls the **"what if" game** as an important component of his pre-sale preparation. He and several of his associates try to come up with the **toughest questions** that a prospect could possibly ask, and then they brainstorm the issue and try to devise the best possible answers. And they write down these answers in the form of scripts and then practice them. Sometimes they even videotape the responses to make sure they are delivered with perfect intonation, eye contact, and emphasis.

For almost any question the prospect brings up, this sales professional has not just two or three powerful responses but 15 to 20—and he delivers them perfectly. *The prospect never knows all the work the sales pro did.* All the prospect knows is that her needs are being met and that the sales professional is the most knowledgeable, self-confident, friendly, and helpful of any other salespeople with whom she has spoken.

For example, one of our client companies recently had some layoffs, and the salespeople were already being bombarded with questions such as, *"We're concerned that your company has been laying people off. How do we know you'll be in shape to handle an account like ours?"*

This is a perfect **"what if"** question. As the group brainstormed, more than one dozen ideas were generated. We helped them clarify their thoughts and perfect the best responses. We combined scripts and fine-tuned them. Not everyone liked each script, which is fine because different salespeople sell in different ways. We believe that diversity brings strength. However, we knew that each and every salesperson needed at least five to 10 responses he or she fully believed in.

As we perfected the responses, salespeople began practicing them. The real artistry in sales is in a natural, down-to-earth delivery. We all listened and observed when the company's most successful salespeople delivered their best responses. As sales coaches, it was our job to make them even more powerful and persuasive. We suggested a change of wording here, a change of intonation there. All of the other salespeople modeled the behavior of the superstars and reported they found the individual coaching particularly helpful.

One of the most popular final responses was:

"I'm glad you brought that up. With the change in the economy, our company is doing some **streamlining** to help keep costs low for our customers. Some of our people are taking early retirement if they want, some are going part-time, and some are going to school part-time to gain even more knowledge to **help our customers**.

We've also promoted a few people into higher level positions and have hired some great new talent. The **best news** is that our customer satisfaction levels are way up, product quality continues to be outstanding, and we're coming out of all of this a much **stronger** company."

As one of the company's best salespeople finished delivering these lines, the room broke into applause. Everything stated in the script was 100-percent true and it was persuasively delivered. Now all the salespeople knew how to handle this objection that had been troubling them. They felt empowered and several reported they couldn't wait to hear the objection again. They now knew they had a response that was much more powerful than the question being asked.

An analysis of this response is revealing. The opening statement about being **glad** the question was raised instantly frames the salesperson's response in a positive context. Instead of showing any fear of this question, *he welcomes it.* The person asking the question might be a little surprised at this self-confident opening response. It makes the prospect eager to hear more.

This response is supportive and it keeps the salesperson in an **agreement mode** with the prospect. The salesperson agrees with the prospect, says in essence, "you are right," and then adds persuasive information that will be taken in along with the previous statements.

The next sentence describes a troubled economy *without using a negative word* that could cast a pall on the rest of the presentation. Notice that the salesperson does **not** describe the economy with such terms as **recession**, **decline**, or **slowdown**, but rather refers merely to a **change** in the economy.

The same type of thinking leads to the use of the word **streamlining**. It has an instant positive visual appeal, and the idea is that the company is becoming sleeker, faster, and more effective. Obviously this is a much better choice than more commonly used words such as "downsizing" or "layoffs." By adding some company-specific information about the nature of the staffing reduction by mentioning early retirement and part-time work, the salesperson is giving **factual data** to the prospect, which increases credibility. It also effectively shows that the company is not just unilaterally slashing positions. This portrays the company in a positive light and shows how it is using some progressive human resources techniques in handling the current economic situation.

With the mention of *hiring new talent*, the message is that the company is **rebuilding**, and this is a clear indicator of confidence in its future and ability to serve its customers and clients.

In addition, by describing the progress in customer satisfaction and product quality as **good news**, that is exactly how the prospect will recall them. And, finally, by saying that the company will be much *stronger* when it emerges from all of this, the unspoken message is that the company is **already strong**, and it is now being further strengthened.

This is the kind of strategic sales thinking, scripting, and rehearsing that sales superstars do for **every** difficult question that they can imagine a prospect asking. During a very challenging time in the economy, our client company set sales records in its industry.

Do It Yourself

We also work with many sales professionals who not only anticipate the toughest questions and script the best responses to them, but they actually ask the tough questions themselves during the presentation. This is one of the most powerful and persuasive steps that a salesperson can take.

When you bring up the kinds of questions that would cause a lesser salesperson to quake and quiver, you are simultaneously demonstrating several compelling positive attributes to the customer or client.

Here is an example of how a sales professional might handle the layoff situation mentioned on page 147. If the prospect had not brought it up first, the sales pro could say, *"If I were in your position right now, I'd want to know about the company's ability to provide high quality service in light of the recent streamlining of some of our operations."*

The prospect's immediate reaction will most likely be to nod in agreement. And obviously, the more agreement during the presentation, even minor agreement, the greater the likelihood of major agreement at the end. In addition, the prospect is likely to feel that she thinks just like the salesperson, and this sense of commonality and compatibility helps to further build a bond of trust.

And further, by bringing up the tougher questions, the salesperson is demonstrating a high degree of confidence and honesty. When prospects sense and literally see these qualities in a salesperson, it is much easier for them to make a decision to buy.

Notice in the statement made by the salesperson that the words *"the company's ability to provide high quality service"* were used. Use of the words "high quality" is a powerful **presupposition** that the service will, in fact, be high quality. Notice also that reference is made to streamlining operations rather than to layoffs. If the prospect says she was concerned about that, you can answer her concern with the powerful response you have already prepared. If she says they are not concerned about this issue, *you have also won.* This is one less thing to worry about and you are one step closer to making the sale. Using the powerful technique of bringing up any objections the prospect fails to bring up leads to a situation where you win no matter what the prospect says. In addition, the prospect wins because soon she will be enjoying the benefits of your company's products and services.

What Do You Want to Know? *Discovery*

During this pre-client contact stage, sales superstars also start to frame a powerful variety of questions that they will plan on asking during the presentation. With these data-collection and need-building questions, the idea is not to assume you know all the answers. Rather, the best approach is to learn as much as possible about the prospect's needs, and then demonstrate how your products and services can more than meet them.

The pre-sale data that the sales pros gather on the prospect and company will help them identify the key areas in which they want to ask questions. Many of these inquiries will be what we call **TNT Questions**, which stands for **Then, Now, and Tomorrow.** The idea is to gather as much sales-relevant data as possible from the prospect regarding key issues from past situations, the current situation, and projections for the future.

Some of the **Then Questions** you can use include:

"What did you like most about that product or service?"

"How did you decide to buy it?"

"What kinds of problems did you experience with it?"

When you have the answers to these questions, in some cases you almost know enough to close the sale. When you find out what they liked most about a product or service they bought in the past, show them how they can get **more** of that with your products or services. When you find out how they made a purchase decision in the past, make sure your *learn the exact mental steps they went through in deciding to buy*. Then, use those **same steps** to help them buy your products or services today. When you find out the problems they had with a previous purchase, show them how or why they will not have those problems with your products or services. If you do all of this, many people will be ready, or nearly ready, to buy.

Samples of **Now Questions** include:

"What are you looking for right now?"

"How happy are you with what you have right now?"

"What problems are you having with your current products or services?"

"What is the **ideal** outcome you're seeking?"

These are also extremely powerful questions. Upon learning what they are looking for right now, do your best to supply it. When you learn what they are happy with, attempt to give them even more of that. When you learn about their problems, offer real solutions. When you learn of their ideal outcome, do your best to help them enjoy it.

The **Tomorrow Questions** include:

Ask "yes" questions.

"What will you need to meet your future goals and objectives?"

Upselling —

"What problems do you anticipate down the road?"

getting agreement

"What needs do you think you and your business will have in the future?"

to buy again...

When you receive answers to these questions, there is a high likelihood that you will obtain not just current business, but also future business. When you learn what they will need to meet their future goals, do your level best to supply it. When they talk about problems that may be encountered down the road, offer solutions that will **prevent** or **mitigate** those problems. When you learn anticipated future needs of their business, do your best to fulfill those needs at the earliest possible date.

Note that these are open-ended questions that call for more than a yes or no response. If you ask a question such as, "Do you think you will have any future needs in this area?" you are handing the prospect or client a loaded gun. Not only is the gun loaded, but you have pointed it at your own head and have cocked the trigger. By using such close-ended questions, you are setting up the prospect to say, "Nope," and then your discussion is over. Using the open-ended questions we have recommended above puts you in a much more powerful position to gather high quality data.

By using questions that start with who, what, where, when, and how, the salesperson is far more likely to generate responses that engage the prospect in a high quality conversation and provide real insight into his or her buying style, needs, and objectives.

Not all open-ended questions are created equal.

When doing our coaching work, we tell our clients to be cautious in their use of "why" questions.

Certainly there are instances in which you would like to know the prospect's reasons for making a particular decision, but an excessive use of the word "why" can potentially turn off prospects.

When you ask a person why she took a particular action or made a decision, there can be an implied criticism of the behavior. It is almost as if the person asking the question knows more than the respondent and is looking down on the respondent. Upon hearing a question starting with "why," some people presume you are asking, "Why in the world…." This is because some people feel that the word "why" requires a justification as well as an explanation. Others feel that the word "why" has an implied criticism.

To get around this challenge and still find out why a prospect made a particular decision, we suggest **reframing the question** into a softer and gentler (though still very effective) form. Start with a mild compliment and then a reframed "why," as in, *"That's interesting. How is it you decided to do that?"* or *"That is fascinating. Can you tell me more about what you were looking for when you made that decision?"* You want to know why. We want to know why. But, in many cases, there are better ways of getting to the information you want and need than by directly asking why. By using more positive language patterns, such as those illustrated above, you are much more likely to get the information you desire.

Is It Ever Acceptable to Ask Close-Ended Questions?

Some books on sales and persuasion will tell you that a salesperson should never ask a close-ended question. We disagree and we just did it in this section heading. The answer to the question we asked is yes. Open-ended questions get their prospects talking. However, *you don't need to have prospects talking about every little thing.*

> **If you want to rapidly build a climate of agreement,
> ask a series of close-ended questions that
> will elicit yes answers. Okay?**

You can do this by placing a brief confirming question at the end of a statement. For example, on a gorgeous day, an average salesperson might break the ice by simply saying, "It's a beautiful day." Sales superstars are far more likely to say, "It's a beautiful day, isn't it?" Automatically, *the prospect will not only agree, but will also use one of the most powerful words in the persuasive process—yes.* And this, as simple as it seems, begins the process of building a climate of agreement with the prospect.

In fact, throughout the sales presentation, many of the statements used by sales millionaires are followed with questions such as, "Isn't it?" "Don't you think?" "Right?" and many more. As a result, the prospect will be getting into the **habit** of agreeing with the sales professional. Of course, that makes it much easier for the prospect to say yes at the conclusion of the sales call, doesn't it?

More Contact Options Than Ever

Today's sales pros do not go into the planning mode with only one sales contact strategy in mind. The assumption that when the preparation is done, the salesperson sets up a face-to-face meeting with the prospect is gone. We now have many powerful alternatives to face-to-face sales calls, and today's sales millionaires scan them all and pick the options that best fit the needs of the client and their own needs.

In selling a management development program to a medium-sized company with a leadership team that communicates almost exclusively via e-mail, all of our initial contact and sales presentation were via e-mail, too. We offered to meet with them in person but were told it wasn't necessary. They actually prefer e-mail contact in most cases! Because this was the way they liked to buy, that is exactly what we did, and it led to a successful sale.

It's not as if the traditional sales meeting is about to be placed on the endangered species list. However, vast numbers of companies are rethinking the need for salespeople to get in cars or get on airplanes to meet with prospects, especially in the early stages of the sales process.

Today there exists a major emphasis on cost containment and efficiency. Combine this with heavier workloads as a result of tighter staffing and significant delays associated with travel in the wake of the September 11 attacks, and you will understand why *alternative means of client contact now make even more sense for both sellers and buyers.*

One of the technologies enjoying exponential growth in this area is **Web conferencing**. Most of us already have all the hardware and software we need to hold a Web meeting. You simply sign on with one of the many companies that provide secure virtual space for these meetings, such as *placeware.com* or *meetingplace.net*, and you are on your way. Most of these companies have or provide any extra software you may require.

In using these types of services, you can meet with your prospects, interact with them in real time, and go as far with your virtual sales presentation as you would with your face-to-face presentation. You can demonstrate your products, review sales materials, create documents, give a PowerPoint demonstration, share visuals, answer questions, and continue to interact with the customer and actually conclude with a final agreement from the prospect that she will buy. And you can do all of this without jumping in a car or hopping on an airplane. Some Web conferencing solutions even allow the prospect to place her order and to pay online.

Without much additional expense on either side, you can even take the step to video conferencing, which includes the use of affordable digital cameras on both sides of the presentation so that you and your prospect can each see each other in real time as you interact and view the actual presentation and demonstrations.

In addition to offices, hotel conference rooms, restaurants, and golf courses, the World Wide Web has become a major sales venue. It is also an excellent way to further screen and qualify prospects, let your prospects see how your products actually work and the benefits your services can offer, and it can save a tremendous amount of time and energy for all who are involved. This clearly translates into major personal productivity gains and increased sales effectiveness. That's an outstanding outcome for using a tool that's already sitting on top of your desk.

In some cases, you may still find that you need or want to meet face-to-face to actually close the sale. However, by using Web conferencing to lay the groundwork, the entire process is greatly accelerated.

The Final Countdown

If you study great athletes just before they are about to compete, you will notice that many of them go through a ritual. It may be to take a deep breath, stretch in a particular way, jog in place for a certain number of minutes, close their eyes, engage in positive visualization, or any number of habitual actions. In all cases, *they are priming their minds and their bodies to achieve world-class results.*

We have found that sales millionaires engage in a similar process. Before they are about to meet with a prospect, whether online or in person, they to tend to go through what we call **the ritual of success**. What is your ritual of success? *What mental and physical steps do you engage in when you are at your best?* Do you review your most powerful sales presentations? Do you go over your elevator pitch? Do you repeat affirmations? Do you practice smiling, deep breathing, or nodding your head?

**Become consciously aware of whatever you do prior to
your most effective sales presentations.
Then do it consciously. Do it more frequently.
Make your ritual of success a habit.**

There is no specific pre-sales routine that is best for everyone, but we have found that every sales millionaire does have a success ritual (even if he or she is not yet consciously aware of it).

**Remember that awareness is the
first step to growth.**

We cannot change anything without awareness of the current situation. We cannot learn or grow without awareness. Increased awareness provides the rocket fuel for the highest levels of sales success.

Our purpose in writing this chapter and in sharing all of these attitudes, strategies, and techniques with you is to increase your awareness of some of the most powerful components of the pre-sales planning process. As in so many aspects of life, it is awareness that makes all the difference. Sales millionaires start with increased awareness during the pre-sales planning process and it is a key building block for others who aspire to be sales millionaires.

7

How to Use the Media to Sell Your Products and Services

As sales consultants and sales trainers to salespeople around the world, it is our belief that many salespeople work too hard for the rewards they receive. How can we say this? We have proof.

Messages From the Media

Most salespeople make between several hundred and a few thousand telephone calls each year to prospects who may be interested in what the sales professional has to say. Salespeople drive or fly thousands of miles each year to visit prospects who may be nice but might also be rude or disinterested. Salespeople spend untold hours writing proposals that go unread or responding to routine RFPs (request for proposal), RFQs (request for quote), or e-mails. Much of this so-called "sales activity" produces absolutely no results. There must be a better way.

Fortunately, there is. Instead of spending all of your time and energy trying to sell yourself, your company, your products, and your services, you can have the media do your selling for you. That's what sales millionaires do, *and you can, too*. Media-based selling through articles, books, radio, and television appearances takes place every day in thousands of cities and towns all over the world.

You just need to get into the media loop.

In this chapter, we will show you how.

You may be surprised to learn that many sales millionaires do not work as hard as you do. They just work smarter. In many cases, they have the media do some of their selling for them. Instead of begging and pleading for prospects, they have the media **send** clients to them. Willing clients, motivated clients, respectful clients. If those are the kinds of clients in which you are interested, read on.

In this chapter, we will reveal the media marketing secrets of sales millionaires, as well as secrets of our own. As you will see, we have also used these techniques to make several million dollars in the field of sales and marketing training, which is an incredibly competitive field. We know these techniques work because they have worked for us and for hundreds of our clients. These techniques are simply too good to pass up.

This is a book about Ultimate Selling Power, and perhaps the greatest selling power of all is to have the media do your selling for you. It is so powerful that many salespeople think they cannot do it.

Do you think media-based selling is beyond your reach? *Think again.*

By following the relatively simple step-by-step format laid out in this chapter, you will learn how to:

1. Get articles published in trade journals, magazines, on Websites, and in the popular press.

2. Use the articles to get on talk radio shows and television shows (we have been on a combined total of more than 200 talk radio shows all over the U.S. and Canada and on several major television shows).

3. Combine your articles to publish an e-book (electronic book) or regular book.

You will learn how publishing and media appearances can make you THE expert in your field and can get huge numbers of prospects to flock to you.

As you are about to see, these strategies are all linked together. Once you tap into one media outlet, others are likely to follow. For example, a good article can lead to a radio appearance, which can lead to a TV appearance, which can lead to magazines and Websites asking you for additional articles, and those additional articles can lead to a publisher or an agent asking you to write a book. The momentum builds with each article published and with each media appearance.

Getting Into Print

One day, Dr. Lloyd received a phone call from Bill Cunningham, coordinating producer for *Good Morning America*. Bill asked Ken if he would like to appear on a segment dealing with the most common people-problems at work and the best strategies to resolve them. There's only one answer to that question: a big, fat "YES!"

In a matter of weeks, Dr. Lloyd appeared on the show and gave advice that was seen by **millions** of viewers around the world. Before the show aired, Bill told Dr. Lloyd that this appearance was going to change his life.

Indeed it did, as it led to numerous consulting assignments, additional television appearances, and many speaking engagements. In addition, there is a tremendous cache associated with having been a guest on *Good Morning America*.

How did this happen? It came as a result of Dr. Lloyd's workplace advice newspaper column, which appears in dozens of newspapers around the country. Written in an upbeat and positive style, yet filled with hands-on advice, the column grabbed Bill's attention, and things rolled quickly from there.

When you publish one or more articles in a newspaper, magazine, or on a Website, not only are you establishing and demonstrating your expertise, building your credibility, and making countless readers familiar with your name, you are also literally getting into the hands of the very people who can give you lots of orders.

How do you get there?

Dr. Lloyd has not always had a newspaper column. He used the very skills revealed in this book to get one. He sold himself. Around eight years ago, he cold-called the *Los Angeles Daily News*, the second largest newspaper in the greater Los Angeles area and asked to speak to the business editor.

The conversation went something like this: "Hi, my name is Ken Lloyd and I'm a subscriber to the paper and I think it is great." Instantly, the editor viewed Dr. Lloyd as a customer and, of course, he had to agree with what Dr. Lloyd was saying.

Dr. Lloyd continued, "I'm a consultant and writer, and I've noticed that you have columns on automobiles and electronics and other timely topics…." Again, all the business editor could do was agree. "As you know, readers spend more hours on their jobs than in any other waking activity, and the main issues that they deal with at work are people-related." The editor had to agree with these pacing statements.

They talked a bit further about work-related issues, the problems people have at work, and then Ken asked, "Do you think your readers will be interested in a column that helps them handle some of the toughest problems that they ever face at work?" Notice how his question had a presupposition imbedded in it, "…your readers **will** be interested…."

Dr. Lloyd then focused on his expertise and writing skills, and offered to send some writing samples to the editor. It's always good to get the product into the customer's hands. The business editor agreed to read them.

Dr. Lloyd maintained regular contact with this editor. After a few more weeks, the editor asked him to write a couple of columns on some popular workplace issues, such as leadership and motivation, just to be used as trial columns. It took another two months, and then these original articles ran. The reader response was positive, and then the readers were invited to send their questions to Dr. Lloyd for future columns. This was the beginning of his workplace advice column, a column that is now syndicated by the *New York Times* Syndicate. It all came from one cold call. Does cold-calling work? You bet.

All of this happened as a result of selling. Some people think that lawyers, CPAs, M.D.s, and Ph.D.s cannot sell. Dr. Moine cold-called the prestigious Morningstar company in Chicago to suggest a column for stock brokers, financial planners, and other financial advisors on how they could best grow their practices through the use of modern sales-manship and marketing techniques. Donald placed the call in August of 2001, followed up with some e-mails, and was hired in September of that year. To make it even more of a win-win situation, Dr. Moine has re-ferred several thousand financial planners, stockbrokers, and money man-agers to the MorningstarAdvisor Website. To date, he has published more than 16 feature articles on *MorningstarAdvisor.com*, which has become the premier Website in the world for financial advisors. If a couple of Ph.D.s such as Dr. Moine and Dr. Lloyd can get on the phone, make some cold calls, be persistent, and get some articles into the media, surely you can, too!

The Marketplace for Your Articles

The first step is to find the right home for your articles. Fortunately, today there are countless media outlets looking for articles. From the hard copy standpoint, there are thousands of newspapers, industry magazines, journals, and newsletters looking for articles. For example, if you want to see a listing of more than 1,900 magazines, complete with submission guide-lines, take a look at the incredible reference book, *The Writer's Market*. This book, which is updated each year, can be purchased in many book-stores and on Amazon.com and other book-selling Websites.

Before submitting an article to a given magazine, journal, or Website, carefully study that publication. It is a complete waste of your time to send articles to publications that have no likelihood of accepting them. You do not want to try to sell an article on square pegs to a magazine that special-izes in round holes.

To prevent this from happening, take a look at the magazines and jour-nals that interest you most and study a sampling of articles *over a several month period*. Look carefully at the topics covered by the articles, along with their style, article length, and voice. Does the publication like to use case studies? Stories? Interviews? Product reviews? Is the **ideal** length of an article 700 words or 3,000? Respect the style of the publication and submit an article that fits their guidelines.

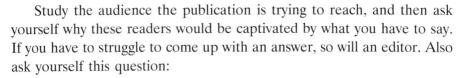
Study the audience the publication is trying to reach, and then ask yourself why these readers would be captivated by what you have to say. If you have to struggle to come up with an answer, so will an editor. Also ask yourself this question:

**Are the readers likely to be interested in
and willing to buy
my product and/or service?**

While you will not be directly selling it in the article, even indirect mentions can lead to a flood of business.

If the first publications or Websites you study do not seem like exact fits, or if they turn you down, do not fret. *There will be many other publications and Websites interested in what you have to say.* Do not let a few rejections discourage you. All writers get rejected. Hemingway got rejected. Stephen King got rejected. The authors of this book have been rejected— but we have persisted and have published hundreds of articles. When you get rejected, we have just one thing to say to you: *Welcome to the club!* Rejection comes with the territory. Just move on and you are likely to find an *even more ideal* publication or Website in the near future.

There is a true art to submitting an article. Some publications have their guidelines listed in a front or back section or on their Website. If you cannot find what you are looking for in these sections or on the Website, look for submission guidelines and contact information in *The Writer's Market.* Or just send the managing editor or a senior editor an e-mail and ask them how they prefer to have articles submitted. At the same time, send them a brief, one paragraph summary of your article idea. This is called a query letter.

If you can't find any information on how to submit an article to a newspaper, magazine, journal, or Website, there's an item on your desk and probably another in your pocket that can help you. It's called a telephone. Just pick it up and call the editor.

"Hello, my name is Ken and I really enjoy your magazine. I have an idea for an article that I think might be of great interest to your readers. It is about some great advances in X technology and how to cut costs and increase productivity with it. Who's the **best person** to talk to about this?" In most cases, the person who answers the phone is going to give you the guidelines on the spot or send them to you. However, sometimes you will actually be hooking up with someone who can make editorial decisions himself. You want to be prepared!

This could be your opportunity to **pre-sell** your article. Have some additional exciting details ready if they want to know more. However, don't overdo it. Keep the editor a little hungry. *Ask if he has any additional suggestions.* Ask about their editorial calendar. Some magazines are collecting articles now that will be published in six months! Others are working on a three-month calendar. Some newspapers might publish your article a few days after it is submitted!

Listen carefully to the editorial guidelines and suggestions. Take notes! Don't just rely on your memory. If you are contacting three or four publications, it can be almost impossible to remember the different guidelines, article lengths, and other submission details for each. If an editor sounds especially interested in your piece, prepare it immediately and send it off as soon as possible! If you incorporate any of the editor's excellent suggestions in your article, be sure to mention that fact in a cover letter when you submit your piece. People are much less likely to reject their own ideas.

By the way, almost every editor today likes to receive articles via e-mail, as a Microsoft Word attachment. With this form of submission, articles can be easily and quickly edited and prepared for publication.

Opportunities for Online Articles

Beyond the thousands of hard copy publications, there are more than 10,000 Websites seeking articles in the very areas that interest you. If you think that writing articles on the Internet is beyond you, just remember what is always said about Websites: *Content is king.* The only reason people visit Websites is for content.

**Good Websites are always looking for
great content.**

They seek the eyeball stickiness that can only be obtained by having fantastic content on their Websites. Present yourself as a source of the kinds of information that will keep bringing the users and readers back for more. If you can deliver on this promise, it is virtually guaranteed that you will be publishing on that Website.

Just about every Website has a "contact us" feature. Use that or directly contact the editor if you can find his or her personal e-mail address. Some Websites do everything via the Internet. In fact, it may even be a mistake to phone them. E-mail is their preferred mode of communication, so use it!

Just as you screened the hard copy publications carefully, you should do the same with the Websites to find the best possible outlets for your articles. Look carefully at their content, style, and level of sophistication, as well as their extent of penetration into the marketplace. If you are just starting to use the media, do not be overly selective. Getting published almost anywhere is better than not being published at all. As they say in Hollywood, "There is no such thing as bad publicity."

Also, do not insist on being paid. Many newspapers, magazines, and Websites—even some of the most prestigious—only pay their regular staff members. Early in our careers, we wrote dozens of articles for no financial compensation. Who cares about receiving a few hundred dollars for writing an article when you can receive tens of thousands to hundreds of thousands of dollars in publicity and sales from some of your pieces?

Some salespeople and professionals write articles and post them on their own Websites. This is an acceptable approach, but it is slower and in many cases, you are preaching to the choir. It is likely that the people visiting your Website are already customers or clients. It is nice to offer articles to them, but you often get much more bang for your buck when your articles are published on major Websites, industry portals, or highly respected trade Websites. Plus, those articles are likely to be seen by thousands or tens of thousands of prospects who might never otherwise visit your site.

How to Pick a Topic for Your Article

You have far more subjects to write about than you may realize. Importantly, you **don't** have to directly write about your company's products or services to sell them! You can write about your industry itself, about market trends, new technology, or how the economy is affecting your industry. Of course, it is perfectly fine to mention your products and services—but only as solutions to bigger problems that readers may have.

**It is most important to pick a topic that is timely,
of interest to the readers, and in which
you can share some
highly useful and enlightening information.**

You cannot merely write an advertisement for your company's products or services and expect it to be published. To be an article, it must offer true value beyond that of describing benefits of your company's offerings—no matter how great they are. How often have you read an article and come away with a real gem of information? It's that one gem that can make the whole article worthwhile. Make sure that your articles contain several true gems. If not, why should anyone want to read it? Or tell a friend about it? Or remember it? Or save it? By offering information of true value to the reader, you do both yourself and the readers a great service.

Sometimes you can write an article that has nothing to do with your company's products and services and it can still generate business! Take the example of an electronics marketing consultant who had a strong interest in international commerce. He wrote a column about international relations that ran in a local newspaper. Remember, some papers actually invite their readers to write columns on timely topics. What an incredible opportunity!

The electronics marketing consultant's column led to a call from a guest coordinator for a major radio program. Soon enough, the marketing consultant was on the air. And when he was introduced, he was described to the tens of thousands of listeners as an electronics marketing consultant, followed by the name and location of his company. Many of his customers heard the broadcast, as did several new prospects who later placed thousands of dollars in orders.

A Few Style Points

When you submit your article, make sure that there are no spelling or grammatical errors, and that the writing is crisp, clear, and to the point. It is fine to be clever, but don't try to be too funny. Most business publications are **not** looking for laugh-out-loud material, and if they are, they will probably want material from someone who specializes in humor. It is not much fun to be asked by an editor, "Is this supposed to be funny?"

It is also important to avoid long-winded sentences and overly inflated paragraphs. Editors value brevity. Use all the words you need to make your points, but then move on. When writing articles, remember Mark Twain's comment to a friend. Twain had written a long letter and apologized for its length. He added that *he didn't have the time to write a shorter letter.* Condensing your thoughts to their essence does take time, but the reward you will receive is that more newspapers, magazines, and Websites will want to publish your pieces.

Make sure that you include a byline that will benefit you. In addition to your name, it should include your title, company, and how readers can contact you. The byline is what is going to inform millions of readers how to get in touch with you.

This article and your byline instantly put you miles ahead of your competition.

Capitalizing on What You Write

After you publish your articles, don't just wait for people to happen to read them. Instead, use reprints and mail them out to all of your existing customers and clients and to your best prospects. You can include a brief note, such as "With my compliments" and sign your name. Your customers, clients, and prospects will see you in an entirely new light. You will suddenly be an expert. Some prospects will save your article for months, or longer. They would never do that with an advertisement. We have had some companies hire us to give speeches or deliver sales training seminars years after we published a major article. Why? Because they saved the article, put it in a file labeled "Sales Speakers," and contacted us when their people needed some training to increase sales.

By actively distributing the articles you have published, you can turbo-charge their effectiveness.

This is also a powerful method of further building name recognition and credibility within your industry. If you are ever looking for another sales position, make sure you mention on your resume that you have published articles to promote your company's products and services. You may be the only applicant who has shown such marketing initiative and it greatly increases your chances of getting a top sales position with the highest level of compensation.

Why are articles so effective as marketing tools? Articles have many times the credibility of advertisements. Consider a **paid** advertisement about **you** in a newspaper or magazine. What is the first thing everyone knows about it? You PAID for it. The newspaper or magazine would never have run it except that you PAID for it. Nothing wrong with paid advertising—in fact, we are great believers in it. However, even if it is a great ad, the reader knows that the publication has been paid to say these wonderful things about you.

> **When a prospect, customer, or client reads an article,**
> **they know your content has been accepted on the basis**
> **of merit, and the underlying message is that you are a**
> **person who is worth hearing.**

The content carries more weight, more gravitas. If you are one of hundreds of salespeople within a division of IBM, if you publish an article, *you will probably get more phone calls and e-mails than any other salesperson within that division of IBM.* You may get so many phone calls and e-mails that you have to give some of these prospects and leads to other salespeople. The senior executives are likely to notice your initiative and creativity and may reward you with a promotion.

> **Your article may produce more business than an**
> **advertisement the company paid $100,000 or more to run.**

Think about that!

How effective are articles compared to paid advertising? Think about a newspaper you read today. *Did you spend more time on the advertisements or the articles?* Many people, especially highly successful people, spend much more time reading articles than advertisements, and that further points to the competitive edge that articles give you and your company.

In addition to the fact that you will be sending your articles to prospects, customers, and clients, *many other readers will do the same.* They are your silent salespeople who are sharing your message with countless others. If you write a great article, don't be surprised to find that many people around the country save the article and send copies off to their friends and business associates. We have consummated numerous sales because people we have never met have photocopied our articles and distributed them to friends and business associates who later became our clients. You can enjoy the same destiny if you publish great articles.

Yet another advantage of articles is that there are no out-of-pocket costs associated with writing an article. Even if you hire a writing coach, the investment is usually only a small fraction of what you would pay to run an advertisement. Figure out **what** you want to say, **where** you want to say it, and then pursue that publication or Website just as you would pursue a great prospect. In fact, it may be the highest potential prospect you have ever encountered! The final outcome for you and your company could be millions of dollars in additional business.

Remember that the articles you write will benefit not just you, but also the publication or Website that runs them. There are thousands of newspapers, magazines, journals, and Websites that are searching ever day for good material to publish. That is their job. They have millions of empty pages to fill and if they don't fill them with quality content, they don't stay in business! You and your articles help!

At this point, you may be starting to see the incredible marketing potential inherent in publishing articles and in using the media to sell for you. However, you may still be put off by a fear of rejection.

We have found that the fear of rejection is the single biggest stumbling block that prevents salespeople and marketing people from submitting articles for publication.

Think about how important it is to overcome this fear of rejection. Successful people deal with rejection **every day**.

Don't let a few rejections stop you. In order to be successful in life, you need to put the rejection in perspective. *If you fall off the bike, get back on the bike and learn to ride*. Just because your article was rejected by one publication does not mean that another won't grab it, and thank you profusely for it. And maybe feature it on the cover of their magazine. The only thing that rejection means is that you need to send your article elsewhere.

All of us who write get piles of rejections—make that **mountains** of rejections—along with little molehills of acceptances. It doesn't matter.

The acceptances you get can help make you one of the top sales producers in your industry or profession, just as they have for countless other salespeople, marketers, and businesspeople who have the courage to continue to submit articles. Later, believe it or not, you can sometimes even laugh about the publications that rejected an article of yours that was later published in the top magazine in your field.

Always be polite and treat editors with total courtesy and respect. They have a difficult job to do: they have to fill their newspaper, magazine, or Website with fascinating new material every day, week, or month. Editors and their staff work under deadline pressure that few of the rest of us can even imagine. If an editor rejects your work, don't take it personally. It might simply mean that it was not right for their publication. It could very well be perfect for another publication. It could be just right for their publication at a later date.

Keep in touch with editors you meet and with whom you correspond. Sometimes an editor who did not accept your publication for magazine X then moves on to magazine Y and he may be looking for an article (or a column) in **your** area of expertise. If you keep in touch, yours will be the first name they think of when they move to that new magazine, journal, or Website.

Use Your Articles to Get on Radio and Television

You can also send your articles to producers and hosts of radio and television programs. In your cover letter, tell them that you authored the enclosed or attached article and that it has generated a great deal of interest. Inform them that you would be available to discuss the subject on the air. Be sure to let their guest coordinators clearly see how your presentation will be interesting, entertaining, and informative for the viewers or listeners.

Leveraging your articles for television is also going to call for some creativity on your part. But that is the fun of the process. When Dr. Lloyd wanted to leverage his column for television, one producer told him that they needed something more visual. Of course, Dr. Lloyd responded with,

"I **see** what you are saying." Television is a visual medium, and it is helpful to use visual words when selling in this arena. Had Dr. Lloyd been dealing with a radio producer, he may have responded with, "I **hear** you."

Dr. Lloyd then suggested combining his case studies of problem employees, such as a boss who screams, and brief movie clips to illustrate the problem. That was all it took. Ken has now appeared with this format several times on KABC Television in Southern California, a station watched by millions of people every day. These television appearances have generated a great deal of publicity, referrals, and business.

Getting on radio and television is a common goal of many of our financial planning clients. When they hear the Motley Fools on radio or see Suze Orman on PBS, they wonder, "How can I do that?" Millions of Americans are addicted to financial advice shows (a fact not lost on radio and television program managers) and an appearance on one of these shows can boost a financial planner's professional stature and assets under management. When a person is featured on a talk radio show or television show, from that moment on, he is viewed as the "*expert.*"

Many television and radio programs will tape your appearance and give you a copy of it. This is something you should ask about **before** you go on the air. After all, you can use the exposure from this type of appearance for months or years to come by mailing out tapes to prospects (cassette tapes only cost about $1 each to duplicate and mail). You can also post the interview on your Website. You will always be **The Expert**. You can use this media exposure to get appointments, build credibility with prospects and customers, and book even more media appearances.

Radio vs. Television

It is usually much easier to get on a talk radio show than it is to get on a television show. The only form of television where you can be booked rather easily as an expert guest is community access cable TV. While the size of the audience may be small, you still might pick up some customers or clients and *this type of appearance can be good practice before you get to the major leagues.* Make sure that you get a copy of the tape, and be brutally honest when you review it. Show it to your friends and solicit their honest feedback. Going over these tapes several times is the fastest way to improve your media performances.

How long does it take to convey your message? It is frequently possible to get booked for 30 minutes on a talk radio show. With the intros, exits, bumps, and commercials, you may speak for 20 minutes. If they take call-ins, you may only speak for 10 to 12 minutes. In some big cities, you might only be featured for five minutes or so during drive time. However, if it is a gigantic station, hundreds of thousands of people could be listening to you, and thus, such an appearance can be very worthwhile.

For example, Dr. Lloyd was booked on a major New York radio program for a 10 minute interview at 6:30 a.m., right in the beginning of the commute. This meant being interviewed at 3:30 a.m. West Coast time, but he did it because of the tremendous reach of this particular station.

While it is possible to get booked for 30 minutes or one hour on talk radio shows, television is an entirely different matter. Unless you are on some obscure cable channel, you should be absolutely delighted if you can get five minutes of air time on television. Don't be discouraged: remember that each minute on television is worth at least 10 minutes on radio. In fact, the wider the reach of the show, the greater this multiplier will be.

Whether you want to get on a talk radio show or television, you have two choices as to how you can reach your goal: you can either hire a public relations professional or you can try to get yourself booked. We have done it both ways and we hope you can benefit from our experience.

Hiring a Public Relations Professional

In 1991, we hired a major Hollywood public relations firm to help us promote our book, *Unlimited Selling Power*, which had been published by Prentice Hall in 1990 and continues to sell well, even today. This firm, which dealt primarily with bona fide movie stars, assigned our PR work to a young intern who seemed to know little about business (or about promoting business books).

First Lesson Learned

If you are going to hire a PR firm, select one that works primarily with business professionals rather than movie stars, politicians, or some other group.

After receiving minimal publicity during the first several months of the expensive retainer we had to pay, we asked for a meeting with the president of the PR firm. To our surprise, we got the meeting. Although he hadn't read our book, he found our concepts and our business fascinating. He told us his firm would do better by us and that he would personally meet with the representative handling our account.

Second Lesson Learned

If you aren't happy with the results you are receiving from your PR firm, voice your displeasure and clearly tell senior management what you expect. The sooner you meet with senior management, the better. Don't hope that things will magically improve on their own.

The intern handling our account kept her position, but she seemed to work with a newfound passion. Now, instead of just sending out news releases to radio and television shows, she also called them! This made all the difference in the world. We started getting bookings on several talk radio shows around the country.

Third Lesson Learned

Insist that your PR agent follow up mailed press releases with phone calls. If he or she refuses to do so, it may be time to find a new PR firm.

Emboldened, we then asked the firm to begin contacting newspapers to get our book reviewed. At first they didn't want to do so, thinking it was an impossible task. Further, they explained that their expertise was in radio and television. However, we persisted and used the power of positive thinking to overcome their negativity. To everyone's surprise, the *Los Angeles Times* did a brief, but very positive, review of our book. This review spurred on many more sales and helped us get booked on some additional talk radio shows.

Fourth Lesson Learned

Ask your PR firm to contact **all** media outlets: radio, television, newspapers, magazines, and major Internet sites. You never know who is going to pick up on your story!

If your budget is limited, or if you are paying by the hour, select the services that you think will have the biggest payoff for you and your firm.

We were able to request all of the above services because we were paying a monthly retainer rather than an hourly fee. If you are paying an hourly fee, tell them exactly what you want and get an estimate as to what it might cost.

The Most Important Lesson We Learned About PR Firms

One of the greatest benefits of working with this Hollywood PR firm is that we were able to hang around the office for a few hours at a time. This behind-the-scenes look at the machinery of a major PR firm took much of the romance out of it, but was a great education.

We learned that public relations work largely involves stuffing piles of envelopes and informational packages, addressing them, and sending them out. About every two weeks, the firm we worked with might send out 20 or so packages in a given day for us. Then, approximately one week later, our PR agent would attempt to reach as many of the recipients as possible by phone. This could involve several hours of phone work and telephone tag. They really only worked a few hours per month on our behalf. Nowadays some of this is done via e-mail, but an amazing amount of it still comes down to one human being calling another on the phone. Public relations people love their telephones!

**Perhaps the most important step in good PR
is doing research.**

For example, when we work with financial planners who want additional media exposure to build their businesses, we remind them that not all talk radio shows or television shows will book business guests. Some shows specialize in human relationship problems, others in astrology, health, sports, religion, or some other area. While positive thinking has its place, it is unlikely that any businessperson will be the first expert guest on the nationally syndicated *Art Bell Show* (which specializes in extraterrestrial life, UFOs, and related topics). A PR firm would just be wasting its time and your money by contacting such a show.

We further advise these planners that, surprisingly, many financial shows do not book financial planners, stockbrokers, or others in the profession as guests. A perfect example is *MoneyTalk* with Bob Brinker. This highly popular ABC syndicated show is heard by approximately 7 million people each Saturday and Sunday, proving the popularity of the financial advice format. Yet in the 15-year history of this show, we don't believe Bob Brinker has ever had a guest. It is essential to do your homework and save time and money by eliminating these types of programs from your prospect list.

Doing Public Relations on Your Own

Public relations is a profession unto itself and its master practitioners are highly skilled and quite expensive. Can you book yourself on radio and television shows? Absolutely.

You are probably more dedicated to your success than anyone else, and no one will be as concerned about meeting your goals as you. There are many PR firms and agents who have rather short attention spans, and if they cannot place you quickly on a show, they'll move on to someone else. As a result, we encourage salespeople and other professionals to be their own PR firms. We've done it for ourselves numerous times, and we have helped many of our clients do it by using the following strategies.

Your first contact with a guest coordinator or program representative is crucial. Sometimes it is just a phone call, and other times it is by good old-fashioned written communication. For the mass approach, you may need to go with the direct mail approach. In such a case, we recommend right at the outset that you take a very careful look at your stationery. *Will a person who gets 50 or a 100 letters a day even want to open your envelope?*

With this in mind, we have suggested to our clients that they do *not* use their conventional stationery—no matter how beautiful it is. A letter or even a package from "John and Joan Smith Financial Planning" or from "ABC Semiconductor Manufacturing" will likely get little attention. Instead, we have suggested that our clients have some new, **less expensive** stationery printed. The difference can be as subtle as using abbreviations for the firm, perhaps "JJSF, Inc." or "ABC SM, Inc." In fact, there are people who have set up publicity or media divisions **within their own companies** and use the names of those PR divisions on their stationery.

In putting together a package to send to present yourself to the media, it is not a contest to see how much money you can spend. Some companies spend tens of thousands of dollars on brochures, catalogs, etc. that are given to their prospects, customers, and clients. These brochures may be effective with prospects and customers, but they usually will not impress the bookers at major talk radio shows or television shows. Such slick packages usually go right into the wastepaper basket.

Your first challenge is to get your envelope or package opened. A great way to do this is to have a provocative headline or "grabber" on the outside of your envelope. Study the envelopes you receive in the mail. Which letters or packages do you open? Read the intriguing messages on the outside of their envelopes. You can tap into the same motivations to get the bookers at top talk radio shows or television shows to open your packages, read the contents, and then contact you.

The Best Contents for Your Promotional Package

You will need to tailor your promotional package to the media outlet you are contacting. For example, if it is a radio program, be sure to include a tape that includes one of your great interviews. If you do not have one, make a demo tape on your own in which you present the kind of information that you would like to air. Then be sure that your package has solid data that shows your expertise, credentials, and, importantly, endorsements.

For your television promotional package, it is advisable to provide a brief videotape that shows how terrific you are. If you don't have such a tape, seriously consider having one made. All of your support materials should be very visually appealing, including the envelope. Most television shows are going to want a good photo of you as well.

Yes, it sounds like a lot of work, but, here's the good news: Once you have been on radio or television once, you are far more likely to get on again and again, particularly as you develop your on-air skills. You can use the tapes from one show to market yourself for other shows. Importantly, as soon as you have a few appearances under your belt, you should have a promotional tape made that features **highlights** of different radio or televised appearances. This tape should be made by a professional (rather than your cousin who just bought a digital camera and a CD burner) and it should have some flair to separate you from others seeking airtime. Any professional can do a job like this for you at a reasonable cost.

Even with a great promotional tape, *your best place to go for television appearances is any station where you have appeared in the past*. We stay in touch with all of the stations that have interviewed us on the air. In fact, it is amazing how many times a producer will say something like, "We were just talking about you. Can you do a segment on...."

If you give the media the same high quality follow-up and service that you provide your customers and clients, you can expect a good number of repeat performances.

What works best?

**We have found that the two best forms
of content for obtaining
bookings on radio and television shows are
newsworthy topics and other media stories about you.**

Let's first examine newsworthy topics. Not long ago, there were many stories about reading difficulties among children in Los Angeles. Dr. Lloyd noticed one of the major articles on childhood reading problems and he spoke with a producer at one of the local television stations where he had appeared in the past. It just so happened that they were about to do a segment on this issue and were sorting out different approaches. Here is where the creativity comes in. Ken is not an expert on childhood reading problems, but he is an expert on solving problems at work. Dr. Lloyd mentioned that these reading difficulties were going to spell job-related problems in the future, and he was immediately invited to be part of the broadcast.

The moral: Read the newspapers and you will find areas where you are a natural guest for TV or radio. Be creative. Think of any possible relevant connection to you or your business. Then pick up the phone, make a call, build the interest, and send out your package.

At the same time, remember that whatever you send to the media **must** have some solid news value or benefit to the listeners or viewers. *It cannot be fluff!*

We would estimate that 85 to 90 percent of the promotional packages that business people and professionals send to the media are composed primarily of fluff. For example, anything along the lines of "Here is why we are so great, we make the best widgets, we are the best lawyers, the best plastic surgeons, etc." While such material might interest potential customers and clients, it is of utterly no interest to those looking for interesting topics for radio and talk shows.

We've had companies and professionals hire us to analyze why their 1,000 piece mass mailing did not garner even one media appearance. Almost invariably, they sent out glossy puff pieces or product pieces in which the media has no interest or almost no interest.

How Can You Generate Newsworthy Topics?

Study newspaper headlines. Ask yourself, "What is **everyone** talking about **now**?" For example, for our financial planning clients, if the newspaper headlines are crying deflation, we suggest that they send out a piece on "How to **Profit** in Deflationary Times." When the headlines roared about the meltdown of Enron, we suggested to one of our clients that he write a piece on "How to Make Sure You are Not Enroned in the Future." He now has a regular column in the newspaper that ran that article and has picked up millions of dollars in additional assets under management.

The idea is a simple one: If there are topics **already** in the news in which you have expertise, that is your inroad to the media.

You Can Show the Audience How

In addition, one of the most powerful ways to get yourself on radio or television is to provide "**how-to**" information. We have consistently found that "how-to" stories are perennially popular with TV and radio bookers.

Think about what human beings **most want to achieve** or **experience** and then tie your story line to that deeply felt motive. For example, when our financial planner clients ask about how-to stories, we suggest topics such as, "How to Retire 10 Years Earlier Than You Ever Thought Possible," "How to Become Debt-Free in Record Time," and "How Average People Can Become Millionaires With Their Investments."

Lawyers can pitch stories on avoiding lawsuits, protecting your assets, how to have an amicable divorce, and how to protect your estate from taxes.

CPAs can pitch stories on how to slash your taxes and on hidden tax deductions no one knows about. Medical doctors have hundreds of different "how to" story lines ranging from "How to Look 10 Years Younger" to "How to Avoid or Manage Diabetes" to "How to Lose that Last 10 Pounds" to "How to See Better Without Glasses," and hundreds more. There are numerous "how-to" angles that automobile salespeople, insurance professionals, computer professionals, Website designers, food professionals, interior decorators, and others can use.

For our residential real estate sales clients who want tens of thousands of dollars of media exposure, we suggest they contact the show bookers and pitch how-to topics such as "How to Buy a Home for Less than What You're Paying in Rent," "How to be First in Line for the House that Everyone Wants," "How to Know if You're Paying Too Much for that House," and "How To Avoid Getting Burned in Today's Hot Real Estate Market."

**If you tap into a timeless human desire—
one probably held by the media gatekeepers
themselves—your odds for success go up dramatically.**

It is important that you select a topic in which you have true expertise. An accountant should not go on a television show to talk about "Breakthroughs in Open Heart Surgery," even if he has had open-heart surgery. Why get a booking on a show to discuss mortgages or health insurance if these are not your areas of expertise? Even if listeners or viewers contacted you, what would you be able to do with the leads? Obtaining media bookings in **your** area of expertise is best for the public and for your success.

Use Your Previous Media Stories As a Springboard

One of the most powerful public relations techniques we have developed for salespeople and professionals is to use *prior* media appearances to generate *new* bookings.

Here is just one brief example. The *Los Angeles Times* interviewed Dr. Moine and published a fascinating article about some of his work. In fact, he picked up a few coaching clients from the article.

He then took the article, reproduced it on two pages, added some interview questions, and sent it out to about 150 talk radio shows. Donald

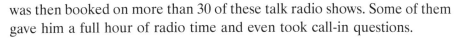

was then booked on more than 30 of these talk radio shows. Some of them gave him a full hour of radio time and even took call-in questions.

Advertising rates on these shows can go up to $2,000 per minute. Dr. Moine received hundreds of thousands of dollars of advertising for free! If you have a fascinating service or product, you could do the same.

And further, many shows allowed Donald to mention the name of his book and phone number. A few interviewers even commanded their listeners, "Folks, go out and buy *Unlimited Selling Power* today!" Dr. Moine brought in only a few clients from the original newspaper article. However, when he mailed it to talk radio shows all across the country, they booked him as a guest and he received hundreds of thousands of dollars worth of free publicity and several dozen new clients. He actually obtained more clients and more business than he could handle! That is the power of getting the media to market your products and services.

Why Is This Strategy So Effective?

We have learned that many media outlets have a follow-the-leader mentality. They follow the ringing bell of those in front of them. If they see that another highly respected news outlet has done a story on a given topic or person, and if it looks interesting and of value, they are likely to follow along and jump on board. Upon reading a previous news story about you, they will call and ask, "When can we interview you?" Send them that story so that they will get the idea themselves to interview you.

What was the cost to Dr. Moine for obtaining hundreds of thousands of dollars worth of publicity? Only a few hundred dollars. Instead of sending out glossy $10 brochures that would end up in the trash, he mailed out a two page photocopy of a newspaper story about himself, along with contact information and some sample interview questions. His cost per piece? Not $10, but maybe 40 cents. Instead of having a success rate of 1 percent or less from mailing out glossy brochures, he had a success rate of more than 25 percent.

We have now helped a number of our clients use these same strategies to get media bookings, become *experts*, and get more business. Using these strategies, you can do it for yourself.

The Importance of Staying in Touch

The most valuable asset a public relations professional owns is his Rolodex or Palm Pilot. These names, addresses, and other contact information are worth more than their weight in gold. *As you make contacts in the media, stay in close touch with them.* Send Christmas cards, Thanksgiving Day cards, and a few notes throughout the year. Let them know what you are thinking about or doing. You never know when a story line might grab their attention and suddenly you will have another chance to speak to their huge listening and/or viewing audiences.

Media bookers and talent coordinators make fairly frequent job changes. The booker for *The Morning News* this year might be working for *Oprah* next year...next month...next week. Who knows—if you stay in touch with her, you might get booked on Oprah. In the public relations ballpark, that is a home run, often good for sales of more than 500,000 copies of a book!

You're Going on the Air Tomorrow. Yikes!

You're excited because you've just gotten yourself booked on your first radio or TV program. Then the reality hits. What have you gotten yourself into? What will it be like? Can you really do this? Don't worry. We have a few pointers to help you set the stage for a successful first appearance.

When you are being interviewed on radio, keep your responses fairly brief. Fully answer the questions and provide a few fascinating stories. However, do NOT deliver any sermons! Clearly enunciate your words, and try to keep your responses positive and upbeat. Try to have a smile on your face as you speak, as this can have a positive impact on the tone of your delivery. And that smile can help you relax, too.

The host or hostess who interviews you may have briefly scanned over your article or book and *may know absolutely nothing about it.* Don't take it personally. Always be courteous and helpful in responding to whatever he or she may ask, no matter how off-the-wall the inquiry may be.

This doubly applies if the radio program has a call-in format. If a caller totally disagrees with you, do not get into a verbal joust. Tell the caller that his point of view is interesting, and then politely and **persuasively** express your points. Let the host or hostess deal with a caller who wants to argue with you.

If possible, *try to listen to the actual radio program before you go on the air.* At the very least, go to the program's Website, if there is one. Many radio and TV Websites now have parts of previous shows that you can listen to or view online. This can help you pick up some of the show's style and attitude.

However, when you go on the air, you are going to have to be flexible, calm, and cool, no matter what the host or hostess may throw at you. Sometimes you will encounter surprises, but that's just part of the fun. For example, when Dr. Lloyd was booked on one of the largest radio stations in Southern California to talk about *Unlimited Selling Power*, he was escorted from the green room to the studio by an assistant producer. As they chatted along the way, the assistant producer casually mentioned that the regular host was sick and that a guest host was filling in. And this guest host wants to talk about the California senatorial election—not the book. As she closed the door to the studio, she said, "Good luck!"

This could have been a real mess. However, Ken found an angle that fascinated both the host and thousands of listeners. *Ken spoke about how candidates for elected offices can use sales and persuasion skills to get their messages to the voters more effectively.* The board lit up with calls from listeners, and everyone had a great time. And the hostess mentioned the book at least half a dozen times during an hour that sped by.

If you are going on television, the same pointers apply, along with a few more. First, just about everyone connected with the TV show wants to help you succeed. If you come across well, it adds to the success of their show. Because they want to help you, if you have questions, just ask.

When you are on the air, look at the person who is interviewing you and not at the camera, unless you are told differently. This is the time to be brief and clear, and remember that time can pass very quickly when you are on TV. In fact, a minute can easily slip by, and that is typically about the longest you should be talking before giving the host a chance to speak again.

Take a deep breath and relax your shoulders just before things go live, and then make sure that you are sitting still and not swiveling in the seat or fidgeting. All that fidgeting or extraneous movement does is distract the viewers, and viewers do notice everything!

Make sure that you know the interviewer's name and use it in the course of your answers. Listen carefully to the interviewer's questions and make sure you answer them. Watch his or her body language and make sure your body language is in alignment. If you pay careful attention, your interviewer can guide you smoothly right through the interview. And that can literally help set the stage for a return visit.

Most importantly, be yourself, be natural, be informative, and have fun.

Turning Your Articles Into a Book or E-book

Would you love to write a book but find the entire process overwhelming? A great shortcut to writing a book is to first publish an e-book (electronic book). If you have 20 pages or so of great material, you can publish it as an e-book and advertise it on your Website. If you have published two or three articles, you can combine those, write an introduction and a conclusion and you have an e-book!

At first you might want to give your e-book away to collect the names of prospects interested in your products and services. Some of our clients have collected the names and e-mail addresses of more than 10,000 prospects by offering a free e-book!

As inspiration strikes, you can add another 10 pages to your book here, and 15 pages there. Once you have 50 or so pages of great material, you can start charging for your book (and you will continue to collect the names, phone numbers, and e-mail addresses of people who buy your book). As you continue to add to your book, you can increase the purchase price. Soon, you will have 200 or so pages of great material and you can then take your book to a major publisher.

As previously mentioned, you can advertise your electronic book on your Website. When people log on to your site, an ad for your e-book will pop up in the upper left hand corner, complete with a picture of the cover. The text will say, "Order Joe Smith's powerful new book now! Click here!"

When visitors click on the button, they will be instructed to enter their name, address, e-mail address, and credit card number (or you can just give the book away for all of the prospects it will generate). If you send the book by e-mail, your computer can do ALL of the work, from promoting the book on your Website to taking orders and sending the book. You won't have to lift a finger (besides writing the book).

Some salespeople and professionals are now using e-books to make thousands of dollars in extra income each month and to generate thousands of new leads and prospects. There are many consultants around the country who can help you set up an e-book on your Website. One of the best we have found is Robert Imbriale of *UltimateWealth.com*.

The Bottom Line

One of the most powerful ways to market yourself, your products, and services today is to have the media do it for you, and that's exactly what will happen if you dedicate yourself to writing articles, making radio and television appearances, and writing a book or e-book. The publicity that comes from these efforts is widespread, credible, compelling, and will be working for you 24 hours a day. When you have books and articles in print, you (and your products and services) are being actively marketed around the world all the time—even when you are sleeping or on vacation!

Most salespeople could never afford to pay for this kind of publicity. It is literally possible to obtain **free** media publicity that would cost hundreds of thousands to millions of dollars if you paid for similar advertising. Sales superstars recognize that they cannot afford to ignore this incredible opportunity. Such publicity has minimal out-of-pocket costs. And in the case of a book, you just might write a best-seller that brings you hundreds of thousands of dollars in royalties, in addition to incredible publicity and thousands of prospects.

The main investment in media marketing is going to be your time, but even if you can only spend a small amount of time each day on this effort, you will be very richly rewarded. Most people can easily find an extra 15 minutes to 30 minutes a day for just about any activity they deem important. It would be hard to find any daily 15 to 30 minute activity that could produce more satisfaction and wealth than this one. Using the mass media to market and sell you, your products, and your services is truly one of the most awesome forms of Ultimate Selling Power in existence.

8

The Power of
Seminar Selling

If you are like most salespeople, you spend the majority of your time selling one-on-one. You call one person on the phone, you send an e-mail or a fax to another person, and then you drive out to visit another person. While one-on-one selling can be very effective, it is also quite inefficient.

Sales millionaires try to get in front of as many highly qualified prospects as possible in as short a period of time as possible. Their passion to meet and interact with many high quality prospects leads them to discover and then master seminar marketing.

You have heard it said that sales is a numbers game. We have updated that truism.

**It is our belief that in the 21st century,
sales is a numbers game and a quality game.**

You cannot just focus on getting in front of a large number of people. You must also deliver an amazingly good presentation when you are in front of those individuals. When you have both a system for getting in front of a huge number of high quality prospects and the skills to do a first rate presentation, you truly have Ultimate Selling Power.

If you have a high quality product or service offered at a fair price, if you get in front of a large number of highly qualified people and do an outstanding job of telling your story, the odds are high that you will achieve the status of sales millionaire.

Entire books have been written on the mechanics of seminar marketing, selection of mailing lists, target marketing, PowerPoint presentations, etc., and yet only a relatively small number of top sales professionals use seminar selling. What sets these sales millionaires apart from the legions of average salespeople who have never tried seminar selling? More than the techniques employed, it is the **mindset** of some sales professionals that empowers them to succeed at seminar selling. In this chapter, we will share with you the attitudes, mindsets, and beliefs of sales seminar millionaires. Acquire these beliefs and attitudes and you will be well on your way to high-level success in seminar selling.

"I've Tried Everything"

The owners of a high technology business contacted us asking for help in raising venture capital. Raising money for a business is one of the more sophisticated forms of persuasion. The CEO of the company claimed that they had "tried everything," to raise funds, but had only been moderately successful. They had used up all of the funds raised in addition to most of their life savings. They were desperate. With the addition of about $2 million in new capital, they would reach critical mass and begin to turn a profit.

The owners of this company had flown all over the United States to meet with potential investors. Sometimes they flew cross-country to meet with just one individual who might invest in the company. Obviously, with the cost of airfare, hotel rooms, meals, etc., this was a very expensive way to attempt to raise money.

We asked if they had ever conducted seminars for groups of potential investors. "That would never work in our industry," the starving CEO claimed. "The kind of people who invest in companies like ours need personalized attention." Yet all the personalized attention they had lavished on individual investors had done little good. It was time to consider a much more efficient way of selling and raising money: seminar selling.

We wish we could say these entrepreneurs met with instant success using seminar selling. They did not because they didn't know how to do it. They didn't know how to get mailing lists, design brochures, and invitational pieces, select a location and, most important of all, they were not skilled presenters. However, after a couple of months of hard work, preparation, assistance, and coaching, they offered their first seminar and raised some much-needed money. Their seminar marketing got better and more sophisticated with each attempt and within six months they had the funds they needed to expand their business and hit their profitability target. Had we not convinced them of the power of seminar marketing and shown them how to do sales seminars, it is likely that their business would not have made it.

Do you think seminar marketing won't work in your business? Unless you change this belief, seminar selling won't work for you. Negative attitudes about seminar marketing become a self-fulfilling prophecy that kills almost all chances for success. Sales millionaires use seminar selling in almost every area of business and industry and in most of the professions. If you aren't aware of this mega-trend, it is because you either aren't paying attention or it could be due to the fact that some companies try to keep this highly profitable method of marketing a secret.

The Wide, Wide World of Seminar Marketing

Seminar selling is used in almost every **high-tech field** and in most of the **basic industries**. It is also used in:

The travel industry	Publishing
Software sales	Food and beverages
Clothing and fashion	Commodities
Real estate	Financial planning
Insurance	Stocks and bonds
Golf	Education
Motivation	Venture capital
Law	Medicine
Psychology	

And countless other fields and professions.

Hundreds of billions of dollars of goods and services are sold each year through seminar selling. If you are truly serious about becoming a sales millionaire (or multimillionaire), tap into the power of seminar selling.

If you do not yet believe in seminar selling, you must open your mind to its possibilities. Look around your industry to find those who excel at seminar marketing. Study and model what they do.

Learn from the best.

Attend their seminars. You might be amazed to find that it is possible to assemble dozens or hundreds of qualified prospects into one room to listen to you explain the virtues and benefits of your products and services. Sales seminars are taking place every day in hundreds of cities and towns all over the U.S. Someone is getting the business from these sales seminars—*it might as well be you*. To give you just some idea of the power of seminar selling, our client Ted Thomas of Orlando, Florida, sometimes brings in $90,000 to well over $100,000 from a one-day seminar. His total costs are, at most, 50 percent, and therefore, he earns $45,000 to more than $50,000 a day from those seminars.

Seminar selling takes many forms. By whatever name, it involves you speaking to a **group** of highly qualified prospects. Seminar selling can take place at conventions, workshops, classrooms, churches, hotels, restaurants, colleges, golf courses, ski lodges, casinos, at your company, at a trade show, or even on cruise ships. It also takes place on the Internet in the form for Web-broadcasted seminars. The only limiting factor in where and how sales seminars are conducted is the imagination of the sales professional.

"But Seminar Selling Costs Too Much!"

Another limiting belief that prevents some sales professionals from trying seminar selling is the false assumption that seminar selling is expensive. In fact, when properly conducted, seminar selling is one of the most cost-effective methods of personal selling in existence. Telemarketing usually costs less, but telemarketing limits what you can show prospects and the impact your presentation can have.

Nothing is more expensive than personal one-on-one selling where a salesperson gets in her car and drives out to see an individual prospect.

Figures vary industry by industry, but it usually costs somewhere between $250 and $300 for each in-person individual sales call. The cost of a live one-on-one sales call can vary from about $25 to well over $1,000 (when air travel is involved). For most industries, the cost averages out to between $250 and $300. When you have a large number of people coming to see and hear you at your sales seminar, costs are frequently just a fraction of that.

Action Step

Before you read any further, *determine how many sales calls you make in an average week*. We define a sales call as a face-to-face meeting with a prospect or customer. You might be shocked at how **low** that number is. Multiply that number by about 45 to determine the number of sales call you make each year.

Now, imagine that *five times more people* saw you and heard your story each year. Such an increase is usually easily attainable with the power of seminar marketing. Imagine that 500 percent more people learned the **benefits** of your company's products and services. How much more successful do you think you might be? Many of our clients have been able to double or triple their incomes by using the power of seminar marketing. Even more remarkable is the fact that they are often able to get these major sales increases while working **fewer** hours per week.

In addition to saving money, sales seminars save you a tremendous amount of time and energy. How long would it take you to call on 300 individuals? Perhaps several months. Why not see them at one or two or three seminars? *Even if you had the time to call on them individually, do you really want to?* Think of how exhausted you will be after giving the same presentation 300 times. Think of how much more **refreshed** you will be if you only have to tell the story three times, in front of 100 prospects each time. Even if you have to do the seminar 10 times with 30 people at each seminar, you will still have avoided 290 repetitive sales presentations.

Burnout is a major problem in the sales field. It costs American corporations tens of billions of dollars a year when burnt out salespeople leave and new salespeople must be attracted, hired, and trained. Why do salespeople get burned out? One of the major reasons is that they get sick and tired of giving the same presentation, the same pitch, over and over again to hundreds of new prospects each year. With the old-fashioned one-on-one selling, salespeople are essentially turned into human tape recorders. Who can blame them for getting burned out? By reducing the number of individual sales presentations and also increasing the number of people learning about your products and services, seminar selling helps to solve the problem of salesperson burnout.

Let's make this personal. Are **you** stressed out by selling? Have you considered quitting? In our experience, many burned out salespeople are *overly dependent upon one-to-one marketing.* How many times have you given your sales presentation? Giving the same presentation several thousand times frequently does lead to burnout. Why not explain all the basics to **groups** of people rather than to individuals?

> **You will not only make more money,**
> **but you will have less stress and**
> **more free time if you use**
> **seminar marketing to become a sales millionaire.**

For all of the above reasons, seminar selling has become the strategy of choice for many sales millionaires.

Turning Seminars From an Expense to a Profit Center

Despite all the financial, time management, and personal advantages of seminar selling, the myth persists that it is an expensive method of marketing. Recently, a financial planner contacted Dr. Moine and tried as hard as he could to control his voice as he recounted what had happened at his most recent seminar. This financial planner was NOT one of our clients. At a cost of more than $14,000, this financial planner had sponsored a seminar at a luxury hotel in his city and had attracted nearly 190 attendees. His featured speaker (the main draw of the night) was a retired high-level government official who charged $7,000 per speech. The financial planner himself spoke for only about 15 minutes and the government official spoke for nearly an hour. The financial planner booked 17 office appointments and ended up getting only two small clients from this seminar. "Seminars just don't work," the financial planner said. "They are too darned expensive and don't produce much results."

"Seminars **do** work," Donald explained to him, "if you do them right. And they don't have to be expensive." In fact, almost all of the sales millionaires we are currently working with are using seminars to attract new clients and to get more business from existing clients. Some top salespeople use seminars as their **only** marketing tool.

We began working with this financial planner and found that he had made many mistakes in seminar marketing. First, he didn't need to spend $7,000 to hire the speaker. The financial planner himself should have been the star of the show. Second, the financial planner had spent too much money on glossy full-color invitations to the seminar. We have found that for this particular type of seminar, simple black-and-white invitations work just as well. The financial planner had rented the wrong mailing lists and also needed help with his newspaper advertising.

When we corrected those mistakes, his cost per seminar fell to below $2,000 and he began bringing in an average of $500,000 in new assets under management from each seminar. Because this financial planner charges an average of 1 percent per year on the assets he manages, he was making more than $3,000 profit from each seminar he offered. The actual figure was much greater than that because his new clients brought in additional assets over time and also referred friends and relatives to this planner. The planner learned that if you do seminar selling properly, it is not an expense, it is a profit center.

Every few weeks we get a call from a salesperson who informs us that "Seminars don't work." Thanks for the advice, but please don't tell that to the salespeople and professionals who are rapidly bringing in massive amounts of new business through seminar marketing. We know salespeople and professionals who have brought in more than $300 million in new sales through seminar marketing. Please don't tell us that seminars don't work or that they are too expensive. We know better.

One estate planning attorney with whom we have worked has acquired more than 4,000 clients through seminar marketing. An insurance agent client of ours earns about $750,000 a year working only from November through March and she acquires almost all of her clients through seminar marketing. Another one of our clients, Craig Meyer, working with first-time home-buyers, combined an infomercial with seminars around the United States to bring in more than $10 million in one year. This is not the value of the homes he sold, this is the revenue generated by selling educational programs, books, tapes, and advanced seminars. What do the seminar selling successes of all these people in these vastly different industries have in common? They all started with the mindset that seminar selling could work for them.

But What About Personal Attention to Clients?

Why is seminar marketing such a powerful sales and marketing tool? It is much more effective to market to a group of people than to market to individuals one-on-one. As we previously explained, individual marketing is extremely time consuming and hampers productivity. Selling through the use of seminars is like selling bananas—you want to sell them in a bunch rather than individually. Of course, prospects do deserve **personal** attention.

> **Once prospects become customers and clients, you can give them all the personal attention they want and need.**

How to Save Money in Conducting Sales Seminars

Seminar marketing does not have to be expensive to be successful. Some of our clients do workplace seminars. What do we mean by workplace seminars? Instead of calling on just one person or two people at a company, you offer to do a seminar for all who might be interested. For example, our client Mark Mendez at Salomon Smith Barney has recently conducted workplace seminars for employees of Boeing and Arthur Anderson. It is no accident that Mark and his two superstar financial advisor partners, Michael McDonald and Tony Coelho, now have more than $200 million in assets under management.

What are the advantages of doing workplace seminars? First, you don't have to rent a hotel room in which to hold the seminar. Your prospect or client will frequently provide a room at their site. It might be a large conference room or a small room or even the cafeteria. Sometimes you can do a workplace seminar at a local restaurant that is convenient for all the company's employees. Either on-site programs or those at a local restaurant can work very well. However, when you are on the prospect's site, people are less guarded. Being on their own home turf, they are much more comfortable. In addition, they think you have been stamped with the "Good Housekeeping Seal of Approval," because the boss let you come in and do the seminar.

Frequently, people who would never come to your office for a seminar will attend one held at their company or at a nearby restaurant. Obviously, they don't have to fight traffic, drive to a strange location, etc.

When you make it as easy as possible for prospects to attend your seminar, the enrollment goes up.

Remember, sales is indeed a numbers game. The more high quality people you see, the more you are likely to sell.

Another advantage of workplace seminars is that you often do not have to mail out flyers or brochures. The company at which you are doing the seminar will promote the program themselves on their Website, in their employee newsletter, and on bulletin boards. Sometimes they will ask you to do a mailing, but the cost will be reduced because they will give you the mailing list for free and the list will be much smaller than if you were mailing to the general public. Our client Marc Mendez frequently faxes or e-mails seminar invitations to employees of a given company.

When designing a flyer or doing a mailing piece for employees and executives of a company, there is seldom any need for a glossy brochure. In fact, a brochure that looks too slick can sometimes backfire. You want your brochure or flyer to look like something the company might have produced itself for its own in-house programs. Many of the most effective seminar invitations we have designed for our clients are simple one-page black-and-white invitations listing benefits of the seminar, biographies on the speakers, and seminar dates and times.

For all of the above reasons, workplace seminars are powerfully effective and they save you a great deal of time.

When you do workplace seminars, make sure your programs have educational value.

Don't just beat your chest about how fantastic your company's products and services are. Make sure that you share some knowledge and wisdom with the seminar participants. Focus on helping them solve one or more of their problems. Of course, you can use your company's products or services to solve this problem, but do focus on finding solutions.

Sharing the Costs of Doing Seminars

Another powerful strategy for reducing the costs of doing seminars is to share those costs with another salesperson or another company. If you are a wholesaler or manufacturer's representative, have two or three of the companies you represent pay the expenses (mailing lists, brochures, seminar handouts) for the seminars you conduct. After all, they will be the beneficiaries of all that you sell. If they won't cover all the costs, have them pay for a fair share. Over the course of a year, this could lead to savings of $10,000 or much more.

Professionals can also use this strategy. For example, we do a great deal of consulting and coaching work with financial planners, CPAs, and attorneys. We have frequently encouraged these groups to **work together** in promoting powerful seminars. In the first hour of the seminar, the financial planner might cover his investment outlook, the best current mix of investments and strategies for reducing risk and maximizing returns. In the second hour, an estate planning attorney might talk about how to slash estate taxes, avoid probate, and provide for the next generation. The financial planner and the estate planning attorney are complimentary rather than competitive with one another.

Someone who might have been attracted to the seminar to hear the estate planning attorney will also hear the financial planner and may very well become a client of that planner. The same is true for people who were attracted by the topics offered by the financial planner—some of those will become clients of the estate planning attorney. This is truly a powerful form of win-win marketing because the costs of the seminar are reduced by 50 percent and at the same time, an even larger group of people is attracted.

Action Step

Before you go any further, write down a list of several other sales-people, companies, or other professionals you can do seminars with. Look for individuals or companies that are complimentary rather than competitive. Now, pick one or two of the **best prospects** from that list and call them to propose the idea of doing a joint seminar. These types of alliances and joint ventures can take the fear and expense out of seminar marketing and can dramatically increase your chances for success.

What if you want to do more **high-end seminar marketing**? There are still ways of saving money. Some of our clients use wedding style seminar invitations printed on heavy rag paper and some have used embossed or gold foil printing. Other clients have used full-page newspaper ads to attract seminar participants. How can you save money when doing such high-end marketing?

If you are doing expensive printing, one of the best ways of keeping costs down is to print up all or nearly all of your wedding style invitations for the year **at one time**. By doing so, you will get a major break on price due to the quantity discount. The biggest expense is just to set up the presses and print the first 1,000 sets. The second 1,000 invitations cost just a fraction of the first and the price drops rapidly with further increases in quantity.

How can you print a year's worth of seminar invitations at one time when you don't know the locations and dates of future seminars? When you are ready to do a mailing for a specific seminar, *you can have a small slip of paper included that has the date, time, and location of that seminar.*

Many people think that advertising your seminars in newspapers is expensive. It doesn't have to be. Start with smaller ads in smaller regional papers. Some of our clients have had outstanding results by advertising their seminars in newspapers serving affluent smaller towns. Others have had great success by advertising their seminars in limited circulation magazines that have low advertising rates but go to exactly the professional group you want to target. Advertising on industry specific Websites has also dropped dramatically in price and enables you to get in front of the exact markets you want to reach.

Don't let the small investment you must make in seminar marketing scare you off. In many cases, you can expect a $5 to $10 return on every dollar you spend on seminar marketing. When was the last time you found a stock or mutual fund that returned five or 10 times your original investment? Besides the financial payoff, seminar marketing will enable you to grow your business much faster than it otherwise would and to have a much more enjoyable lifestyle with more free time.

A lack of money should not prevent you from offering seminars. As mentioned above, you can do workplace seminars at practically no cost. You can also offer seminars through your local community college or adult education group without paying any promotional expenses. In some cases, they will pay you! For example, some owners of computer stores are paid to conduct seminars or classes at local colleges. The students are impressed by the instructor's knowledge, build trust in her, and then shop at the instructor's computer store. In other cases, computer consultants teach these classes and a number of the students end up hiring the instructor as a consultant to assist with various information technology projects.

Don't Let Your Peers
Discourage You

If there is no economic reason not to do seminars, then why don't more salespeople and professionals use this powerful marketing tool? Sometimes a well-meaning peer or associate talks them out of it. Recently an executive from a major company called to ask for help. When we were speaking about seminar marketing, in a booming authoritative voice, he informed us that seminars do not work in today's environment.

We asked him the date of the last seminar he had offered and he told us it was more than four years ago. We then asked him how his business was doing. He told us he had lost a number of clients in recent years and that his income was half of what it used to be. Despite the fact that his business had declined **every year** since he stopped offering seminars, he was absolutely certain seminar marketing would not work for him. He told us that seminars used to work in his city but that he didn't offer them anymore because his partner had told him that people were "seminared out." They were both wrong and, as a consequence, their business suffered severely.

As Henry Ford once said, "Whether you think you can—or you think you can't—you are right." We told this caller that we knew of someone in his profession in his city who had doubled his business over the past 18 months through seminar marketing. The caller was dumbfounded.

The belief that "seminars don't work" is widespread today (especially among the less successful salespeople), *and that is good news*! It means that you now have fewer competitors when you offer a seminar. In traveling around the country working with businesses and professionals, we study all the seminars advertised in local newspapers. Seminar offerings have declined in number and frequency. Many cities and towns that used to have a large number of seminars now have relatively few. That spells opportunity for you! In the first chapter of this book, we wrote about the mindsets of sales millionaires. When it comes to seminar selling, the very best salespeople in the country have the mindset that, "There is always room for another truly outstanding seminar!"

Proof of the Public's Desire for Seminars

We all love seminars. You have probably attended dozens of seminars, workshops, and classes. You might have even attended one of our seminars!

The general public loves seminars as much as salespeople and professionals do.

**When you can't, or won't,
fulfill the public's thirst for seminars,
others will rush in to fill the void.**

Donald was recently contacted by a financial advisor who said that people no longer want to attend seminars on how to invest. Donald shared the following amazing case study with the caller and it gave him an entirely new perspective on the public's desire for seminars.

Wade Cook is one of the most prominent (some would say notorious) investment seminar leaders around. According to SEC filings, his seminar firm lost 89 percent on its recommended trades during 2000. Did that hurt the seminar business of Wade Cook? Not at all. Wade Cook is not a financial planner yet he does seminars around the country on various financial topics such as picking stocks, investment strategies, and how to save on taxes. How much has Wade Cook made from his seminars? According to Securities and Exchange Commission documents, nonfinancial planner, noncollege graduate, ex-cab driver Wade Cook has made more than **$28 million** from people who have paid money to attend his seminars. He has made this $28 million since 1996, a period of five short years. The $28 million is not his gross receipts, it is the net income his company has paid him. Do you still think that no one wants to attend seminars anymore?

We are not recommending Wade Cook or his methods and he is not a client of ours. We are also not criticizing him. The public definitely seems to have a desire to attend his seminars. Wade Cook is exhibit number one in establishing that the public has a *deep hunger for seminars*. Why else would thousands of people pay him up to $7,995 to attend his two-day programs? If you think you cannot offer a free seminar and get dozens of highly qualified people to attend, you must readjust your thinking (or what you are doing to promote your seminars).

In the early 1990s, one of our clients hit the mother lode with his seminars. They became so popular that he had to hire several other people to conduct them. Eventually he had more than 40 speakers on the road each week conducting his seminars in cities and towns all across the U.S. It was our job to train and coach his speakers on how to use the most powerful forms of persuasion. At that time, many of his competitors were saying that no one wanted to attend seminars anymore. He proved them wrong and brought in millions of dollars each month in extra revenue from his seminars.

People in every area of business love to go to seminars as much as you do. If you don't do seminar selling, someone else in your industry will. One of our purposes in writing this chapter is to encourage you to try seminar marketing. It is truly one of the most powerful sales strategies ever developed.

The Pros and Cons of Pre-Packaged Seminars

Some industries and professions now offer pre-packaged seminars. We do not sell any of these pre-packaged seminars and, therefore, can be objective in writing about them. While we will not comment on individual seminars, properly used, these "ready to go" seminars can get you up and running in seminar marketing much more quickly than a seminar designed from scratch.

Designing a seminar from scratch is a lot of work. We know this from personal experience because we've designed, written, and redesigned dozens of seminars for our clients over the years. Today, a major part of our consulting practice is helping our clients redesign and customize their existing seminars or pre-packaged seminars they have purchased. We work on between four and seven of these seminar redesign and customization projects each month, so we have become known as experts in this area. Even though we know many time-saving and effort-saving techniques to produce a high-quality compelling seminar, it is still a lot of work; and thus, the allure of pre-packaged seminars that you can customize.

Tips for Success

If you are going to buy or use a pre-packaged seminar, we strongly suggest you **customize** it. Many pre-packaged seminars are rather bland. Some are downright boring. A sales professional working for a large company called us last year to ask for help in redesigning a seminar he had just used. He had decided to use this pre-packaged program because his company had already approved it.

Note: Many companies require you to get approval **before** delivering any seminar. This approval process is frequently referred to as compliance.

This seminar had already gone through all of the compliance checks. The lawyers at his company found that the pre-packaged seminar did not make any false claims, did not exaggerate, and was not offensive, and therefore, they approved it. There were no compliance problems because the seminar was bland, boring, and gutless. The sales professional spent a fair amount of money on newspaper advertising to promote this boring program. Do you know how many people registered for his heavily promoted seminar? Exactly one.

The bland, pre-approved seminar and its bland advertising copy was so nonpersuasive that only one of the 10,000 or so people who read the newspaper advertisement decided to register for the seminar! When we showed him how to customize the ad and the seminar content (and get compliance approval), his success rate soared in future seminars.

Evaluating Pre-Packaged Seminars

To effectively customize a pre-packaged seminar, you must **first** objectively diagnose its strengths and weaknesses. If you use a pre-packaged seminar, ask yourself these questions:

1. Would I attend this program?

2. Why or why not?

3. What are the *strongest* parts of the seminar?

4. What are the *weakest* parts?

5. What is most in need of improvement in this seminar?

6. What can I leave out of this seminar?

7. What do I need to add to this seminar to make it maximally effective?

By answering these questions honestly, you will know what to concentrate on in re-designing and customizing the seminar. It is also a good idea to *practice delivering the seminar to several of your friends and/or business associates*. Don't just trust your own judgment on how great you are and how great the seminar is. You need some additional sets of eyes and ears to honestly evaluate the program and your own skills in delivering it.

We know. This all sounds like work, and it is. However, seminar selling has created many sales millionaires. Some of our clients have become multimillionaires (in only a few years) from seminar selling. If you seriously work at developing your skills in seminar selling, you will be very well rewarded.

Make sure that whoever gives you feedback on the seminar is **objective**. Without honest feedback, you won't be able to make the program as powerful and effective as it needs to be.

Recently, a local company hired us to redesign and customize their seminars. Because most of our clients are out-of-state (and a few are out of the country), it is always a special pleasure to work with someone close to home. While this company's seminars had received positive reviews from attendees ("Great speech! I loved it"), the seminars were not bringing in the business.

One of the owners of the company called and said, "Well, we are ready to get criticized. Come analyze our seminars." We corrected her. "No," we said, "you are not ready to get criticized. You are ready to get better."

**In our opinion, feedback on your seminars
is only beneficial if it leads to
an increase in business.**

It is nice that 1,000 people told you that they loved your seminar. *How many of them actually became clients or customers?* You should focus on turning seminar attendees into clients and customers. After all, that is the main reason you are offering seminars. That is what we focus on when we help our clients set new sales and profitability records with seminar marketing. Happiness ratings, smiles, applause, and pats on the back are nice, but they do not pay the bills.

If you can, **tape-record** or **videotape** your seminar. Studying and analyzing those tapes can lead to rapid improvements in your seminar performance and your own success. Recently, we've been rewriting seminar brochures and PowerPoint presentations for an attorney in Colorado who earns several hundred thousand dollars a year in extra income through his seminars. We knew he was serious about his seminar success when he informed us that he had videotapes of his seminars that he wanted us to analyze. It is this type of analysis (or even better, analysis of a live seminar) that leads to quantum-level performance improvements.

Do not take the above comments on pre-packaged seminars as criticism. In fact, we have found that **most** pre-packaged seminars are fairly good. *Usually about 80 percent of the material in most pre-packaged seminars is worth keeping*—and using that already assembled material can save you a great deal of time and money you would otherwise have had to spend if starting from scratch in creating a seminar. If you customize the other 20 percent of the seminar, you will usually have a very powerfully effective program. Just don't expect to buy a seminar off the shelf and bring in hundreds of new clients or customers by using it.

If it were that easy, then almost anyone could become a sales millionaire. Be realistic. It does take a little time and work. But you will be handsomely rewarded for the expertise you develop in seminar marketing.

Additional Tips

Tip 1: If you are considering buying or licensing a seminar from one of the pre-packaged seminar companies, make sure you find out exactly how many other licensees they have in your area. "Business Success Secrets," "Breakthroughs in Internet Backbone Technology," or "Steps to Real Estate Riches," may look like hot seminar offerings to you—until you find out that 13 other people in your town have offered the same seminar during the previous two years.

Tip 2: Before you buy a pre-packaged seminar or seminar franchise, make sure you ask about both current **and previous** seminar licensees. Some companies will tell you they only have two licensees in your city. That's **now**. What they won't disclose (unless asked) is that they have had 27 licensees in your city in the past few years. The seminar you are so excited about is old hat in your area.

Tip 3: Make sure you get the seminar packager's claims **in writing**. Some pre-packaged seminar companies will tell you almost anything over the phone ("We've only got three licensees in your area."). Yet, if you could see their files and the facts in black and white, you would note that they have had 39 licensees in your city over the previous several years offering the very same seminar. *This tip alone could save you $10,000 or more and help you avoid the mistake of buying a canned seminar that people in your area will see as a rerun.* If you do buy such a seminar, you need to extensively customize it.

The best seminars combine **education** and **group involvement** with **trust-building** and a little **entertainment**. An effective seminar must offer content of **genuine educational value**. Product specific seminars or sales oriented seminars usually turn off prospects and lack effectiveness. While it is perfectly acceptable to have a goal of bringing in many new clients from each seminar, you should make sure that **everyone** who attends—even those who do not become clients or customers—receives something of lasting value.

You have much wisdom to share. Share your wisdom in a seminar with dozens of prospects instead of explaining it one-on-one. You will save time, energy, and money. You will be able to help more people more rapidly. This is the win-win benefit of seminar marketing. When you master seminar selling, you are likely to become a sales millionaire or multimillionaire.

Seminar selling is a process of sharing your wisdom and insights with a group of people who are highly interested in what you have to say. Of course, you also get to explain how your products or services can help the attendees **solve problems** and **enjoy great benefits**. Through sharing your wisdom and interacting with the groups of people who attend your seminars, you are likely to have your best year ever as a sales professional.

9

Strategies and Tactics for Dealing With Challenging Prospects and Customers

One of the major problems with conventional sales training is that an assumption is made that prospects and customers do what they do for logical reasons and, therefore, certain universal "laws of selling" apply to all prospects and customers. In fact, emotion plays a very strong role in all buying decisions, even when those decisions are being made by engineers, doctors, lawyers, and other well-educated professionals. The problem with the "universal laws of selling" is that many of them contradict one another. Some sales laws or principles that work brilliantly with one prospect will doom you to failure with another.

Individual differences between customers must not only be considered, they must be respected.

We are a diverse nation with many wonderful nationalities and religions and many unique human beings! *Diversity is our strength*. The U.S. is not really what some people call a "melting pot," but is more like a salad bowl, and it is our unique differences that contribute to our greatness. In this chapter, we will share specific tactics and techniques that will lead to sales success with some of the most challenging prospects and customers you will encounter in your sales career.

Dealing With Different Customers

As part of the process of maintaining positive expectations in dealing with prospects and customers, we encourage sales professionals to refrain from derogatory labeling of people who are not as cooperative as a salesperson might like.

For example, if there is a prospect who trudges along the decision-making path rather slowly, there is nothing to be gained by labeling this type of prospect a **slug**. That expression implies a lack of respect and trust toward the prospect and *thinking in such terms can actually have a negative impact on the way you deal with the prospect or client.*

Remember that every so-called resistant behavior tells you something valuable about the client or prospect.

Every resistant behavior is also saying, *"What you are doing now is not working. It is time to change."* What valuable information! Your prospect is **not** criticizing you. The so-called "difficult customer" is giving you clues and tips in how to sell him.

Unfortunately, it is true that **we learn little from the "easy" customers** (also known as "lay-downs"). Although it is wonderful to have customers who immediately buy from us, those customers teach us nothing. In fact, easy customers put salespeople into the role of order-takers. How much are order takers paid in our society? Not much.

When we are hired to speak at seminars, we sometimes hear salespeople say that they wished they had more easy customers. Don't. If a large percentage of your prospects immediately agree to buy whatever you were selling, and to pay full price, why would your company need you? They could probably get almost all of those sales through advertising, the Internet, and direct mail. When selling gets too easy, salespeople end up in the unemployment line.

**Therefore, celebrate your different or difficult customers.
They are the ones who make you stronger.**

They are the ones who truly develop your sales and persuasion skills. They are the ones who keep you gainfully employed and earning a high income. Without challenging prospects and customers, you are little more than a clerk.

There are many different types of challenging customer behaviors and sales millionaires have proven strategies on how to deal with each. Let's take a closer look at some of the challenging prospects and customers and the best ways of working with them.

The Deliberative or Procrastinating Prospect

This is a prospect that some salespeople would have referred to as the slug noted previously. This prospect literally and figuratively moves at a slow and cautious pace. You can sometimes see it in his gait and slower physical actions, and you can certainly hear it in his speech patterns. The extreme form of the deliberative prospect is the procrastinator. The techniques that work well with deliberative clients also work well with procrastinators, and so we shall deal with both in this section.

Some salespeople believe that there is a fairly large sampling of deliberative prospects in the South. Maybe—but you will also find many deliberative clients in the Northeast and every other part of the country. We have even encountered slow decision-makers in the heart of fast-paced New York City! Let's start with an example of one of our clients who was transferred from the Northwest to the deep South. A very successful salesperson from Seattle, he was transferred to a new territory in Texas, and struggled mightily. In an attempt to get his sales numbers up, he called on more and more prospects each day and shortened each sales call. At last, one of his Texan prospects, with boots propped up on the desk, stared him in the eye and said, "Y'all gotta slow down."

And therein lies a message in selling to a deliberative prospect. If a salesperson comes in a warp speed, hyper, or overly animated mode, he is going to be perceived as slick, aggressive, and even untrustworthy. When sales millionaires deal with deliberative prospects, they begin more slowly and get in step with the prospect. They subliminally send the message, "I am like you are. I will not threaten you. You are safe with me." After they have paced the prospect and have built a deep level of trust, they can then begin to speed up the sales process somewhat.

This is known as pacing and leading. First you pace, match, and mirror certain key client behaviors to build trust. After you have paced, paced, and paced, you can then safely lead the client. We call this the "dance of the sales millionaire." They match the client, match the client, match the client, and then lead the client. It truly is like a dance rather than a battle. Once you get in step and synchrony with the prospect, when you change the beat, they are much more likely to go along with you. When properly done, the process is nearly effortless and always elegant.

Another very powerful way of dealing with the most deliberate clients is to use **mental judo**. With mental judo, you do not resist what the client is doing. You do not fight the client. Rather, *you tell them to do even more of it!* It is ironic that when you stop pushing against a client, they will frequently stop resisting you. When you use mental judo, there is nothing for the client or prospect to push back against.

In the case of a deliberate client who is slow to make decisions, you could use mental judo and say, *"Take all the time you want in making this decision. If you want to go slow in making this decision, you can. Don't be bothered by the fact that some of your competitors already have this new high-efficiency system. Just take all the time you want."*

While you are giving the prospect permission to take all the time he wants, you also remind them that some of their competitors already have the new system. The message is that you don't care how long they take to make the decision, *but they may care.* Another powerful message you can slip in using mental judo is that there may be price increases in the future. However, make sure you give them permission to take all the time they want. Their subconscious mind will get the message that you do not care if they delay the decision, but it could hurt their company and they may have to pay a much higher price in the future. When skillfully used, mental judo will lead the prospect to change his behavior (in this case, to speed up the decision-making process), without any pressure from you.

Procrastinators take deliberation to the extreme. The favorite decision of procrastinators is to make no decision at all.

Don't assume procrastinators are not interested in what you are offering.

They may be very interested, but they are stuck on the fence. Mere patience does not usually work with procrastinators—unless you have all the time in the world. Some of these prospects have shown staying power that would impress the Rock of Gibraltar.

What can be done with procrastinators? Give them encouragement and support throughout the decision-making process. Show them that it is **safe** to make a decision, especially a decision to go with you. Find out what their fears are and *address each and every individual fear*. Leave no stone unturned.

Another technique we teach in our seminars is to help procrastinators set **guidelines** and **deadlines**. *Most procrastinators have a lifetime history of procrastinating* and it is a major problem for them. They don't just procrastinate with you. They may have procrastinated on asking someone to marry them (and that person today might be married to someone else!). Procrastinators delay filing their income taxes and get into trouble. They put off the decision to buy a house and may today still be living in an apartment because now, with rising prices, they cannot afford to buy. Many procrastinators know they have a problem and if you help them solve it, or even partially solve it, they can be quite grateful (and can become loyal clients). **Guidelines** and **deadlines** work with procrastinators.

Recently, Dr. Moine was working with one of his coaching clients on the East Coast. Donald's client was calling on a very wealthy man who was an extremely slow decision-maker. Despite having all the facts, the prospect could not make a decision. The salesperson thought the situation was impossible and was ready to give up. Donald coached the salesperson to ask a series of powerful related questions. The first new question was, *"Have you ever made a decision quickly that worked out well?"*

To the salesperson's surprise, the prospect said he had. The salesperson asked the prospect to talk about that and noted what contributed to the prospect's ability to make a rapid decision. Donald then coached the salesperson to **compliment** his prospect on his ability to make a smart decision quickly and then to ask for another example of rapid decision-making that worked out well. Again, the sales professional took notes as to what conditions permitted the prospect to make such a decision.

Donald then showed the salesperson how to **recreate** those same conditions to make a sale happen today. The "impossible client," the procrastinator whom the salesperson thought would "never make a decision," ended up buying a very large life insurance policy from this salesperson. The salesperson received a $79,000 commission and the wealthy prospect bought a high quality insurance policy that solved all of his estate planning needs. Everyone won in this situation because the sales professional learned how to deal effectively with a severely procrastinating client.

In dealing with a procrastinating prospect, make sure that before you leave any sales presentation, you have a **commitment** for some further action. At a minimum, get the prospect to agree to another meeting. Even better, get the prospect to agree to try a small **sample order** or a **trial use** of your services. If you can't get that far, try to get the procrastinator to bring in another decision-maker to your next meeting. You can probably close the other person and he might be able to motivate the procrastinator to take action.

> **One of the greatest keys to success with procrastinators
> is to get them to start making decisions—
> even if they are only small decisions at first.**

In an ironic way, it is the salesperson's procrastinating on getting a commitment from the prospect that is actually enabling the prospect's procrastination. If you want your prospects to stop procrastinating, *make sure that you're not procrastinating in getting a decision from them.* You can be a powerful, positive role model of *someone who takes action.*

The Silent Prospect

There will be times when you encounter prospects who are very quiet. In some cases, they are rather introverted and are simply not inclined to engage in much banter or formal discussion. Or perhaps, they are thinking about what is being said and are trying to digest it and figure out what to do.

In other cases, the silent prospects are using their silence as a negotiating strategy. The theory behind it follows the old sales adage, "Whoever talks first loses." Some prospects know that many salespeople hate silence. They use silence as a tactical weapon to break salespeople down.

When sales millionaires encounter these quiet prospects, they become more quiet. Remember that we trust and take to people like ourselves. If a prospect is on the quieter side and you come across as a chatterbox, the prospect will think to himself, "This person is really different from me. We don't see things the same way." That prospect will not trust you as much and is less likely to do business with you.

Being a little more quiet in the sales presentation is often difficult for many salespeople. One of our coaching clients recently told us, "I feel a strong need to fill that blank time." When that silent prospect leans back to either think about the product or simply wait out the salesperson, the best salespeople will also sit back. They might smile, too.

Faced with a prospect who retreats into silence, some inexperienced salespeople will get into trouble. They may sit back, but then say something like, "So, what do you want to do?" This typically opens the door for the prospect to extract a major concession from the salesperson. In contrast, the sales pro will sit back quietly, smile, and beam self-confidence.

Perhaps after a minute, which in sales time feels like a week, the prospect may say something like, "I like to really think about things before I make a decision." The sales professional might say, *"I fully understand. I am confident that the more you think about it, the more you will see that we are offering you the best solution."*

The previous example is actually a form of **mental judo**. Let's analyze this linguistically to determine what is really going on here. The prospect says, "I want to do X" (quietly take my time). Instead of saying, "No, you can't do X," the sales millionaire says, "Yes, go ahead and do X, because *the more you do X, the more I know you will do Y* (buy from us). This is the inner structure of a very powerful method of persuasion.

Another method we teach in our seminars is to actually go one step further and **command** the silent prospect to be quiet. You can say, *"I would like you to sit here quietly and think of all the many benefits our products and services offer. I know the longer you sit here quietly and think of those benefits, the more you will want to become a client."* In using this powerful persuasion technique, you actually tell the prospect that the more he thinks he is resisting, the more he is likely to buy. Upon hearing this and thinking about it, many prospects suddenly lose a great deal of interest in being quiet.

One of our favorite mental judo strategies for working with this kind of prospect is to say, *"I like quiet, thoughtful people like you. I find that quiet, thoughtful people like you end up becoming my best customers and buy the most from me."* This appears to be a very gentle strategy but is actually incredibly effective. You are **complimenting** the prospect's so-called "difficult behavior," *showing absolutely no fear of it* (unlike other salespeople) and then inform the prospect that people like him become your best clients.

As you can see, you **don't** have to resign yourself to being totally quiet with quiet prospects. You do want to be patient and more quiet. When you speak, make sure every word counts by using some of the powerful strategies above.

Another step that can also help silent prospects open up is to use questions that call for more than a yes or no answer. For example, the question, "Are you happy with their product?" is going to generate little more than a word or two from a silent prospect. However, you can open the door to a dialogue by rephrasing it as an open-ended question, such as, "What do you like most about the product you are currently using?" After the prospect speaks and reveals his buying criteria, *show how the prospect can get even more of that with your products and services.*

The Fast-Talking Prospect

Every salesperson has had encounters at one point or another with a prospect whose mode of speaking is in permanent fast-forward. In fact, these prospects typically do everything at full speed. They are a whirlwind of energy and activity, and they want everything to move more quickly— and that includes you.

Some salespeople believe that the best way to approach these prospects is to speak slowly and softly to "slow them down." The idea is that by doing so, you will be able to induce them to focus more on what you have to say. Unfortunately, such an approach is usually counter-productive. Chances are good that many other people before you have tried to slow this person down—and to no avail. Parents may have tried to slow him down. A spouse has probably tried. His boss might also have tried to slow the person down. *What makes you think you will succeed in slowing this person down when no one else has?*

One definition of insanity is doing the same thing over and over again and expecting different results. If numerous other people have been unable to slow down the fast-talker and have been unsuccessful, what do you think your chances are? Not very good.

A much better approach is to communicate with the fast-talker at his pace. If you can't match it, at least get closer to it. Bridge the gap between you and the prospect. Communicate, "I am like you are," by speeding up your speech rate. The prospect will not know what you are doing. All he will know is that you seem like a sharp person, someone who is on the ball. You will be more trusted because we trust and like people like ourselves.

Fast-talkers and high-energy people like to buy from people like themselves.

When your prospect is on the fast-track, the best step for you is to get on it, too. When you speed up your delivery of your sales presentation to a fast-talker, he senses you are a person worth hearing. After you have moved at this prospect's pace for a while, you can **then** start to slow things down just a bit, and you may see him following you. This is the highly successful pacing-pacing-pacing and then leading formula we shared earlier in this chapter.

**The key to making it work is to first pace (or match)
the other person's behavior
before leading them to another behavior
(in this case, slowing down a little).**

By pacing this individual from the start, you will have quickly built up trust and credibility, and this will allow your messages to be truly heard.

One of our California clients had an interesting experience with a fast-talking prospect on a sales call in Philadelphia. As the salesperson continued her presentation, the prospect paid her what she regarded as a real compliment. The prospect said, "You're different from the people we've been dealing with from California. You're not laid back. I'd actually guess you're from the East Coast." Our native born Californian felt very good about blending in so well with the environment in Philadelphia, and felt even better when the sale was made.

Sometimes the fast-talking prospect can be at the extreme end of the continuum and get into a hyper mode. You obviously do not want to pace or match this, but do try to understand it. He may be undergoing significant problems at work or at home, or perhaps this is a tactic to throw you off.

Put some passion in your voice but do not try to match the amplitude of this truly hyper or frenzied type of prospect. Let the individual know that you, too, are concerned and try to find common ground. If you try to calm the prospect down before he is ready, the cork is only going to pop again. If you can endure the catharsis, you may be in the catbird seat. Few salespeople can effectively handle this type of prospect and by demonstrating your patience and understanding, you may separate yourself from all of your competitors. Your hard work and professionalism may be rewarded with a big order.

The Dominant Prospect   IN vs C4

**This is the prospect or customer who   —Less m C4.
has all the answers.**

In fact, this customer even has answers when there are no questions. Some salespeople react negatively to this style and feel intimidated. As a result, they try to top this customer or at least shove back. Because the idea is to consummate a sale and not to fight the prospect (or win a fight), this aggressive approach needs to be shelved.

A much better approach is illustrated by a successful salesperson in the medical community with whom we have worked. He spoke to us of his dealings with a particularly dominant doctor. In fact, this doctor once implied to the salesperson that he could learn his entire business in a matter of a few minutes! In reality, there is a great deal of complex technology associated with the CT scanners and MRI machines this person sells. However, the salesperson did not argue with the doctor.

Instead, he used mental judo. He agreed with the doctor and complimented him by saying, "You are indeed a very brilliant man." What could the doctor say? He tried to push against the salesperson and there was nothing to push against. The doctor had to smile, just a little. The salesperson went on to say, "And your time is very, very valuable, isn't it?" The doctor had to agree. An overall climate of agreement and rapport was being built.

The salesperson then said, "It is my job to keep totally up-to-date on this complex machinery and the best ways of using it. By spending a great deal of time and energy studying it and going to conferences on it, I can save you a lot of time. My job is to help you solve problems and to make your life easier." This highly dominant physician was now nodding his head. After a few more sales calls, the salesperson sold a $500,000 medical diagnostic imaging machine to the hospital where this doctor worked.

In dealing with a dominant prospect, there is certainly no need to grovel. You do not want to be quiet or retreating with strong, highly dominant people. You need to be strong.

> **Remember that strong people like strong people.** —Compliment
> **Show respect to this dominant person,**
> **but also show that you are knowledgeable and powerful** —Agree when
> **in your own right.** appropriate

What should you do if you encounter a prospect who is dominant to the point of attacking you? Be respectful, if at all possible, but do not allow yourself to become a doormat. In fact, if you become overly deferent, you will be perceived as weak, wishy-washy, and not deserving of respect. In this scenario, either there will be no sale, or you will give away the farm.

When dealing with prospects who come on this strong, project strength and professionalism. You can use mental judo by saying, "You are a strong person. I like that. I find that my best customers are people just like you. I like working with strong people." You can also add, "*I am a strong person myself. I think we will see eye-to-eye on many things.*" Then, give him or her an example. Look for common ground and when you find areas of agreement, focus on them.

Show that you are a confident, knowledgeable, and decisive person. You should speak forcefully, make direct eye contact and demonstrate your expertise. Let the prospect see that you know your stuff and can help him. We coach our sales millionaire clients to let dominant prospects know they are highly successful. You can say, "Sir, **you** are at the top of your profession and **I** am at the top of my profession. It might make sense for us two winners to work with one another." Because we both trust people like ourselves, you can rapidly accelerate the trust-building process with this type of approach.

The Inaccessible Prospect

Some of your prospects are moving targets who seldom respond to your phone calls, e-mail, or any other inquiries. Ironically, these prospects may like you and want to buy from you but they are busy and distracted. Their behavior, while not courteous, is becoming increasingly common.

**If you want to sell to these moving targets,
you need to use a combination of
creativity and persistence.**

Obviously, you need to try your telephone calls at varying hours, particularly early and late in the day when the gatekeeper may not be screening the calls. You may even want to try making some calls on the weekends. We have been surprised at how many people are now putting in at least a few hours at the office on weekends. Part of this trend is due to flextime, which allows some employees, for example, to take off Wednesday to play golf, as long as they make that time up somewhere else in the week. Another factor contributing to employees working on weekends is that it is more quiet and there are fewer distractions on the weekends.

However, even if the gatekeeper is out, you will most likely have to deal with voice mail. For some salespeople, this is a major source of frustration. They tire of leaving messages that are not returned. A participant at one of our recent seminars asked, "I wonder if the messages I leave are doing more harm than good." That is a possibility—depending on what kind of messages you are leaving.

The most successful salespeople don't mind voice mail at all. In fact, we have many clients who now see it as an opportunity to present a well-crafted and compelling message to their prospects. Voice mail is actually often a far superior alternative than leaving the message with a gatekeeper who waters it down to a few words before passing it on to the prospect. You would be surprised at how many gatekeepers leave messages like, "Joe from Xerox called. He probably wants to sell you a photocopy machine." The recipient will immediately throw a note like that into the trash. Sometimes your phone number is not even written down because the gatekeeper assumes the boss already has the number. Rather than leaving your messages with such gatekeepers, you can do a much better and more persuasive job with voice mail.

The real challenge, and one that some of our salespeople have actually described as "fun," is to come up with a brief compelling message to leave on a prospect's voice mail. You will never hear them say, "Hi, this is Joe from XYZ Company and I wanted to give you some information on our new machine."

Rather, the sales superstars' messages are given with confidence and enthusiasm in their voice, but never to the extreme that you hear on canned cold calls. The tone is professional, and the salespeople play any power cards that they might have, such as mentioning that a particular individual referred them. In fact, the referral's name is often the first two words of the message. For example, "George Anapolis suggested I give you a call...." If the prospect knows and respects George, the chances your call will be returned have increased dramatically.

Another great opening line is: "Mary Robbins said you would be a great person to speak with about this." In addition to the credibility associated with using the name of an individual known and liked by the prospect, notice the compliment implied by using the words "**great person**."

When you leave a message on voice mail, make certain you have a smile in your voice. If you sound needy, tired, or the least bit angry, your message will be ineffective. If you have any doubts at all about the quality of your message, play it back (you are now able to do this on most voice mail systems). Use this feature for a quick one-minute rehearsal. If anything sounds weak or off-key, take a second and record it again. Leave the best, most positive message you can and you will be well rewarded.

Your message should also be focused on getting the prospect excited about calling you back. One of the worst things in the world you can do is to say, "Hi, this is Fred Foster from XYZ Company and I am just checking in." Effective voice mail messages have a **purpose** and, therefore, **urgency**. Without purpose or urgency, the recipient of the voice mail is likely to hit the "erase" feature within seconds. How can you add some urgency? If there are any special savings, financing packages, closeouts, or special quantity deals available, be sure to mention them.

If there is some great news about your company, briefly and positively mention it and in the same breath send your wishes that the prospect is doing well. For example, you might say, *"Hi Tom, this is Jonathan Washington at the Superior Technology Company. You may have heard we just moved into our big new building and to celebrate, we are having a 10 percent off sale for the next three days. I hope you are doing great. If you are interested in saving several thousand dollars, please give me a call at (555) 555-1212. I look forward to speaking with you!"*

That is it: short, sweet, to the point, and offer a benefit. If your company or one of your products has won a special award, mention that. But *always include some special benefit or reason for the recipient to call you back.*

You can also use voice mail to, in a very subtle way, let prospects know how successful you are and to pace them. Leave a message such as, "Beth, this is Robert Atlams at Ohio State Company. I've been meaning to call you but I have been incredibly busy. We have some really fantastic deals right now that we are offering to new clients. Give me at call at (800) 777-1212 and I will share these unadvertised specials with you. I know you are busy, just as I am, and I promise you I will make this worth your while." In a low-key way, you brag about yourself by letting Beth know you have been incredibly busy. Then you share a positive benefit she can enjoy. Then you pace her by establishing the commonality that you and she are both very busy and you promise to make her call worth her time.

How can you make sure the voice mail messages you leave are as powerful as possible? Do what sales millionaires do and *write out your message*, practice it, record it, critique it, and then pick up the phone and make the call. The few minutes you spend doing this could help distinguish you from all other salespeople leaving voice mail messages with that person. Your professionalism will come through.

For additional ideas on how to craft powerful voice mail messages, read the section of this book on elevator speeches and also read the chapter on Unique Selling Propositions.

Remember, if you sound like every other salesperson, you cannot expect to be any more successful than other salespeople. You must have one or more Unique Selling Propositions.

Don't overdo your voice mail communications. Generally speaking, short messages are better than long ones. And do not leave a large number of voice mail messages. Fewer is usually better. If you call early in the morning, in the evenings, or on the weekends, your hope should be to reach the individual—not voice mail. If your prospect is not in, do not leave a voice message at these times. Only leave voice mail during business hours. Don't tip your prospect off that you might be calling him before or after regular business hours.

Use your day planner, contact management program, or CRM system to set a tickler file to follow up on prospects. Persistence does pay off, but it must be the right kind of persistence. If you are going to leave several voice-mail messages over a certain period of time, strive to say something **new** or **different** in each one. Give your caller a reason to listen. Few people want to hear the same message repeated over and over.

In addition to voice mail, remember to use regular mail to reach out to inaccessible prospects. In this day and age, many salespeople make little use of regular mail and this is a mistake. Remember that 24 percent of the people in the United States are primarily visual thinkers. They prefer to read rather than listen. A brief, personal, written note can be more persuasive than a voice-mail message for visual thinkers.

Another great benefit of sending a brief letter or memo to your inaccessible prospect is that these people sometimes read their mail at home, or on airplanes, or in taxicabs. You may have their undivided attention at this time and might get a more favorable audition than if they are simply listening to your voice mail in their noisy office. Moreover, you can send the prospect a special discount certificate or other offer that cannot be transmitted via voice mail.

A technique many sales millionaires use is to send articles of interest to prospects and customers, along with a brief note. "Hi, George, I saw this and thought of you. I think you might find this new technology and these cost savings of interest. –Ronald Johnson." Include your business card and send the article off. Make sure the article truly does have information of value and that it is not a fluff piece. We have sent articles to many of our prospects and clients and have found them instrumental in generating phone calls and then business.

One of the techniques we especially like is the use of post cards. This is a technique that few salespeople use, yet we have seen post card campaigns generate tens of thousands of dollars in sales. Post cards are inexpensive, you can write them quickly, and they tend to get read by several people in the office because they are not sealed in an envelope. As you know, many people now throw away much of their mail without even opening it. A post card with a great headline or benefit statement has a much better chance of being read than letters that have been stuffed in envelopes.

And finally, there are places that these inaccessible prospects tend to frequent. If the prospect is not at the office to take your call, **where is he**? Call on your sources and contacts to gather intelligence. Is he at the golf course? Does she like to go to a certain nearby restaurant every day for lunch? With this knowledge, you can "happen" to run into them at such venues as well. In using such a strategy, make sure you have a great elevator pitch and Unique Selling Proposition ready to go. The last thing in the world you want to do is finally get the chance to meet this prospect and then end up tongue-tied. If the prospect is too busy to meet with you then, use your Unique Selling Proposition and *set a date* for a real meeting.

The Complaining Prospect

Let's face it, some prospects are chronic complainers. In fact, if there were nothing to complain about, they might just complain about that! Some salespeople can easily become frustrated with these customers and assume that they are impossible to please. That need not be the case—if you have the right approach.

Sales millionaires deal quite easily and comfortably with complainers. They listen carefully to their complaints, and they actually deliver compliments for any observations that are particularly astute. If possible, do not refer to the complaint as a complaint, but instead **reframe it** as an **observation** or a **concern**. That immediately takes much of the power out of the message.

Let the complainer know that you care about their thoughts, observations, and feelings. Let him know that you care about what he wants to say.

> **Just being a good listener makes it much easier for these prospects to make a purchase decision.**

After all, you have done something for them (listened respectfully to them) and now *they owe you*. They can repay you by buying.

Some complaints can be outright dismissed or ignored and others need to be tended to. As an example of the former, consider the prospect who complains that your company's products are too expensive. You know that your company's prices are moderate: higher than some competitors, lower than others. The prospect's complaint has little validity. An effective way of dealing with such a complaint is to express surprise and to *even use that word.* "I am surprised to hear you say that. Most people are amazed at how inexpensive our products are, especially considering the high quality we deliver."

Notice that you have not only addressed the so-called complaint, but you have also used it as an opportunity to brag a little about your quality. An outstanding follow-up to the example is to go on to say, "Do you know of any company in our industry that offers quality this high at a lower price?" Your prospect will probably fall silent. Then say, "What other concerns do you have?"

Notice again that you asked for mere "**concerns**," and made no reference to complaints. What you have effectively done with the above powerful responses is to have quickly and gently dismissed a pseudo-complaint and have focused the attention of the prospect on "other concerns." It is in the other concerns that you will find the real issues.

Here is an even stronger approach to the above situation where a prospect brings up a pseudo-complaint or a false issue. You have to be careful how you use this because it is incredibly powerful. Remember that strong people like to deal with strong people and, therefore, this approach is best used only with strong people.

When a false issue is raised, call the prospect's bluff.

Assume the prospect complains that your prices are too high and you know that your company is the low cost solution provider in the industry. With a strong person, you can say, "You are kidding me, aren't you? You're pulling my leg. What is your real concern?"

With the above 15 words, you have shown the prospect that you know this could not be a real issue. You have communicated that you know what the real issues are and that you can quickly identify a phony issue (without calling it such). This is actually a very truthful response and it is incredibly effective with strong people. This approach also saves a great deal of time because you can both settle down to dealing with the real issues.

If you are dealing with a **valid** complaint, ask your prospect to be specific. Sales millionaires don't deal with vague generalizations. Once you know **exactly** what the specific issues are, you can deal with them and solve them, but you must get beyond the level of generalizations. For example, if the prospect says, "I hear you have had some quality control problems in the past," you would want to know **who** he heard this from, **how long ago** it was, and **what** the specific quality control problems allegedly were. Be patient and deal with them *one at a time*. Being a sales professional, you can most likely address and solve each one. But you cannot "solve" generalizations.

What if you cannot solve the problem or address the complaint? We have a solution!

Ask the prospect to give you suggestions.

Ask, "What would you like to see done in this area?" or "What would you like to see us do?"

As psychologists, we have been trained to look for reasons, causes, and motivators of human behavior.

One of the reasons complainers complain is that they want to create a forum wherein they can propose their brilliant solutions.

Give them the audience they want! Listen to their solutions. If you can use their solution or even part of it, you are both likely to win. They get the product and solution they want and you get the sale. This can be an incredibly effective way of dealing with complainers.

Here is an example of how one sales professional used this technique to handle a particular complaint. His prospect would not buy and voiced vague complaints about what he had heard about the company's financing and billing system. First, the sales professional took these generalizations and got the prospect to speak in **specifics**. However, even after getting the specifics, the salesperson was not certain what he would do or what he could do.

The salesman then remembered something we had covered in one of our coaching sessions. When all else fails, ask the complainer how he would like the problem solved. *Ask the complainer to solve the problem!* In the next sales call, that is exactly what the sales pro did. The complainer said he wanted a written contract saying the first payment would not be due until 90 days after the products were delivered and that the financing would be at the prime rate.

Right there in the prospect's office, the salesperson took action. He asked if he could use the prospect's phone and then called his company's legal department. They agreed to the terms and said they would put it all in writing. Because the prospect worked for a very strong company with excellent financials, there was minimal risk. Other safeguards were built into the contract to protect the sellers. The complainer suggested a solution to his own complaint, the sales professional took action, and in doing so, booked one of the largest sales in his career.

Psychologically, using the above technique puts the salesperson on the same side of the desk as the complaining prospect or customer. It is then no longer you versus me, but *you and me versus the problem*. With the prospect and the customer working together so closely, *the problem does not stand a chance*. The problem will be blown away and the sale will be consummated. It is this partnering and collaboration with the customer that is so vitally important in successful selling.

Out With the Old Adage

There is an old adage that "the customer is always right." As insightful and responsive as top salespeople are in their dealings with the broad range of customers whom they meet, there will always be some with whom they cannot work. For a good number of salespeople, this is a bitter pill to swallow, particularly if they have been brought up to believe that the customer is always right.

However, like so many other adages, there are exceptions to the rule. The customer is not always right. For example, there are customers who make outrageous demands, burn up hours of your time merely to leverage a present supplier, or even expect kickbacks. Sales millionaires try to identify these customers as quickly as possible and then move on. Life is too short and there are too many other fantastic prospects and customers to justify wasting time on tire-kickers, looky-loos, or game-players.

**Rather than naively believing that
"the customer is always right,"
sales millionaires today have created a new adage,
"I always do what is right for my prospects and customers."**

When you know in your heart and mind that you always do what is right for your prospects and clients, you need not be concerned if you have to let a few non-serious prospects go. After all, such a course of action is probably what is also best for the prospect.

There are a few people in this world who are genuinely toxic. If you happen to come across one of them in your sales work, the best thing to do is to get out of their presence as soon as possible. It is extremely unlikely that you will be able to change or reform a toxic person and it makes much more sense to simply move on.

If you internalize the insights we have shared with you on dealing with challenging prospects and customers and if you practice using the techniques and the sales scripts provided, you will soon find that you will be able to close sales that previously seemed impossible or unattainable. You will be well on your way to becoming a sales millionaire or multimillionaire.

Remember, anyone can sell the easy prospects. Your special skill and the reason you are rewarded so handsomely is that you can also close sales with the more challenging ones. Some customers are indeed different, but that simply calls for a different sales approach, and perhaps using more creativity and insight. Such creativity and insight will make you a great deal of money and being creative adds a lot of fun to the sales process.

10

Capitalize on the Power of CRM

One of the most effective ways to enhance your selling power is to have a solid system of Customer Relationship Management (CRM) assisting you, backing you up, and turbo-charging every sales and marketing effort. With its unprecedented range of services in the areas of sales force automation, marketing automation, and customer relations, CRM literally puts more sales power at your fingertips than you may have ever imagined possible.

As a result of CRM, selling will never be the same. Salespeople who continue to relegate customer relations to outmoded systems or even no system, along with those who suffer from CRM phobia, are fated to be looking at their competitors' taillights.

We are now in a greatly enhanced age of customer service. Customers not only expect more, they demand more. And in today's marketplace, they can get it—if not from you, then from your competitors.

Just put yourself in the customer's position. Would you prefer to buy from a sales professional who tells you that his or her company has a state-of-the-art CRM system to cater to all of your needs 24 hours a day, seven days a week, or a salesperson whose idea of customer relationship management is a pager? The choice is indeed a simple one. CRM not only helps you make the sale, but also helps you **retain** customers, build accounts over the long term (sell more to each customer and client), and generate huge numbers of new accounts.

If you want Ultimate Selling Power, you need to provide your customers with the ultimate in service and support. And that comes down to three letters: CRM. At the same time, with all of the praise being heaped on CRM, many salespeople still have little understanding of what it is, how it works, and how to benefit from it. Some think CRM is only for large companies, that it requires large investments in hardware and software, and that it is time-consuming to implement. As you will see, none of these preconceptions are true.

There is no mystery to CRM. It is no longer an experimental technology. CRM has been perfected and has grown into a multibillion dollar industry. In fact, the only mystery is why some companies and some salespeople are still not using it.

An Introduction to CRM

There seem to be as many definitions of CRM as there are Websites that deal with it. In fact, if you go to *google.com* and enter CRM, you will be see that there are over 2 million listings that are ready to tell you all about it! However, because you are not planning to spend the rest of your career going from listing to listing and site to site, the best way to understand CRM is to develop an overview of its two major components.

First, CRM is a *philosophy of doing business*.

According to the CRM philosophy, the customer is viewed as being of primary importance, and a company (YOUR company) should be organized from top to bottom to meet the customers' needs.

As a business philosophy, CRM is premised upon organizing a company around the customer, providing the customers with products and services that meet all of their needs and specifications, and then standing behind these products with first-rate 24-hour customer service and support. The best way to describe this philosophy is through the term **customer-centric**, meaning that everything about the business revolves around building and supporting the customer base.

At the same time, CRM is a *business strategy and technology*.

Today, CRM is typically conceived of in terms of three primary areas: sales force automation, marketing automation, and customer service.

By applying state-of-the art technology, software, and Internet capabilities, CRM helps a company manage **every** aspect of customer relations, with a broad base of integrated applications to acquire customers, provide outstanding service, retain customers, expand the customer base, sell more to each customer and client, and ultimately dramatically increase sales revenues.

CRM at Every Contact Point

CRM plays a central role whenever and wherever customers interact with your company. With a CRM system in place, your customers get clear, **consistent**, and accurate information, along with excellent treatment, whether the contact point is you, customer service, shipping, or any other department, and regardless of whether such contact is via telephone, e-mail, the Web, voice mail, or any other channel.

For this to work, it is apparent that all of these interactions need the support of every other business process. For example, a company's inventory and shipping operations will need to be integrated with the CRM service so that customers who call in can accurately find out the status of their orders, and inventory and shipping must be integrated with billing, so that customers can find out if they have paid all of an invoice or part of it, what their financing rate is, etc. Billing must be integrated with collections, which must be integrated with accounting, and so on.

The better CRM services can directly link dozens of systems and functions within a company to one another. In fact, with these types of linkages, all, or almost all, of a company's processes can be integrated with the CRM system so that customers receive the *highest quality, most up-to-date information available* on sales, products, service, order status, and all other related information, regardless of their original contact point with the company.

We have worked with salespeople who are very concerned over the loss of customers due to inadequate, inaccurate, or inconsistent information being provided when these customers contact the company regarding product availability and choices, prices, and/or shipping dates. Customers rely heavily on this information, and if your company cannot provide it and another company can, your customers' loyalty will be sorely tested. Sales forces that do not have CRM systems are hearing more and more of their customers say, "So long—it's been nice knowing you."

Other Powerful Benefits of CRM

No matter what you are selling, you will find that an effective CRM service can help reduce the stress of selling and can help you dramatically increase sales. Here are some of the key benefits of CRM that can help make you a sales millionaire.

Sales Force Automation

The sales force automation (SFA) functions that accompany CRM will support you in the core sales processes that make up a great part of your day. This includes **contact management** that will keep you informed of **exactly** where you are with each and every one of your prospects, leads, and customers.

Sales force automation will also show you where every deal is in your pipeline, while giving you information on all of the most important players, previous sales figures, potential areas for additional sales, and any changes, updates, new developments, trends, or news concerning the company or industry. In this way, SFA helps you manage the sales life cycle all the way from the generation of leads to actual closing of sales, and then booking repeat orders. And further, you can use your CRM system to do customer data mining to identify the **very best opportunities** for additional sales and service.

SFA also includes all of your calendar and planner functions, complete with prompts, cues, and ticklers to help you organize your time and set your priorities. It can remind you to make every necessary call and will specify **when** and **how** to follow up on each and every account. You will never again have a prospect or customer "fall through the cracks." As a part of the calendar function, some CRM services also provide you with a tremendous amount of support when you are traveling. This can include travel arrangements and even automatic changes to your travel plans if work-related delays or snags develop!

We all have known salespeople who love customer interaction but find it almost impossible to file reports, write proposals, or do much of anything they consider "paperwork." CRM can be a fantastic aid. It is almost like having your own personal administrative assistant to do many aspects of the "paperwork part" of the job that you would rather not do. In addition, the SFA function can help you better organize your time, keep records of everything you learn about a prospect or client, and almost instantly access and analyze every relevant piece of sales data about each prospect or client.

Problems with the "paperwork side" of selling can easily lead to dissatisfied customers and lost sales. In the past, some salespeople and sales managers may have been willing to live with these drawbacks, often viewing the associated losses as one of the costs of doing business. Collectively, these lost sales have totaled billions of dollars. In today's highly competitive business world, companies and salespeople can no longer afford to ignore such lost sales. CRM makes it easy to acquire needed proficiencies in these crucial areas.

Streamlining the Contact Center

CRM gives you and your contact center the ability to give your prospects, customers, and clients far more support and higher quality support. If you are in a telemarketing position, your CRM system can direct you to the best prospects and customers, can (in some cases) auto-dial for you, and provide you with a broad range of up-to-the-minute information to help you sell more effectively. Such information can include powerful, persuasive sales scripts, product information and upgrades, and late-breaking stories on the client company itself.

The customer service people behind you are also going to be able to provide you and your customers and clients with far more support as a result of CRM. All of the information that your customer service associates need is made available through the CRM system. As a result, the customer service team can instantly access whatever information the customer may seek from the company database, whether it deals with warranties and guarantees, defective products, returns, additional available inventory, and much more.

Importantly, when you are making your sales presentation, you can raise your prospects' comfort and confidence levels by mentioning that your company has a powerful CRM system that is designed to **quickly** respond to all of their inquiries, take care of their problems, and get them what they need, all on a 24-7 basis.

Another advantage of CRM is its automation of the field service process. With CRM, your customers' requests for service are far more likely to go through a process that is both **user-friendly** and **expeditious**. Your customers' inquiries will be managed and tracked from the first contact all the way through scheduling, service calls, and fulfillment.

It is very nice to tell your customers how service-oriented your company is, but when you walk them through your CRM system that is *specifically designed* to take care of all their service needs, you go a long way toward building a deep level of trust and high credibility, as well as building further interest in your products, your services, and your company.

Marketing Management

Your company's CRM system will also be integrated with applications that oversee the marketing programs and marketing packages. These systems can actually automate much of the marketing campaign and then provide compelling offers to prospects and customers based on their requests, needs, and interests. In addition, at scheduled intervals or as a result of your sales contacts, a constant flow of exciting new offers can be sent to the customer or client, which will result in a large number of additional orders.

Notably, these applications can track all the responses from the recipients, and this can be very valuable data for you on a number of levels. First, it will provide your company's marketing staff with quality information from the trenches as to what the customers really want. Second, once you are armed with this type of customer feedback, you will be in a much better position to **customize** your sales strategy to best meet the needs of your individual customers.

E-commerce and E-service

Through the Web, companies can now market, sell products and services, and provide outstanding follow-up service. We have all used virtual shopping carts and ambled down the cyber lanes tossing products into them. We can check order accuracy, shipping dates, return policies, and learn anything we want to know about our order. CRM makes all of this possible.

What's in it for the sales professional? Plenty. CRM gives you a humongous number of new leads and prospects, advertises you and your products and services, and can even set appointments for you! CRM provides your prospects and customers with a great deal of information, which saves you time when you go on your sales calls.

CRM does not replace the sales professional but sets the stage for you to be a real star.

CRM sells the prospect halfway, and you come in and close the deal. It sets the stage for you to come in and do a much more productive sales presentation that takes less time.

With all the time you save with CRM, you can call on **more** prospects and customers, close more deals, and make more money. CRM applications are best seen as a complement to the salesperson, and not as a replacement.

There is no question that the most important element in the sales process continues to be the human element.

For many customers, online purchases are merely an adjunct to their typical buying habits. After all, many customers prefer and need the support, guidance, and personalized collaboration that a sales professional (you) can provide. In addition, many companies with substantial online business still have their **best accounts** handled personally by the sales force, as such accounts typically respond optimally to the individualized attention and support that sales professionals provide.

CRM also provides knowledge of the online buying practices of your customers and can help you put together a powerful in-person presentation that is based on hard data rather than mere hunches. As a result, you will be able to focus more directly on your customers' real needs and buying patterns.

Knowledge Management

Your company's CRM applications can hold a wealth of information that can greatly enhance your sales effectiveness. It is often said that knowledge is power. Adding to this adage, we often say in our seminars that *quality knowledge is selling power*. What makes CRM so effective is that it provides you with quality knowledge in numerous key areas and integrates all your back-end services and databases.

CRM enables you to directly access every bit of information on your products, services, and marketing programs. This knowledge is priceless in meeting all of your customers' standards, specifications, needs, and expectations. Everything you need is in your CRM data warehouse, including the size, shape, configurations, capacities, additions, old models, new models, changes, add-on's, prices, upgrades, warranties, and just about anything else a prospect, customer, or client might want to know. And you don't have to call Bud in the warehouse in Minneapolis and be placed on hold for 20 minutes while he tries to find the information. With a few keystrokes on your computer, you have the information your customer needs—and that you need to close the sale.

If there are special packages, programs, discounts, or incentives in place, you can quickly and easily stay on top of them as well. Your CRM system will keep you fully informed of every discount and incentive you can offer a prospect or customer to close a sale.

The data warehouse also contains complete information regarding your customers' **past buying practices**. You can instantly check out your customers' prior preferences regarding quantities, prices, makes, models, reorders, returns, pay practices, and the like.

> **When you know how your customer or client has
> purchased in the past, you have a very
> good idea how to sell to him or her today.**

Research shows that almost everyone buys today in the ways they have purchased in the past.

One of the techniques we have become famous for teaching in our sales training seminars is what we have labeled the "instant replay technique." The first step is to learn everything you can about how someone made a decision to buy in the past. Having this information helps you develop a deep understanding of the prospect's buying habits and buying style. In our coaching and seminar work, we show the sales professional how to craft a presentation that fits exactly into the prospect's past buying behaviors. In essence, we create all the conditions that previously led to a decision to buy. Properly done, this is one of the most effective sales strategies in existence and consistently results in closing ratios of more than 90 percent. Being able to use CRM to access all the knowledge stored in your company's data warehouse, the replay is already there for you to watch in advance. Using the instant replay saves a great deal of time and sets you up to close the sale much more quickly.

Your CRM system will also track **every** customer request and inquiry— even the ones that your prospects and customers don't tell you about (such as when he or she logged on to your company's database at 11:30 p.m. a couple of days ago to check on the availability of 170 gallons of a certain chemical). In one powerful CRM database, all of this knowledge is stored—and you can access it any time you want!

By reviewing your prospects' and customers' prior contact with the company, you can gain great insight into their needs, values, standards, and expectations **prior** to any sales contact. With this knowledge, you can tailor a presentation that is far more likely to meet their needs.

> **This level of insight and understanding into your customers is also going to send them a powerful message that you understand them better than any other sales or marketing professional.**

It also sends a message that you can be trusted. You really do understand them and what they want—all thanks to your CRM system. This quickly builds and enhances relationships with prospects and customers, and builds revenues just as rapidly.

A very successful life insurance sales professional with whom we have worked **always** checks the client's prior buying behaviors, inquiries, and any other information that the company CRM system stores. Then, when meeting with the client, he says, "You currently own such-and-such a policy..." to which the prospect says, "Yes, I do." The sales professional then continues, "And I noticed that you invested in some additional coverage earlier this year...." This elicits another "yes." The sales professional continues, and during the first two minutes of the presentation, the client frequently ends up saying "yes" or agreeing with the sales professional many times. This state of frequent agreement not only builds trust and lets the client see that the sales professional has a good deal of insight into his or her needs, but these early "yes" responses set the stage for even more "yeses" and *further agreement* during the rest of the sales presentation.

Tracking Your Inputs

As part of the CRM process, the data warehousing function also keeps track of all of the information and reports you and your fellow sales and service associates submit. This is vital intelligence on many levels. This information can be analyzed and reviewed by your manager, who can then use the findings as a basis to implement appropriate changes in marketing, service, support, or other areas that will benefit you and the company.

In fact, some CRM systems contain analytical tools that can be used to dissect the information that salespeople submit and then highlight key problem areas or **opportunities** on a sound factual and statistical basis. This means that your manager does not have to try to labor through the data and look for or guess about trends, but rather can generate the desired comparisons, ratios, trend figures, forecasts, and analyses *on a scientific and fully automated basis.*

CRM also makes your life easier. In the past, your sales manager might have asked you to complete clunky and time-consuming reports or surveys on each of your prospects or customers. If you hated to fill out these forms or complete the surveys, **relax.** Your CRM system will do it all for you. If you want to get rid of those cumbersome old reports, you need to fully support your company adopting a CRM system. Think of all the time you will save!

When your management acquires and implements a CRM system, you profit in two additional ways.

1. The barriers that may have been preventing you and your fellow salespeople from meeting your sales goals can be clearly identified and hopefully removed or solved. When this occurs, at least some of the obstacles along the path to your sales goals will be removed.

2. There's no question that when employees have an opportunity to voice their ideas and have them heard, there is a positive motivational impact. When you see that your reports have actually led to some significant changes in your company's sales and marketing practices, you are going to feel more energized. This is a cause for celebration! It will become much easier for you to sell (and to increase your income).

When you combine the **removal of sales obstacles** with **increased motivation**, the ultimate outcome is increased sales and increased profits. This benefits both you and your company. That's not a bad deal, especially when compared with the countless hours you used to spend on reams of reporting that served as little more than wallpaper for the interiors of file drawers.

More Powerful Communications Through CRM

CRM helps to dramatically improve communication within your company as well as with your prospects and customers. For example, CRM can provide a capacity for you to communicate **directly** with all of the key individuals who play a direct or indirect role in the sales process itself—all the way up to the president of your company in some cases. Through CRM, you can share notes and other information with the rest of your sales force, with your sales manager, sales associates, customer service representatives, and other key players or departments relevant to the sale.

Your CRM service can also help you generate **creative proposals**, complete with prompts and guidelines to greatly facilitate the preparation process. If you hate to write proposals, you may see CRM as a godsend, as it makes proposal preparation almost effortless. It can also provide you with all the resources to make a compelling presentation, including any necessary charts, graphs, or graphics. Currently, few CRM systems have many sales scripts but you can add those yourself using the script writing and polishing techniques we presented in Chapter 3. Be sure to include the best scripts of the sales superstars within your company. Once a few CRM companies begin including these kinds of powerful scripts in their offerings, they will make billions of dollars in additional revenues from CRM sales.

Many CRM systems now also include a training component, showing you how to quickly master CRM. Some of these training systems are even tied in with real-time training with live instructors. If your CRM system does not already offer it, you can easily add links to additional sites or your Web favorites that provide crucial information on your industry, prospective customers, and the sales process itself. Once properly set up, your CRM system may be the only site, or one of the only sites, you ever need to log on to. It can become a portal of choice for you and all of the other employees of your company.

How Do You Profit From CRM?

CRM can revolutionize the way salespeople organize their day, prospect, make sales and follow-up calls, close sales, and complete the administrative side of their jobs. There is a learning curve involved during the start-up phase, which does take some time and energy.

Is it worth the effort to implement and learn CRM? Most experts respond with a resounding "Yes!" In many cases, there is no alternative. If your competitors acquire and master a good CRM system, they will take away a large portion of your business unless you too have this incredible tool.

There is a vast array of benefits that accrue directly to the salesperson as a result of a first-rate CRM service. Some of these benefits include the following:

> **Sales confidence.** With CRM, you can walk into a sales presentation with a secure feeling that you can readily handle **any** questions that your prospects may raise.

> **The right customer.** With the data and analyses that you can access via your CRM system and associated applications, you can clearly identify your **best** prospects and customers and know that you are focusing your efforts in the most productive and profitable arenas.

> **General efficiency.** As a result of CRM, you are going to be better organized, and you will be spending less time backtracking, searching for information, and working in less profitable areas. Your days of missed appointments or other related mix-ups will be over. CRM is a seamless system, and, by definition, nothing can fall through the cracks if there are no cracks in the first place.

> **Greater insight.** With all of the data and analyses that your CRM service can provide, you are going to have a far greater understanding of your customers' buying practices, needs, standards, and objectives. The precision of this information can help you build trust and guide your sales presentation into areas that truly meet the customers' needs.

Staying on track. You are also going to know exactly where you are with all of your customers and prospects. Instead of having to make any guesses about their position in the pipeline, CRM allows you to know precisely where you are with each prospect and customer and what you need to do **now** to further the sale or close it.

Useful feedback. The increased feedback that CRM generates brings in countless useful suggestions for product improvements, service improvements, and new products and services. This ultimately leads to new sales.

The bottom line. Importantly, with this broadly-based automated focus on the customer, the likelihood of fully meeting the customers' needs increases dramatically. As a result, you should see equally dramatic increases in sales revenue.

The 10-Point CRM Checkout System

For some companies, CRM services have not been a bed of roses, but have actually been little more than a bed of thorns. There are several reasons for this outcome, and every one of them is avoidable.

Several of our clients have asked us to review the CRM systems that they are considering and as a result, we have looked over a broad range of available systems.

Among the better CRM providers, we often include Saleslogix 2000 v. 4.02, eCMS, Onyx 2000, Vantive Enterprise V. 8.5, Applix iEnterprise, Siebel Sales 2000, Pivotal eRelationship 2000, and e-Point 5. You can easily spend several hundred hours or more examining these different CRM systems.

At the same time, we are often asked which CRM service is our favorite. Which is the one that we recommend most frequently? The answer is *salesforce.com*, a fully integrated *online* CRM service that fully supports all sales, service, and marketing efforts. With a mantra that proclaims, "The end of software," *salesforce.com* quickly and easily delivers the benefits of customizable CRM without requiring your company to buy, install, upgrade, or maintain additional hardware or software.

We put *salesforce.com* through our 10-Point CRM Checkout System, and it passed with flying colors. You can use the same system in evaluating any CRM service that you or your company is considering. If the service falls short under scrutiny on any of these points, it would make sense for you to seriously examine another service.

Point #1: The Features

The first point to check with any CRM service is content. If the service does not cover the content areas you need and is not customizable so that it can do so, then you should move on to another service. And further, if the services can only be provided at substantial additional costs, that too is your cue to move on.

Salesforce.com delivers powerful, scalable, and reliable CRM applications at a fraction of the cost of comparable services. Its key components, namely Sales Force Automation, Customer Support, and Marketing Automation, provide state-of-the-art service for virtually every conceivable CRM function.

For example, *salesforce.com*'s *online customer CRM service* provides everyone in sales, customer support, and marketing with tools such as:

Account and contact management.

Opportunity and pipeline management.

Forecasting and lead management, complete with point and click forecasts.

Customer support case and resolution management.

Knowledge-based management that allows all departments to interact with customers in a consistent manner.

Campaign and sales cycle analysis.

Detailed reporting, with enhanced sharing of information between individuals and departments.

Salesforce.com's new Enterprise Edition enables larger and more complex businesses to rapidly deploy a single, integrated solution across multiple departments and divisions, all without purchasing or installing a single line of code. The Enterprise Edition also offers several advanced functions, including the capacity to do the following:

Track and model complex revenue streams.

Deflect customer inquiries to an online self-service channel.

Customize for various workgroups, departments, and divisions.

Integrate with other key business applications using industry-standard APIs.

Easily administer usage across hundreds and thousands of users.

Update opportunities, accounts, and contacts offline.

With *salesforce.com*, all of the sales, marketing, and support processes can be standardized, deals and customers can be prioritized based on revenue potential, and marketing expenditures can be optimized by understanding which marketing initiatives perform best. The system truly sets the stage so that all departments can interact with customers in a consistent manner. When your customers experience this high level of service, both satisfaction and sales increase.

A brief look at even a few of the many services offered in each of the three *salesforce.com* components shows how powerful this service is, and how it can give you Ultimate Selling Power. With *salesforce.com*'s **Sales Force Automation** component, you can have immediate access to real-time forecasting, reporting, and pipeline management. You can have direct lead capture and routing from your Website to *salesforce.com*, and you can upload leads from trade shows, seminars, direct mail, and other sources. This automated process gets your leads routed and qualified quickly and lets you focus on what you do best, namely making presentations and closing sales.

Through *salesforce.com*, you can access a complete customer history in one place, and you can capture every piece of important information about your customer, all the way from the initial contact point through every contact up to the present. The system even provides up-to-the minute news and information about your clients, their industries, and their partners, as well as breaking news on key accounts and competitors. This is the type of information that can help generate numerous up-selling and cross-selling opportunities.

This component has many features that can specifically help you make better use of your time. In the past, many of the administrative and coordinating responsibilities of salespeople burned up far too many hours, and still were replete with errors. With the calendaring, scheduling, and account management features of *salesforce.com*, it is as if you have been given one of the greatest gifts any salesperson could ask for: **more hours to sell**.

To help make better use of your time and make life a little easier, Sales Force Automation even offers such integrated services as travel reservations, e-mail, business gift ordering, and online conferencing. In fact, if you're working on an international basis, you can even get sales tracking, forecasting, and reporting in multiple currencies. Sales force automation not only helps you get where you want to go in terms of sales, but it can literally help you get where you want to go by generating maps of states, cities, and roads you will be traveling.

Looking at *salesforce.com*'s **Customer Support Component**, you will find instant access to all customer communication, including e-mails, calls, notes, and case resolutions. Customer inquiries are automatically captured, and there are links to back-end systems to look up information such as inventory levels and order and billing status. The service is designed to automatically capture, route, track, and escalate inquiries to ensure that customer concerns are quickly addressed and resolved. In fact, with *salesforce.com*, customers can submit their inquiries **directly** to your Website, and this information will be automatically captured and routed to the appropriate customer support representative or team for quick resolution.

The system also creates a **knowledge base** of customer support issues and solutions so that instead of just solving problems, the issues behind them can be identified and **permanent solutions** can be implemented. Your customers appreciate support that is quick, responsive, and effective, and their high degree of satisfaction not only solidifies their relationships with you, but also sets the stage for increased sales and referrals.

You may be the best salesperson in town, and your company may have terrific products and services, but if your customers sense that you and your company are not responsive to their inquiries, needs, and concerns, all of your best efforts and best products and services will be overlooked. CRM can give you world-class customer and client service and customer management.

With its **Marketing Automation Component**, *salesforce.com* provides your company's marketing staff with a single comprehensive view of all interactions with customers and prospects. The *salesforce.com* system can capture and identify all key customer demographic information and create a standardized central repository of critical customer information. In the broadest sense, the system is designed to track, monitor, analyze, and improve the marketing efforts. It allows marketing professionals to better understand **which** marketing campaigns are succeeding, **why** they are succeeding, and the types of customers they attract.

The system also helps track inquiries from trade shows, direct mail, advertising, and all other customer-acquisition programs. With such data in hand, there can be a quick and accurate determination as to which marketing, promotion, and advertising campaigns are delivering the best leads. By having a system that gathers and analyzes this essential data, your company can develop a more targeted marketing program focusing on your most sought-after customers as well as identifying further cross-selling and up-selling opportunities.

Ultimate Selling Power comes from the skills that you have learned over the years and *that power is multiplied many times over* when your company's marketing program gets you in front of the best prospects. That is the kind of selling power that that a great CRM program, such as *salesforce.com*, provides.

Point #2: Ease of Use

There's no point in having a CRM service that has every conceivable bell and whistle if it takes an information technology (IT) specialist to figure out how to use them. For a CRM system to become widely adopted in a company, it must be easy to use. Because *salesforce.com* was designed for the Web, easy usage is at its very core. In fact, the phrase, "easy to use," permeates most discussions about the site.

This user-friendly quality of *salesforce.com* eliminates one of the primary reasons that salespeople fight and then abandon their company's CRM system: the sheer difficulty of navigating it. If the system is encumbered with technical language, confusing messages, and overly complicated features, salespeople tend to quickly develop a mental block against all of it. And that ends their venture into the world of CRM.

Another key factor that determines if salespeople will actual use a CRM service is whether any of it seems to makes sense. The *salesforce.com* site has a strong intuitive feel for salespeople—after all, "sales" is even a core part of their corporate name. It is amazing how many CRM offerings are all about the "customer" and say little about the sales professional. The language and tools of *salesforce.com* are oriented toward the sales professional. The vocabulary is what salespeople speak, and the site's layout and navigation give salespeople a sense of familiarity and comfort right from the start.

It is also easy to use *salesforce.com* because you can have wireless access by phone or personal digital assistant. In addition, you can have full synchronization with Microsoft Outlook, Palm OS, and Microsoft Office applications so you can work offline and easily upload your work. And further, *salesforce.com* provides easy data standardization regardless of source, simple data importing with easy-to-use importing tools, and easy data exporting for integration with other applications.

All of these inviting aspects of *salesforce.com* make the entire notion of using CRM far more palatable and exciting for a sales professional. The proof of the site's ease of use is that the adoption rates regularly top 90 percent. The reason behind this level of widespread acceptance is actually twofold: salespeople have no problem navigating on *salesforce.com*, and they find that they can sell more by using it.

Point #3: Start-up Time

One of the most important points to consider in assessing a CRM system is the amount of time associated with the installation. We have found that prolonged installation periods are often a source of frustration for the sales team. Many salespeople have told us that they feel that they are part of a costly experiment during this period, and they have a hard time seeing the value that CRM can add if it disrupts sales during installation.

Part of the problem is that many software-based CRM applications take at least six months to implement, and it is not uncommon to hear horror stories of 18-month installation periods. In fact, it is often just assumed that implementing CRM is time-consuming, complex, costly, and requires the diversion of significant company resources and personnel. This is not the case when installing CRM with *salesforce.com*.

Because *salesforce.com* has no software or hardware to buy, install, upgrade, or maintain, a company can sign up online and literally get started immediately. Any necessary customization and configuration can typically be accomplished in just a few weeks at most—*while you are using the system*. *Salesforce.com* fits quickly and easily into a company's existing staff structures, organizational processes, and computing environment, so there is no downtime during implementation. *Salesforce.com* requires no IT resources for implementation, and there is no need for an information technology team to support it once installed. And further, there are no special networking requirements.

With *salesforce.com*, you can sign up online, upload your customer database to a secure server, and start taking advantage of the full range of CRM benefits without any costly commitments or purchases. All you need is an Internet connection and a Web browser.

Sales environments can change quickly, and by the time a company has completed a CRM installation lasting a year or more, it is possible that there have been so many changes in products, customers, services, and the industry itself that the installation may have to be prolonged even further. We know of companies that have been trying to implement CRM for a long time, and they still are no closer to having an operational CRM system today than they were over a year ago—and over several hundred thousand dollars ago.

Point #4: Capacity for Customization

When it comes to CRM, one size does **not** fit all. Each company has its own unique needs, systems, and structures, and some customization of the CRM system is typically necessary. The extent to which a CRM service offers customization, along with the price for doing so, are key criteria in determining if that service is right for you.

The better CRM systems provide as much customization as you need. However, extensive customization is often found only in the more expensive CRM systems. Online CRM services, such as *salesforce.com* have tremendous customization capacity without the steep price tag.

Salesforce.com easily adapts to a company's existing processes, staff structures, and organizational processes, and it can be personalized to meet individual work preferences in many different areas. For example, you can have control over the display of fields and page layouts, and you are also able to create and alter standard fields.

In addition, your company can modify the customer service function to match existing work practices. In fact, a user can personalize and configure this service to create the ideal customer interface.

Your company can keep all key sales information, including marketing data, customer support information, and much more in the same database. And with *salesforce.com*'s customization capacity, your company can create the specific page views in data that the salespeople, support staff, and marketing people most want to see.

Salesforce.com also offers preconfigured and customizable reports, and you can export your reports into Microsoft Excel for further manipulation. With the new Enterprise Infrastructure, there are advanced capabilities for customization, integration, and administration to meet the needs of larger, more complex companies.

Point #5: Training Options

Because the introduction of CRM to a sales team will call for some training, it is important to check out the type of support that is included by the CRM providers that you are considering. It is **both good and bad news** if you find that a CRM service has tremendous training support.

The good news is that the provider has made a bona fide commitment to training the users of the service. However, the bad news is that the CRM service may be so complicated that it **requires** a major training intervention before the users can get up to speed.

As previously noted, *salesforce.com* is premised on being user friendly and easy to learn. With that in mind, it is not surprising to find that *salesforce.com* requires almost no formal training. You can get all the training you need by clicking resources found at the site. The material is easy to follow and absorb, and salespeople are able to get themselves up to speed quickly.

At the same time, it is interesting to note that *salesforce.com* has features that can help train you to become more successful as a salesperson. For example, you can access a great deal of information on past sales successes and **best practices** in your company. This type of information can greatly facilitate the sales process and contribute directly to your sales success. In addition, *salesforce.com* gives you access to powerful customer communication tools, such as e-mail templates and sales presentations, which are excellent resources to build your personal knowledge base and selling strategies.

Salesforce.com provides you with outstanding sales training opportunities right on the site through the integration of Miller Heiman's popular Strategic Selling methodology and Blue Sheet analysis worksheet. Miller Heiman, Inc., is a leading developer and provider of strategic sales process solutions for sales professionals around the world, and more than 500,000 salespeople worldwide have attended Miller Heiman public and private programs. Used by thousands of salespeople today, these programs can help you shorten your sales cycle, collaborate on sales strategies, share best practices, and ultimately deliver more sales. All of these resources to further enhance your sales effectiveness are just a click away.

Point #6: The Accessibility Factor

Another critical element in assessing a CRM service is its accessibility. Certainly the element of user friendliness plays a role here, as the unfriendly systems typically are not easy to access, and most salespeople don't want to access them anyway. Many sales professionals have told us that they have tried to pull up real-time information from their CRM system, only to encounter erroneous data or strange messages. Even if you have a user-friendly CRM system, it won't do you much good if you cannot access data when you need it.

Salesforce.com offers fast access to the data and analyses you need anywhere and anytime via the Internet. *Salesforce.com* offers 24-7 reliability 365 days a year. Further, the information and knowledge you want can be accessed on a wireless basis by phone, handhelds, and laptop computers. With the Enterprise Edition, you can access account, contact, and opportunity data while untethered from the company's server. Then, once you go online and synchronize with *saleforce.com*'s hosted site, an Active X control will automatically update your data.

All of these features enable you to meet changing customer demands and needs anytime and anywhere.

Point #7: The Security Factor

In the world of CRM, security is not a relative factor. There's simply no such thing as a service that's "generally secure," "usually secure," or even "highly secure."

A CRM service is either secure or it is not. If you are satisfied that the CRM solution provider you are considering is secure, you can move on to the next point on this checklist. However, if you have even a scintilla of equivocation in this area, you should move on to another CRM service.

Salesforce.com is a secure CRM solution provider because it uses a world-class security system that protects your data with the most advanced technologies and methods available. This complete security system works whether you're in the office or on the road. The *salesforce.com* security team is composed of experts and engineers with great experience in building large, scalable, and secure hosted systems. Their highly qualified staff deploys the latest security technologies, including proprietary methods developed specifically for *salesforce.com*. They also continuously evaluate all emerging security trends and developments to stay two steps ahead of any potential issues or problems.

Salesforce.com has invested millions of dollars in some of the most advanced technology available for Internet security, disaster recovery, and backup protection. This includes physical security, continuous professional firewall monitoring, the strongest available encryption to protect all customer data provided over the Internet, user authentication, application security, and more.

Also contributing to its reliability is the fact that all customer data is backed up on tape on a nightly basis, up to the last committed transaction. All customer data is stored on disks that are mirrored across different storage cabinets and controllers. As you evaluate CRM solution providers, it is important to take them through a security test that is as thorough as this one. If they don't pass the test, you should pass on them.

Point #8: Testimonials

It is always important to see what current users have to say about the CRM solution providers that you are considering. You should take a careful look at testimonials from these satisfied customers and consider contacting some of them.

When you read testimonials, consider not only their content, but also the company itself and the role of the individual who actually provided the testimonial. Look carefully at the size of the company, its industry, and its standing in its industry. Then try to see if the testimonials line up with the primary claims that the CRM provider is making. For example, if a CRM solution provider makes frequent claims about its ability to quickly impact the bottom line, which should be reflected in some of the testimonials.

A brief look at some testimonials regarding *salesforce.com* are quite revealing in this regard.

Six months and half a million dollars later, companies that chose traditional CRM vendors still had nothing to show for it. With salesforce.com, *we have results.*

—Michael Blumenthal,
Vice President and
Chief Technology Officer
of Essex Corporation

With the help of salesforce.com, *we are a more successful enterprise. It gives us a more coherent culture and makes us more competitive. It has been bottom-line profitable for us within six months. I just don't see how you can help but make money using this product.*

—Donald H. Putnam,
CEO of Putnam Lovell

Adobe implemented and began profiting from salesforce.com's *online CRM in less than 30 days. No new hardware. No new software. Just proven reliability, security, and scalability that now empower Adobe professionals worldwide.*

—Lew Epstein,
VP North American Sales
Adobe Systems

Naturally, the written testimonials that any CRM service provider shows you are going to be positive. For this reason, you need to take a careful look at what is really being said. For example, notice that testimonials from key executives at companies using *salesforce.com* back up exactly what *salesforce.com* has placed at the heart of its services: a positive impact on sales revenues and profit, cost effectiveness, rapid implementation and impact, and solid reliability and security. We've seen and heard many other testimonials about the user-friendliness of *salesforce.com*'s CRM services.

Point #9: Pricing Considerations

Another key element to consider in reviewing any CRM service is the price. Many CRM providers have solutions that can easily run into the hundreds of thousands to millions of dollars. Salespeople and executives wonder how in the world such costly CRM services can ever be considered "solutions." When salespeople and executives have negative feelings about the costs of a new program even before it is implemented, the likelihood of a successful installation is further decreased.

When it comes to cost considerations, *salesforce.com* provides pricing that is uniformly regarded as being among the most reasonable in the industry. Instead of having to spend millions of dollars on CRM, companies that sign up with *salesforce.com* can, as of 2002, spend about $65 per month per user for its powerful Professional Edition, $125 per month per user for its new Enterprise Edition, and its E-business Suite is $195 per user per month. For users of the Professional Edition, the Offline product costs an additional $25 per user per month. There are *no up-front costs* with this system, and the users can pay as they go.

By contrast, the costs of some of the popular entry-level sales CRM software programs start at approximately $200 per license, and prices in excess of $1,300 per seat are not all that uncommon. Of course, prices will change over time, but experts predict that the online services such as *salesforce.com* will always have a price advantage.

Further, *salesforce.com* provides upgrades six times a year, and these are provided at no additional cost. Some of the most dramatic savings arise from the fact that there is no software or hardware to purchase and maintain, no need for IT involvement, no administrative overhead costs, and there is a rapid implementation period.

Point #10: Company Strength

The final point in screening a CRM solution provider focuses on the CRM company itself. Examine the company's history, track record, financial condition, client list, honors and awards, and management. You must believe that you are literally and figuratively in good company.

We have checked out *salesforce.com* thoroughly and on our own dime. When we traveled to examine their operations and offerings, we paid all of our own transportation and travel expenses, and we do not own stock in the company. We were very impressed by what we learned. Founded in 1999, with headquarters in San Francisco and offices in Europe and Asia, *salesforce.com* currently has more than 3,600 customers. Even a small listing of those customers is impressive:

Adobe Systems	First Union National Bank
Alamo Rent-a-Car	Fujitsu Computer Products of America
Autodesk	MicroStrategy
Banker Tanks	Putnam Lovell
Berlitz Global Net	Siemens
Briggs Equipment	Textron Fastening Systems
Broadvision	Thomas Cook Global Services
Dow Jones Newswires	Time Warner Communications
Essex Corporation	USA Today

Salesforce.com is currently ranked as the number one Online CRM Solution Provider, and has received some of the industry's top honors including "Company to Watch" at the Demo 2000 conference (February, 2000), *Upside* magazine's "Hot 100" (May, 2000), and *PC Magazines's* "Top 100 Web Sites of 2000," just to name a few.

The capitalization of *salesforce.com* is strong. Public records reveal that *salesforce.com* raised $52 million in venture funding, and has put together a board of directors composed of a veritable who's who of America's technical and business elite. The company founder and board chairman, Marc Benioff, spent 13 years as a top executive at Oracle. At age 25, Benioff became the company's youngest vice president, overseeing product development for desktop PCs. At *salesforce.com*, he has assembled a large, growing, and impressive team of highly skilled technical, sales, marketing, managerial, and administrative professionals, who have been recruited from the most respected companies in the industry.

Making the Right CRM Decision

In light of the wide range of advantages offered by CRM, it is imperative that many sales forces select and implement the CRM solution provider that is best for them. With the numerous options available today, this may be easier said than done. We have spent several hundred hours researching CRM and you may find you have to do the same.

To save time, we suggest you take each of the CRM solution providers you are considering and walk them through our 10-Point CRM Evaluation System. By doing so, your chances of making the right decision for your company will increase dramatically.

Evaluate each possible provider in terms of its:

1. Overall features.

2. Ease of use.

3. Startup time.

4. Customization.

5. Training.

6. Accessibility.

7. Security.

8. Testimonials.

9. Pricing considerations.

10. Company strength.

As we were writing this book over the past year, we knew we would have to cover CRM, as it is truly one of the major components of Ultimate Selling Power in today's business world. However, we quickly realized that we could not profile multiple companies in one chapter as they each have separate (and sometimes confusing) product offerings, terminology and services. We also could not write about CRM in a theoretical or hypothetical sense as we knew our readers needed specific details. With all the data we gathered from our analyses, we had no difficulty identifying a great CRM solution provider to showcase the most important benefits of CRM. By using the evaluation system we have provided, your search for the best CRM provider for your sales force will be greatly simplified.

The Bottom Line on CRM

The right CRM solution creates more than just a classical win-win situation—it actually creates what must be called a **win-win-win situation**. First, with the tremendous emphasis on customer service through features such as rapid and effective responses to all inquiries and proactive steps to prevent problems in the future, your customers are going to be far more satisfied. As a result of this proven increase in customer satisfaction that results from CRM, winner number one is your customer.

Second, as a result of CRM, **you** are going to be able to sell more to your existing customers and clients, as well as capture additional leads and sell more to them as well. In addition, you will be spending less time on tedious administrative matters and more time doing what you do best: selling. You will be better organized and will be operating with far more insight into your customers. As a result, another proven benefit from the right CRM service is increased personal productivity, increased sales, increased income and personal satisfaction for you. With CRM, you are winner number two.

And, finally, with more satisfied customers and greater sales, your company will enjoy increased revenues and profits. This strengthens your company's competitive position and may help increase its stock price, making your company winner number three.

Whether you work for a large multinational corporation or a small firm with just a few salespeople, you can take your selling power to an entirely new level with a CRM system that is easy to use, affordable, and structured to truly enhance sales force automation, customer service, and marketing. If you truly want to enjoy Ultimate Selling Power in today's demanding marketplace, you need to participate in the CRM revolution and select the best CRM solution provider for your sales force.

11

How Coaching Creates Ultimate Selling Power

Have you ever known an average salesperson who turned his sales career around and became enormously successful? In a *year or less*?

We know plenty of them.

How do they accomplish this remarkable feat? Very few of them fall into some great accounts. Few convince their father-in-law's company to make a huge purchase. Few become mega-successful because their company introduces the world's best new product or because the company lowers prices by 50 percent. Very few are just plain lucky.

Their success is typically due to something far more powerful than simply waiting around for things to improve, or for their company to introduce a great new product or slash prices.

We have seen literally thousands of salespeople make a quantum leap in their careers and their earnings by taking advantage of the newest force in sales development: **a sales coach.** Coaching has actually been used for decades to create sales superstars. However, it has only been in the past few years that sales coaching has become more widely available to average salespeople. In the past, much "coaching" consisted of a wizened sales veteran sharing his wisdom with a younger salesperson. As you will see, coaching has now become much more scientific and makes use of linguistics, psychology, persuasion, measurement, and accountability.

Solving the Major Challenges of Sales Coaching

If coaching is so effective, why don't more of the 18 million salespeople in the U.S. avail themselves of its benefits? First, sales coaching remains mysterious and little understood by many salespeople. Millions of salespeople do not even know what a sales coach does or how a sales coach works. Some think that the range of services coaches offer is limited to teaching "closing techniques," when in fact, coaches work in every area of sales and marketing. **Whatever** your sales challenge, there is probably a coach somewhere in the U.S. who can help you rapidly overcome it!

In this chapter, we will show you the kind of work sales coaches do and the benefits they offer. We will not just be discussing our work in the coaching field (although that is what we are most familiar with!), but will also examine services offered by other coaches. There are many outstanding sales coaches besides the authors of this book! The most dramatic benefits we have seen in terms of improved sales skills have come about from sales coaching.

**Our goal is not just to show what coaches do,
but is also to encourage more people
to enter the sales coaching field.**

There is a great need for skilled sales coaches all over the U.S. Almost every industry in our country is suffering from low sales, and consequently, is suffering reduced profits and a lower stock price. We would like to encourage many readers of this book to enter the field of sales coaching, on either a full-time or part-time basis. The work pays very well and it is quite fulfilling to see your clients make massive improvements in their sales abilities and in their take-home income.

One of the factors that has slowed down the more rapid adoption of sales coaching is the limited availability of top coaches. In any field, whether it is law or medicine or coaching, there are only a few top experts. Despite being expensive, these top experts are in great demand because of the benefits their expertise provides. Most fields, including medicine and law, have hundreds of thousands of other competent practitioners—besides the top experts. Sales coaching is different in that there are only a couple thousand sales coaches (no one knows the exact number) to help the 18 million salespeople in our country.

Sales coaching, like athletic coaching, can be time and energy intensive. No one can personally coach more than a few dozen individuals at any one time, unless group coaching is used. For this reason, we will also cover the ins and outs of group coaching. This work is exciting, demanding, and fulfilling, but it is not for everyone!

If you have a deep understanding of sales and persuasion, if you enjoy working with people and teaching, you may want to become a sales coach. The need is great, the compensation is outstanding and, perhaps best of all, you can help people rapidly improve their lives, lower their stress and greatly increase their incomes. After reading this chapter on sales coaching, you may decide to hire a coach **or** you may decide to become a sales coach! We want to give you the tools to do either or both. That is one of our goals in sharing this material.

If we can encourage another 1,000 or so highly skilled and knowledgeable people to enter the sales coaching field, we believe we can have a major positive impact on sales, business profits and our national economy. One of the reasons companies have laid off more than two million people over the recent (2000–2002) time period is that corporations were not selling enough goods or services to support their payrolls.

**As sales coaches increase
sales for companies
around the U.S.,
they strengthen our national economy.**

As powerful as it can be, coaching is not a panacea or a magic pill. While coaching can produce nearly miraculous results for some salespeople, in other cases the coaching is of only limited effectiveness. Sometimes the lack of success in the coaching relationship is due to the fact that the salesperson simply does not know what to expect from the coach or how to get the most from his or her coach. In some cases, coaches do not know how to work with that particular salesperson or how to set and achieve goals. In this chapter, we will reveal some of the best, most productive, ways of working with your sales coach.

What does a sales coach do? The answer is simple to describe in words, yet challenging to accomplish:

**Whatever is needed to improve the performance
and success of a sales professional.**

For example, a very successful attorney in Denver sent Dr. Moine the PowerPoint presentation for his upcoming seminar. This attorney, William Bronchick, is one of the top experts in the country on real estate law and is also a very successful real estate investor. He decided to take all of his knowledge and write a series of books to share what he has learned with others. Bill Bronchick also has produced outstanding audio and videotapes on real estate investing. Dr. Moine spent about three hours going through Bill's PowerPoint slides, analyzing them, and coming up with ideas on how to improve them and how to use them in seminars.

Dr. Moine and Bill Bronchick then spent about two hours going over his seminar presentation and his PowerPoint slides, with the goal of massively improving the sales of his books and tapes at his seminar. Bill's seminars, always popular, have become even more successful. At several of his recent seminars, Bill Bronchick has sold $15,000 to more than $20,000 of his real estate investing books and tapes. Not bad for conducting a 90-minute seminar. These are just some of the benefits of sales coaching. Just as significant, the people attending William Bronchick's seminars are getting the best real estate investing knowledge that is currently available.

Bill Bronchick's other major area of expertise is asset protection, and he now has a series of books and tapes on that important topic as well. Dr. Moine is currently coaching Bill on the best, most persuasive and powerful ways of marketing this information to the people who need it. This is another win-win solution, as William Bronchick's clients are now learning how to use this knowledge to protect hundreds of thousands to millions of dollars of their net worth.

There are many different ways of doing sales coaching today. Sales coaches now work with clients via the Internet, over the phone, through fax, CD (compact disk) communications, e-mail, PowerPoint and, of course, face-to-face. As part of his coaching role with William Bronchick, Dr. Moine worked with him by phone, over the Internet, through use of PowerPoint, and in person by attending one of his seminars, and coaching him afterwards. In-person sessions are powerful but are not always necessary.

We've worked with clients in Canada, Europe, and Australia via phone, fax, and the Internet and have achieved outstanding sales results. We have never met some of our clients face-to-face and yet we have been able to help them break sales records. There are others with whom we have met, become friends and business associates. We even coach other top coaches. One such super-coach is Geoffrey Pickworth, who is probably the premier sales and management coach in Australia. Working out of beautiful Sydney, Australia, Geoffrey has become the advisor of choice to dozens of top salespeople and executives across Australia. We first met Geoffrey by phone, worked with him in-person in several major cities in Australia and Bali, Indonesia, and then conducted seminars with him. We have also coauthored articles with Geoffrey that have been featured in major Australian business and sales magazines. Geoffrey Pickworth, whose company is Chally Consulting, Pty., is now a famous coaching expert and has been featured on several radio and television shows across Australia.

As you are about to see, the above examples are but two of the emerging waves of the sales coaching movement that is now quietly sweeping across the world of business.

**Wherever savvy salespeople or their managers
around the world seek massive
increases in sales and profits,
they look for a top coach or consultant.**

The coach they seek may be us, it may be someone else, *it may be you*, but top sales coaches have become highly sought-after specialists in the world of business today.

Do you know of any business that can say it has too many sales? NO. Do you know of any business that can say its profits are too great? NO. For this reason, major corporations around the world are seeking out the best sales coaches and are doing everything possible to tie up as much of their time and expertise as they can obtain. For those of you considering a career as a sales coach, one option is to work full-time or nearly full-time for just one company. We have had periods of nearly a year when one company bought up almost all of our time. In some cases, we have had to hire other coaches to assist us on many coaching and training projects.

The need for sales coaches is growing rapidly as business becomes more global and more competitive. If you are considering entering the field, you may wonder how much sales coaches earn. Beginning coaches who are just starting a practice might earn $60,000–$100,000 a year. Experienced sales and marketing coaches make several hundred thousand dollars a year. Top **athletic** coaches earn millions of dollars per year. There are now sales coaches who earn more than $1 million per year. Why? Because they help companies increase sales by tens to hundreds of millions of dollars per year. Companies and individuals are happy to pay pennies on the dollar for these kinds of results.

Do You Really Need a Coach?

Think of some of the best performances that you have ever seen, regardless of the arena. Perhaps it was a basketball player who defied gravity on his way to a monster reverse slam-dunk, a runner who sprints all-out for a mile in under three minutes and 45 seconds, or maybe it was a musical performance that left an audience of thousands spellbound.

In addition to their drive, skills, motivation, and dedication, all of these masters of their crafts have one thing in common, and that is the fact that *they all have coaches*. The coach may be called a coach, a guide, a teacher, a mentor, an instructor, or a guru, but top performers all have them. If the greatest athletes and performers in the world have coaches, what does that tell you about the value of coaching?

If you talk to some of the most successful businesspeople you know, you will be amazed to hear how many of them have profited from the advice and guidance of coaches. Many people in business now brag about their coaches. Coaches have become a status symbol among elite salespeople, top executives, and highly successful corporations. Unsuccessful people cannot afford coaches and, consequently, they do not have coaches. While coaches are becoming available to more and more people in business, it is still largely the elite who benefit from working with the best coaches and advisors and for this reason, working with a top coach has become as much of a status symbol as driving a luxury car.

What Do Sales Coaches Do?

If you are uncertain as to whether you need a coach, just ask yourself if you could use some help in any of the following areas, to list just a few:

Turning certain prospects into clients.

Using powerful story-selling techniques.

Distinguishing yourself from all the other salespeople in your field.

Dealing with prospects who say "I'm loyal to someone else."

Rapidly building trust and rapport with any prospect.

Solving personal problems that affect your business.

Using invisible closing techniques that get the business.

Profiting from audio business cards and CD brochures.

Dramatically improving your closing ratio in seminars and in one-on-one selling.

Hiring assistants and other salespeople to multiply your effectiveness.

Learning how to sell in a down market or a recession.

Overcoming procrastination.

Dramatically improving your time management skills.

Managing and motivate *yourself*.

Getting newspaper and radio publicity for you, your products, and your services.

Rewriting your ads, brochures, and prospecting letters to make them powerfully persuasive and effective.

Conducting powerful, productive sales seminars.

If you heard an internal voice telling you "yes" as you read over the list, then it's time to think seriously about finding a sales coach. Remember, this is just a beginning list of the services sales coaches provide.

Can You Be Coached by a Book or by Tapes?

We will sometimes be contacted by a self-proclaimed "fan" who claims to have read all of our books (more than 10) and articles (more than 300) and to have listened to our tapes. The individual may ask, "Can I benefit from coaching? I have read and heard everything you have done."

This is an outstanding question. If you go into coaching, you are likely to hear this same question. Obviously, only the salesperson can decide if coaching is right for him. However, you do need to understand that there is a world of difference between reading about a skill and actually acquiring that skill. You could read every word Tiger Woods has ever written about golf and it is doubtful that you could break 70 on the course at Pebble Beach. You could read every word Michael Jordan has ever written and listen to every interview and speech he has given and it probably would not give you the ability to shoot a slam dunk or shoot nine out of 10 at the free-throw line.

Books, tapes, and seminars are an outstanding means of acquiring information and of learning about strategies and techniques. However, **to change behavior**, a skilled and caring coach is usually needed. We are not saying this to build up our coaching business, as we currently have almost all the coaching clients we can handle. We are saying this because it is a fact. Books, articles, and tapes are valuable learning aids, but they can only take you so far. Coaches are needed by those who are serious about becoming the best athletes and by those who want reach their full potential as top salespeople.

A coach can help you acquire skills, behaviors, and **self-awareness** that you cannot obtain from any book or tape series. You can also dialogue and problem-solve with your coach (something that is impossible to do with a book or tape). Perhaps most valuable of all, your coach can hear you, see you, role-play with you, and give you **immediate corrective feedback** that no book or tape can provide.

There is one additional powerful reason that many sales superstars and future sales superstars choose to work with a coach. They know that a coach reserves his or her most powerful techniques for clients and does not usually publish them in articles or books. This is not because the sales coach is trying to hold anything back, but is rather due to the fact that it would take tens of thousands or perhaps more than 100,000 words to describe all the sales strategies a top coach knows and to show how they work.

The power of many strategies comes not from knowing the general strategy but from having it totally customized to sell **your** products and **your** services to **your** clients in **your** geographical area. Further, you want to know how to do this at **your** desired prices against **your** competitors **right now**!

This level of customization easily takes tens of thousands of words to describe. Who wants to write all of that out or read it all? Writing it out, with all of the necessary subtle but powerful nuances could take days or weeks. A coach might have to charge $10,000 to write it all out (and we have been paid that much and more to create powerful training programs for our corporate clients). Instead, your coach can explain it to you and coach you in how to do it *in just a few hours*. Think of all the time and money saved! For this reason, you will never find the most powerful, totally customized sales coaching strategies for YOUR business in any book or on any tape.

Even if a coach did write an article or produce a series of tapes at that level of detail (about **your** selling style, **your** products, **your** services being sold to **your** clients, etc.) who would want to read it or listen to it except you? Imagine that the top batting coach in the world spent seven hours coaching your brother-in-law on how to hit a 97-mile-per-hour fastball. Your brother-in-law is 6' 3" tall and weighs 220 pounds. You are 5' 11" tall and weigh 160 pounds. Do you want to listen to tapes of this world-class expert who coached your brother-in-law for seven hours on how to hit a fastball? No. Do you want to read a transcript of this? No. However, *you might want to be coached by this same top expert*. For exactly the same reason, you will never learn the most powerful strategies on exactly how **you** can best sell to **your** clients by reading a book or listening to tapes. *You will learn a great deal from books and tapes*, but to reach your full potential, you will probably have to work with a great coach.

A few months ago, a client from a small midwestern town flew to Southern California to work with Dr. Moine. This client, who is in financial services, has a weekly radio show in his hometown. The radio show had produced a few small clients for this financial planner but the planner knew it could bring in much more business. He had read an article Donald had written on marketing through radio shows. Because both the planner and Donald were very busy, the only time they could meet was on a Sunday. During their five hour session, held in the back corner of a hotel restaurant near the airport, Donald shared a number of techniques that had helped other clients make several million dollars in extra income from their radio shows.

Donald had never previously written about these specific highly customized techniques and to this day has not written about them. Together, Donald and his client further customized them for the client's market and his own radio show. A transcript of this five hour session would have been as long as two or three full length books, but reading such books (even if a coach had the time to write them) would not be nearly as much fun or as impactful as interacting with the coach. In working with this client, Donald also shared some powerful referral techniques that he has never before written about because they are so specialized.

In just the few months since that session, the planner has added millions of dollars in new assets under management and reports that he now has more referrals than he can handle. In addition to his two existing full-time assistants, he is considering hiring another assistant or a junior planner to handle all the business that is now coming in. This planner is making more than $600,000 a year working in a small town. This is the kind of skill that no book or tape series can develop in an individual. As far as we can tell, you can only make these kinds of quantum leaps in production by working with a highly skilled coach.

There are salespeople who say, "Sales coaching doesn't work." Some of them, of course, have never tried coaching. They are similar to the overweight individual who says, "Reducing the number of calories you eat and exercising do not work." However, at least in the case of the overweight person, there may be metabolic issues involved with the weight problem. Salespeople who claim that sales coaching does not work cannot use the genetic explanation.

In the case of a salesperson who has tried coaching and found it to not be effective, we have found that in almost every instance, the problem is that the salesperson had the wrong coach. Maybe this salesperson needed to work with you. Not every coach can work with every salesperson! Sometimes there is simply a personality mismatch. In other cases, the coach may have been uneducated, unskilled, or uncaring. The coach may not have put enough time or energy into coaching his client. If there is a personality mismatch, *do not take it personally.* A personality mismatch is not the fault of the coach, nor is it the fault of the salesperson. It simply means it is time for the salesperson to find a coach who is more attuned to his or her needs and with whom there is a better rapport.

There are many outstanding sales coaches in the U.S. besides the authors of this book. In fact, it is entirely likely that some other coach somewhere in the country could do a better job coaching you than we could. That other coach could have more product knowledge in your field or might have more time to work with you than we have or might be less expensive. If you go into coaching, you may be the best coach in the world for certain salespeople. What is your area of expertise? Publishing? Biotechnology? Carpets? Aerospace fasteners? Radiology equipment? There is a need for sales coaches in all of these fields and hundreds of others.

With all the seminars and sales consulting we do, our coaching practice is nearly full during most weeks. If you want to work with us, and if we have the time, we would welcome the opportunity to help you, or to coach you in how to become a sales coach. However, the vast majority of readers of this book will work with sales coaches besides us and we fully support and encourage that. We want you to work with the coach who is best for you.

When Is the Best Time to Start Working With a Coach?

Before even selecting a coach, you must ask yourself, "Is this the best time to work with a coach?" Unlike some other sales coaches, we do **not** say that every salesperson should be coached or that salespeople should be coached all the time. For example, if you are having major problems in your marriage, this might be affecting your sales career. Rather than seeking out a sales coach, it might be more productive for you to find a great marriage counselor. Once you have successfully resolved the issues in your marriage, then find a skilled sales coach. At that time, you will be able to fully concentrate on the benefits the sales coach can offer and you won't be tempted to ask the sales coach for help in solving your marriage problems.

It is a common assumption that the best time to begin working with a sales coach is when you are just starting out in your career. *Ironically, a coach may be least necessary at that time.* Your sales manager can probably provide you with much of the advice and guidance you need to get started in sales or in a new sales specialization (for example, if you are moving from automobile sales to real estate sales or computer sales). When you are just starting out in sales, or in a new sales specialization, you also need to master product knowledge in your field. This can take some time.

Before hiring a professional coach, make all the use you can of your corporate trainers and your sales manager. They can teach you a great deal! Even when working with a coach, continue to consult with your company's trainers and your sales manager. In real estate investing, there exists a concept of "highest and best use." Sophisticated investors ask, "What is the highest and best use of this piece of property?

The highest and best use of a sales coach is by someone who has already learned the basics and who is ready to make a quantum leap to a much higher level of selling.

If you are making several hundred thousand dollars a year or more and if everything is going great, it is easy to assume that you "don't need a sales coach." However, there is a danger in complacency. We have seen some salespeople go from earning $500,000 a year or more to unemployment as conditions rapidly change in their industry. Don't assume that just because you are currently making a high income that you do not need or cannot benefit from a coach. Some of our clients are making $1 million a year and they work with us because they want to *do even better*, or they want to improve the quality of their lives, or grow their business even more. We also work with some people who are making only $50,000 a year and they just want to get to that $100,000 a year income level as soon as possible. A few of our clients are making more than $2 million a year and their motivation is to help more customers (and maybe make an extra $1 million a year), and that is why they continue to work on their sales and marketing skills.

We have found that the most successful people in sales, as well as in any other endeavor, are those who are motivated to continuously grow and improve.

Take the case of a successful baseball player who is hitting 40 homeruns a season. What does he do to improve further? It would make no sense for him to just go out and hit more balls. All he would be doing is practicing the same old swing over and over. So, he works with a top coach who looks at every aspect of his swing, his posture and stance, his breathing, his grip, his eye movements, his attitude and expectations, and dozens of other variables, and makes powerful suggestions for improvement. In guiding and reinforcing those improvements, the player hitting 40 homeruns per season maximizes his chances for hitting even more.

In exactly the same way, if a salesperson wants to improve his closing ratio, it does not make sense to go out and keep doing what he or she has always been doing. Usually, *if you keep doing what you have always been doing, you will keep getting what you have always got* (or less). Are you satisfied with that? When you want to do even better, coaching is often the answer.

If you keep doing what you have always been doing, in most cases, you will stay in the same place. In order to get significantly more hits and homers, both the salesperson and the baseball player can profit greatly from the services of a top-notch coach.

Do not misunderstand us. We are not against rookies using coaches. It always surprises us when someone new to sales hires an expensive coach, but some do. They tend to be the most ambitious of all salespeople. Why do some sales rookies hire a coach? They want to start out **right** and avoid acquiring bad habits that can be so hard to break later. Some sales coaches specialize in working with beginners in the profession while others work only with very successful salespeople. Most of our coaching work is with highly successful salespeople and sales managers but we do devote about 20 percent of our time to working with newcomers. This is exciting work because some of these newcomers rapidly rise to become the top producers in their companies. When this happens, we have that wonderful feeling of having helped coach a young Babe Ruth. This is truly one of the greatest rewards of all in being a sales coach.

Do salespeople ever have regrets about sales coaching? Of course. Perhaps the most common is that they regret not seeking the skills of a top sales coach even sooner. One of our very successful clients recently said, "I wish I had the benefit of professional coaching years ago. I could have gotten to the top so much faster." While you may not mind slowly climbing to the top of a very high mountain to enjoy the view, some salespeople and sales managers would rather get there sooner than later. Sales coaches are dedicated to serving those people. If you enjoy struggling (it is a psychological fact that some people do), a sales coach may not be right for you.

If you can afford to work with a professional coach or if your company makes coaching available to you, seriously consider taking advantage of it. You are probably going to become a sales millionaire one of these days. Why not use a coach to make that day sooner rather than later?

Who Can Actually Benefit From a Sales Coach?

Selling and persuasion skills are not only important in sales positions, but in countless other professions. We have coached bankers, financial planners, stock brokers, compensation consultants, insurance agents, stock option experts, real estate agents, CPAs, hospital administrators, lawyers, and business owners who are interested in making quantum leaps in their careers and in their businesses. If persuasion is important in your business, a skilled sales coach can probably help you achieve a much higher level of success.

Even corporate executives can benefit from sales coaching. We have coached corporate executives in many different industries and with owners of companies in fields as diverse as semi-conductor manufacturing and distribution, office equipment sales, apparel manufacturing, medical equipment sales, executive search (headhunters), payroll services, and many others.

For example, one of our clients owns and operates convalescent hospitals. The administrators of the various care centers are expected to play a key business development role—in other words, they are expected to sell. However, these administrators are typically strong on technical skills but have had absolutely no interest or experience in selling. In fact, many not only dislike the entire notion of selling, but they often have deep-seated fears of selling. It seemed like an absolutely impossible task to develop sales skills in these administrators. No book or seminar on selling would work. Only coaching could develop the powerful sales skills these administrators needed to help their hospital stay profitable.

We conducted face-to-face group sessions with them and let them share all of their concerns. We then showed them how they are already using sales skills in leading their staff. After all, there is a great deal of trust-building, persuasion, negotiation, and handling of objections in building and managing an executive team. With this **foundation** in place, we continued to coach many of them on an individualized basis and they enjoyed major improvements in their sales skills **and** attitudes toward selling. It was not long before these improvements had a dramatic effect on their bottom line profitability.

Finding a Great Sales Coach

It is difficult to find a truly skilled sales coach and there is a severe shortage of coaches in the U.S. to work with our 18 million professional salespeople. If you believe you have the potential and the aptitude to become a great sales coach, we would like to encourage you to get the training and education you need to enter this exciting field. Due to our busy seminar and consulting schedules, we will only be able to coach a small number of the readers of this book. We'd like to provide you with referrals to some of the other top sales coaches in the U.S. As you will see, many of these coaches specialize in particular areas. We do no receive any financial compensation in providing these referrals, and therefore, we can be objective.

In the areas of goal-setting and sales skills, we highly recommend our student, friend, and associate **Eric Lofholm** of *SalesChampion.com*. To develop skills in selling on the Internet, one of the world's finest coaches is **Robert Imbriale** of *UltimateWealth.com*. In the area of Neuro-Linguistic Programming (NLP), two of the best coaches in the country are **Steve Andreas** of *NLPComprehensive.com* and **Don Aspromonte** (donaspromonte@msn.com) of Dallas, Texas. For financial planners and insurance agents, we give standing ovations to **Tom Gau, CFP**, "the $3 million man" (that is his annual income, not his net worth), **Ken Unger** of *MillionDollarProducer.com*, and to **Larry Klein** of *nfcom.com*. Larry Klein is perhaps the top expert in the country in the area of marketing to seniors.

Jerry Richardson of San Francisco is an expert in both Neuro-Linguistic Programming and sales and is a joy to work with. **Mark Magnacca** of Boston is an expert in Unique Selling Propositions and many other areas of sales. **Dan Seidman** of Chicago can perform detailed autopsies on any sale and also has a wonderful sense of humor. **Peter Lowe** of Tampa, Florida is a skilled coach for people who do seminar selling and is also a true expert on success mindsets. **Ted Thomas** of Orlando, Florida is one of the top coaches in the U.S. on direct mail marketing and the selling of information. **Jay Abraham** of Rolling Hills Estates, California, is a marketing genius who, at $5,000 an hour, may be undercharging for his services.

Roger Pell of Charlotte, North Carolina, is one of the top sales coaches for bankers and mortgage professionals. We have done more than $2 million of consulting in the banking field ourselves and can recognize a true expert when we see one—Roger is one of those experts. In Seattle, we have two favorite sales coaches: **Roy Chitwood**, president of Max Sacks, International, is one of the top coaches of high-technology salespeople in the country; and **Gus Fernandez** is a highly accomplished public speaker and a much sought-after sales coach for small to medium-sized businesses.

A true sales mastermind we wrote about in *Unlimited Selling Power* is **Pat Knowles** of Orlando, Florida. Pat is truly the salesman's salesman and is one of the most persuasive people in the world. Combining an I.Q. that must be well over 170 with incredible honesty, Pat Knowles has the power to find and satisfy needs, educate, dazzle, and entertain all who meet him. Pat Knowles has the exceedingly rare ability to effectively sell to anyone from high school dropouts to CEOs of Fortune 500 companies. Pat has broken sales records selling everything from televisions to multimillion dollar oil and gas fields to huge real estate developments. Pat has also built some of the most powerful and loyal sales forces in the U.S. Any sales professional who ever has the opportunity to be coached by Pat Knowles is indeed fortunate.

While he is not a professional coach, **Gerhard Gschwandtner** has served as a mentor, guide, and unofficial coach to hundreds of the best sales managers and to dozens of CEOs across the U.S. As publisher of the world's most popular magazine for salespeople, *Selling Power*, Gerhard is a walking encyclopedia of everything worth knowing about sales. Gerhard has an uncanny ability to listen to the most complex and seemingly unsolvable sales challenges and then, in a matter of minutes, to solve them. Due to his incredibly busy schedule, you will probably never be fortunate enough to speak with Gerhard, but by subscribing to *Selling Power* and by bookmarking its Website *Sellingpower.com*, you will have much of the benefit of his wisdom on selling.

If you ever have a chance to hear Gerhard speak at a seminar, you are in for a rare treat. Gerhard is a great entertainer as well as a skilled educator. As he speaks, hang on to every word he says—we do. We've known Gerhard for 20 years and we are still learning from him. Gerhard is from Austria, home of Arnold Schwarzenegger, and as strong as Arnold is in body, Gerhard is just as strong in sales and persuasion.

Put Your Career on Fast-Forward

When should you work with a coach? *When you are highly motivated.* If everything is fine and you are more or less contented with the way things are going, you may not want to work with a coach. Will you really follow his or her suggestions? We do not wish to overly romanticize coaching! Sales coaching, like athletic coaching, does involve work to develop powerful skills. Will you do the work? Will you make the coaching meetings, whether in person or over the phone?

**You need to make a commitment to coaching
to get the most from it.**

We know you will achieve your goals **eventually**. If you work hard, gradually, maybe in five or 10 or 15 years, you will meet your income objectives. Why not achieve them sooner and with less stress? Why not achieve them in the next year or two? That's what sales coaching is all about.

Nothing in life is guaranteed, but investing in **yourself** and **your future** is probably the best investment you will ever make. For most people, an investment in oneself pays off much better than does investing in the stock market, real estate, or bank CDs. Investing in yourself is an investment that you can totally control, and if you have the motivation and a great sales coach, the capital gains and return on investment from coaching can surpass that of any other investment you will ever make.

**If you offer a great product or service, working with a
top sales coach can virtually guarantee that you will
become a sales millionaire or multimillionaire.**

Epilogue: Interview With G. Edward Hunt

As this book was going to press, we heard from G. Edward Hunt, who has built a $25 million company in less than two years using many of the techniques you have just read about. Edward is president of Avtech Computers and AmeraFund (a finance company), and he has spent the past 20 years studying and applying success principles. The principles, strategies, and tactics he learned from our writings and us have enabled Edward to build this $25 million business in less than two years starting from scratch.

Edward also hosts a live weekly talk radio show, *The Success Power Unlimited Radio Network*. Billed as the Most Powerful Wealth Building and Self Development Radio Talk Show in America, each week G. Edward Hunt and his noted guests discuss how average people can reach or exceed all of their financial goals. In Edward's words, his mission is "to give back to the community by providing success tips to listeners in Southern California and around the world." His highly popular radio show is now carried live on the Internet.

We stay in touch with our clients and students around the world. Dr. Ken Lloyd had the opportunity to interview Edward Hunt in May of 2002. In the interview, Edward shared many rich examples of how he is using our techniques to break sales records in his industry. We'd like to share a few of the highlights of that interview to give you some additional ideas and strategies you might use to make several million dollars in two years, as Ed Hunt has.

Ken Lloyd:

It's a real pleasure to discuss your rapid success and some of the ways that our sales strategies have helped you.

Edward Hunt:

First of all, I'm absolutely honored to be interviewed by you. This means a lot to me. I picked up your first book, *Unlimited Selling Power* in 1992. I was amazed at all the powerful techniques the book contained. Everything in that book is universal. The techniques you teach don't just work in sales—they work in everyday life, in business, and in advertising. I've used your techniques to write ads for my businesses, *and in just the past two years, the ads brought in more than $25 million in sales for my main company and millions of dollars in sales in another company I've started!*

I've got two copies of the book—one in my office and one at home. I give out copies to the sales team. It's very comprehensive and very powerful. There's just something wonderful about this book. It's just all there. *I live these techniques, and it's truly made the difference between our company being a success and being an also-ran.*

I talk to many other marketers and they all think they know how to sell product. However, since relatively few salespeople and marketers know how to use your techniques, they don't get the results we do. It's not because I'm so talented. It's because of the techniques I've learned from you and Dr. Moine. It really is.

KL: I'm sure our readers would like to know more about your companies. What is their history and where are you today?

EH: We build computers, but we originally started out selling gym floor covers and recreational equipment. Selling to schools, we were always running into budgetary constraints and we were hearing that they didn't have the money for the gym equipment because they have to buy computers. So, we started selling computers, originally from other manufacturers. Then discovered later we weren't getting quite the quality we wanted, so we started building them ourselves. And from there, using your sales techniques, it grew so wonderfully. Now, we are selling to both schools and government agencies.

KL: Can you give us a few examples of some of your favorite techniques?

EH: Sure. Scripting is one of my favorites. The words you use really can make you rich. Most people in sales do not pay enough attention to the words they use. In speaking to teachers, I say, "Resources for teachers are limited," and, later, "Teachers are not given enough credit." These are undeniably truthful statements. They have to agree with me. This helps build a climate of agreement in our meetings. And based on our initial agreements, I show teachers how my company can help them stretch their resources. Using the techniques you and Dr. Moine developed, I now have scripts for everything. Nothing is left to chance. And consequently, we would get a phenomenal response.

KL: Are there any other ways you use scripting?

EH: I even use it in the letters I write. When I write a sales letter, I actually go back through it and ask myself if it has all the persuasion techniques I have learned from you. I ask myself, "Do I have *this* in my letter?" "Do I have *that* in my letter?" and I methodically make sure my sales letters are as powerful as possible. I've got to tell you that a great part of the success of the company is due to using these techniques, without question. We use these techniques in our advertising, and we have our salespeople use a structured presentation in all of their sales calls. We simply cannot have them experiment on prospects and clients. They have to use words that we know are effective and that result in sales.

KL: Do all of your salespeople use a structured presentation?

EH: We have about 25 salespeople, and almost all of them use a structured sales talk. The most successful ones always do. There's no question about it. And the ones who don't use a structured sales talk are not as successful—they usually don't last.

KL: Can you tell us more about how you use the scripting process?

EH: We do so many things we learned from you. We start with undeniable truths, trust-building, and then do a major needs assessment. Then, when we present our recommendations, we tap into their imaginations and create a sense of ownership by saying, "Imagine what you could do with this powerful computer...and all the ways you could help your kids." And then maybe we will tell a story around that, such as, "Let me tell you a story about someone who reminds me of you who's been using our products." We create a structured sales talk through an actual script.

KL: Has your business changed much during the past few years?

EH: We've grown tremendously. We've been selling to the schools and government. The teachers themselves like the computers so much they want them for personal use. So now we are selling on the retail level. Scripts work beautifully there, too. We are also now providing financing, which is another profit center. We have a different structured presentation for that. With all of our scripts, we use your presentation and pacing techniques so the scripts become invisible and sound totally natural.

KL: How else do you use these techniques?

EH: I use them to sell our people on the profession of selling and to build pride in our sales professionals. My job really is to sell our employees on doing an excellent job in sales and service and the techniques you and Dr. Moine have developed are outstanding in building that mindset. We also use these techniques with our telemarketers.

KL: Can you share with us a few successful scripts your telemarketers use?

EH: Sure. We immediately repeat the person's name, such as, "Oh, hi John." If we know the person is a teacher, we'll say, "You're a teacher, right?" And the person will respond, "Yes." This starts building some agreement. And we'll then say, "So you're calling about the special, right?" and the caller says, "Yes...." We continue with, "Let me see if we have any of those available still." So now we create a little anticipation. And then, we'll say, "Okay, we have a few available." Then we do some additional need assessment and say, "What will you be using this for?" We want to make sure they have the right computer for the job. Just as you teach, we believe in highly ethical salesmanship. We only want to sell a product the client **needs** and **can afford.**

So we're creating a little bit of ownership and also doing a needs assessment simultaneously. After that, we say, "That's great. Let me tell you a little about our best products for that application. We build our computers, for example, for NASA and up until now we've made them exclusively available only to government agencies like schools and NASA." We build credibility.

We also anticipate any **objections** they may have. For example, we're not a brand name like Gateway or Dell, so, we say, "You're familiar with brand names like Sony and Intel?" and the prospect says, "Yes." We then say, "We use Intel processors and Sony disk drives, the same way that Dell and Gateway do." This makes prospects feel more comfortable. It's all about credibility and comfort and our sales scripts create that.

Then we explain the technology to them because we want to make sure it is the perfect computer system for their uses and applications. We always present two choices because we never want to force anyone to buy anything. We say, "Would you like the A model at $699 or do you want the B model at $899?" From there, they'll take the A or B, or they'll have some more questions. Using our powerful planned presentation, with your techniques built in, we will answer any remaining questions or objections. We might say, "Well, it sounds like maybe you need the C model. So would you like the C model or the B model?" The sales process we've learned from you and Dr. Moine has made our company incredibly successful.

KL: Do you think your computers could be sold without a script?

EH: Yes, but if we did not have powerful scripts, it would cut down on our closing ratio from one in four (25 percent) to one in 20 calls (5 percent). That would cost us millions of dollars. So, obviously the sales scripts make all the difference in the world. First of all, they keep you **focused**, and you've got to be focused. If you want to drive from here to New York, you need a road map, don't you? If I don't have a road map, well, you may get to New York, but it could take you months or years. We want to get there as soon as possible taking the shortest possible route. That's what sales scripts do for us. It's the shortest possible route to the sales goal you are looking to achieve.

KL: I notice that you used a metaphor in describing the value of scripts. Do you use them often in your sales presentations?

EH: That's something else that I learned from Dr. Moine and you— the power of stories and metaphors. I can now use stories and metaphors very effectively.

KL: What is one of the most common objections you get and how do you handle it using scripts?

EH: I would have to say it has to do with price. Price versus what am I getting for the money? As you know, to overcome this objection, you go to value. How do I show value to surpass whatever the price is? We **don't** want to just equal the price. We want to surpass it. If the price is $900, we want to show them $1200 of value or $1,800 of value. In terms of scripts for price and quality, we might say, "If NASA has ordered this particular model, do you think NASA wants good quality? NASA can afford the best, can't they? Well, don't you think that a teacher like you, and your students, deserve the best—especially at this low price?

KL: How firmly do you believe in the concept of having a sales success mindset?

EH: What you think is everything; you become what you think. Every single self-help book has that common denominator. I walk into a library and look at all the self-help books and they all have one thing in common: your mind. *Your mindset determines your level of success—especially in sales.* It's like a thermostat. If you believe you have the ability, the products, and services, and if you believe you deserve to have a certain level of success, it is likely you will achieve it. If you believe in a different level of success, maybe a lower level, you're going to achieve that. Your level of thinking determines your level of success. Period.

Every single human being out there can improve their mindset, and there are very specific techniques to do it. I am grateful that Dr. Moine and you showed me the way. Actively creating a sales success mindset brings you to a higher elevation and is a great way to do everything better—sell better, communicate better, sell with less effort, create less resistance, make more money, have more fun. If you know **how** to create a sales success mindset, without a doubt you're going to be much, much more successful. Thanks for showing me how to do that. It's your beliefs that determine the outcome of your entire life.

KL: What other strategies have you found to be the most powerful?

EH: Unique Selling Propositions. We do them in several ways: by combining a custom built product at an assembly-line kind of price, which is unique. On top of that, we layer in our financing. The driving force behind our USP is to add more value and is enhance the quality of the customer's business careers and private lives. It's giving them an opportunity they never had before and reaching out to them with the most powerful language in the industry. That is how we have been able to bring in tens of millions of dollars in just a couple of years.

KL: What would you like to tell other people to help them to reach your level of success?

EH: Number one is staying **focused** on an objective or goal. As we talked about, if I want to travel from Los Angeles to New York, I want to find the **shortest direct route** to do this. I'm not going to just meander down the road. Many salespeople say, "Well, I want to have a million dollars." But they don't have an idea of how to create even the first step to get there. You showed me how to do that. Thank you. It's staying focused on what you want. That's number one. Then, it's **constantly improving** yourself, your mindsets, your prospecting, your sales scripts, and everything else along the way because whatever you're doing today, you probably won't have enough skills to get you where you really want to be. And I know that in the past two years, I learned many skills thanks to Dr. Moine and you. Plus, I learned a lot about the computer business. You have to be willing to **learn** and **grow** each day, and **stay focused** on what it is you want and remember that you have to give value before you can get value.

You have to believe you're adding value and believe in what you're selling. Then you want to create a **real connection with the customer**. Dr. Moine and you taught me how to do that. Once a sales professional follows the steps you recommend and teach, the rest of it falls into place.

KL: Is there a Website where people can contact you?

EH: Sure, we can be reached at *amerafund.com* and at *avtechdirect.com*. For our radio program, we can also be contacted at *www.SuccessPowerTalkRadioLive.com* and *www.SuccessPower.net*.

KL: Do you have any final thoughts you would like to share on sales success?

EH: When you know how to sell and be persuasive, you can create a much higher quality life for yourself. Your techniques touch people's lives, and just one of your techniques can make the difference between somebody being an average salesman and a great salesperson, who can truly enjoy life. With these techniques, you truly realize the impact you can have. Have you ever really thought about how beautiful that is? You're creating more commerce and more riches for people, which is great for America.

Post-Script From Dr. Moine and Dr. Lloyd

It has been said that the business of America is business. We believe that to be true. And at the heart of business and profitability is sales. Nothing happens until a product or service is sold. Then, and only then, are all of the contributors in the process rewarded. If you are contributing to making American business stronger by increasing sales and profits, call us, write us, or speak to us at one of our seminars. We may be able to feature you in our next book. We would be very happy if we could help make you, like our other clients, sales millionaires, and help your company book several hundred million or a billion dollars in extra sales. We have experienced and celebrated many of these wins before and we would like to strengthen the U.S. (and international business) by doing it again with you.

Index

About the Authors

Dr. Donald Moine

Dr. Donald Moine is one of the founders of the new scientific discipline of Sales and Marketing Psychology. Dr. Moine is one of the top sales coaches in the U.S. and has served as the personal coach to more than 200 sales millionaires. A popular convention speaker for Fortune 500 companies, Dr. Moine has delivered sales training and motivational seminars on four different continents. One of Dr. Moine's special areas of expertise is helping financial planners, stock brokers, insurance sales professionals, pension fund managers and money managers build multimillion dollar sales careers. He has also appeared on more than 100 major talk radio shows and on several television shows. Dr. Moine is President of Association for Human Achievement in Rolling Hills Estates, California.

Dr. Ken Lloyd

Dr. Ken Lloyd is a nationally-recognized consultant, executive coach, speaker, and newspaper columnist whose syndicated workplace advice column (*New York Times* Syndicate) runs in newspapers across the U.S. and in Canada. With specialties in organizational behavior, employee development, and communication, Dr. Lloyd consults in a wide range of industries, including health care, apparel, financial services, and entertainment. A frequent television and talk-radio guest who has appeared on *Good Morning America* and CNN, Dr. Lloyd has authored numerous articles and six books, including the widely-acclaimed *Jerks at Work: How to Deal With People Problems and Problem People* and *Be the Boss Your Employees Deserve*. He has taught in the Anderson Graduate School of Management at U.C.L.A., and he lectures at various universities. Dr. Lloyd's consulting practice is based in Encino, California, where he resides with his wife and three children.